A Critical Race Approach to Systemic Inequity

A Critical Race Approach to Systemic Inequity

Rory Bahadur
Professor of Law
James R. Ahrens Chair for Tort Law
Washburn University School of Law

CAROLINA ACADEMIC PRESS
Durham, North Carolina

Library of Congress Cataloging-in-Publication Data
Names: Bahadur, Rory, author.
Title: A critical race approach to systemic inequity / Rory Bahadur.
Description: Durham, North Carolina: Carolina Academic Press, LLC, 2025. |
Includes bibliographical references and index.
Identifiers: LCCN 2025027699 | ISBN 9781531033132 (paperback) |
ISBN 9781531033149 (ebook)
Subjects: LCSH: Race discrimination—Law and legislation—United States. |
Race discrimination—Law and legislation | Discrimination—Law and
legislation—United States. | Fairness.
Classification: LCC KF4755 .B34 2025 | DDC 305.800973—dc23/eng/20250610
LC record available at https://lccn.loc.gov/2025027699

Carolina Academic Press, LLC
700 Kent Street
Durham, North Carolina 27701
(919) 489-7486
www.cap-press.com

Printed in the United States of America

This book is dedicated to Professor Stephen A. Plass. He understood human nature and the magnitude of systemic inequity better than anyone else I have ever met. And he went above and beyond what he needed to do to support and ensure the success of people like me who were blissfully unaware of the reality of racism. Without his help I would never have become a law professor. I can never thank him enough for believing in me and telling me what I needed to hear to navigate this world, even when it wasn't what I wanted to hear.

Contents

Preface

The initial purpose of this book was to identify and discuss examples of systemic racism and suggest a formulation for dismantling race-based systemic inequity in America. On the one hand, this book exposes and explores the cruelty and dehumanizing examples of race-based systemic inequity in America. On the other hand, after examining the well-developed research about human cognitive realities, this book explains that systemic inequity is probably an essential reality of all human civilizations. The dilemma in this regard is that achieving more equitable societies than we have thus far been able to achieve as a species requires a complete reformulation of the norms, assumptions, and myths we depend on for the very existence of human societies. Not only is this reality sobering, but the larger obstacle to eradicating systemic inequity is that we have no control over the unconscious and involuntary, double-edged sword of mental processes simultaneously responsible for both societal stability and societal inequity.

Using contemporary examples from American society and research from the cognitive sciences, this book demonstrates both the source and power of American race-based systemic inequity and suggests that current and genuine, well-intentioned efforts to mitigate race-based inequity are doomed to fail because they focus on individual behavior and belief modifications rather than systemic reform. Unfortunately, individual conduct, belief sets, and behavior have no effect on systemic inequity. For example, morality, civility, and religion, while powerful and relevant to individual behavior and well-being, are all mechanisms which reinforce systemic inequity.

Unless we stop underestimating the magnitude of the disruption to norms and belief sets necessary to mitigate race-based inequity, systemic inequity will remain the norm exactly as it has been throughout human history. But, more importantly, even if we acknowledge the magnitude of the task, the question remains whether humans are capable of living in societies without systemic inequity because the solution to systemic inequity requires a fundamental restructuring of humanity.

Acknowledgments

I can never fully express in words my gratitude to my immediate and extended family for their unwavering support, so I will not attempt to do it here. But they know how much they mean to me.

Initially I would like to thank Carla Pratt, Ali Khan, and Janet Thompson Jackson for their grace and forgiveness as they patiently guided me on my long and bumpy journey from blissful and naïve immigrant to grateful American citizen. Thank you for always finding the time to engage with me and help me improve. And additionally, thank you to Carla for your relentless support of my work, your mentoring, and for dedicating so much of your time to reviewing and making suggestions to so many of my publications, including this book.

Thank you to Dr. Jennifer Yamin-Ali, Rodney Yamin-Ali, Michael Hunter Schwartz and Dr. Stacey Hunter Schwartz for your support and feedback. Without your encouragement and our countless discussions, I am not sure this book would have come to fruition. And thank you to Nancy Levit. I don't deserve the support, encouragement, friendship, and guidance that you somehow always find the time to provide for me.

Thanks also to Washburn University and Washburn University School of Law. I am lucky that this municipal university in Topeka, Kansas, took a chance by hiring me in 2007. Even though we all have different views on life, society, and politics, we listen, respect, and support each other. I would specifically like to thank Nancy Maxwell for her compassion and friendship and her genuine interest in my well-being and my family's well-being. Thanks to Bill Rich for his mentoring and for taking the time to ensure I felt a sense of belonging. And thanks to

James Concannon (deceased) for his patience and guidance as I navigated what was then the foreign world of academia.

Thank you to Julie Robinson, Jasonn Weber, and Richard Schiefelbein. We may not speak often but our decades of friendship have been a long source of happiness for me, and your acceptance of me back in the day when Seattle was the cool city we lived in provided me with a sense of belonging that was essential to everything that came after. Our discussions, or "bickerfests" as we called them, helped educate me and to shape, expand, and change my views on countless things. You helped me survive in what was then a place far from home.

And thanks to Dr. Kevin Ruth, who I first met at the University of Miami in 1991, when we were both graduate students there. Your friendship and our ability to discuss, in depth, the things we fundamentally disagree on are indeed privileges.

To my friends from the country of Georgia, David Kapanadze and Eka Oniani, I don't know how to begin to thank you. Somehow the universe brought us together as friends across continents and oceans and gave me another place to feel at home. Throughout the years you have made my heart sing and made me feel grateful to be alive. When so much seems wrong with the world, you remind me of the joy and wonder of this thing called life.

And thank you to the members of my writing support circle of Alex Glashausser, John Francis, and Michelle Ewert. Our discussions were invaluable to this book's publication.

Thanks also to Grace Reiman, my research assistant on this project. This book would never have been published were it not for her amazing work.

A Critical Race Approach to Systemic Inequity

Introduction

In 1991, at about age 21, as an immigrant from the Caribbean island of Trinidad, I began living in the United States of America when I attended the University of Miami and obtained a master's degree in marine affairs. Immediately after that I began what would be almost ten years of biological fieldwork living aboard ships. The first four years were in the Bering Sea and Gulf of Alaska on board commercial fishing vessels, doing work for the National Marine Fisheries Service. This was followed by five years of work for the Army Corps of Engineers from 1996–2001 as an endangered species consultant, working on ships rebuilding beaches and keeping shipping channels deep everywhere from the Texas/Mexico border to Sugar Island in New York. Both jobs involved a fixed period aboard a ship and then as much time off as you needed before getting back on board a ship if you needed to. My typical rotation was three months on followed by one to three months off.

I took advantage of that flexibility to make sure that I traveled to every state in the United States in between ships, and I have spent time hiking, camping, driving through, and just experiencing every region of the country. I can confidently say that I have seen and experienced more of this country than most Americans will in their lifetimes, and I think I love it and appreciate it more than most of the people who knew its freedoms from birth and consider them normal.

Like most foreigners, when I initially arrived, I believed that America was a utopian meritocracy, and the American dream was guaranteed if you worked hard. And because most of this country's wealth is held by white people, I believed they owed their success only to hard work. I reasoned that if I just behaved like them and conformed to their norms, success would be certain. And so, I worked really hard, graduating first in my law school class in 2003, and now, 21 research articles, two books, and countless national and international presentations on effective teaching later, I am a chaired and tenured professor of law.

But I now understand that my impression of America as a utopian meritocracy, uniformly and routinely rewarding hard work regardless of a person's background, is a fiction. However, we find it difficult to unsee this fictional utopia because powerful evolutionary and essentially human, unconscious, cognitive processing mechanisms obscure the reality that American society, like all human societies, is saddled with deeply rooted systemic discrimination and biases.

Unconscious racism versus conscious racism is an excellent example of the difference between unconscious brain function and conscious brain function. To illustrate the difference between conscious and unconscious racism I provide first, an example of when I experienced conscious racism and then an example of when I experienced unconscious racism. Before exploring these examples, you first need to understand what I look like.

Phenotypically, I am mostly East Indian. My father is mostly the descendant of indentured laborers who were brought to Trinidad to replace the slaves in the sugar cane fields after emancipation. I say mostly twice above because three generations ago a white plantation owner "carried away" a 14-year-old Indian girl and had children with her. That 14-year-old Indian girl is my great-great-grandmother.

My mother is Jamaican, Black and white, but that is an oversimplification. She is the descendant of both African slaves and of Europeans from everywhere, in a uniquely Caribbean way. Her mother is the daughter of a Scottish woman who met and married a half Black, half Irish medical student from Jamaica when he was studying in Scotland. Her father was the son of a half Black, half Irish man and a white woman. A robust oral family history indicates this woman was of Jewish descent. For example, my grandmother consistently mentioned that the star of David she wore until her death was a gift from her "Jewish in-laws" and that my grandfather, who was a talented musician, routinely played music in the synagogues in Jamaica because of his mother. For reasons that will become apparent in Chapter 5, it is critical to mention here that my grandmother's maiden name was Dryden.

Early in my prelaw career as a marine biologist I experienced conscious racism. I boarded a ship and was introducing myself to the captain, chief engineer, and cook on the bridge who were all white males. I barely got two words out of my mouth when the chief engineer asked me in a flat tone I will never forget, "Are you a nigger? Because I don't like working with niggers." Just as my Caribbean brain was Mr. Magooing its way through this and leaving me thinking, "Oh cool, real racists! I gotta write home and tell them I've met the people we always see on TV that hate people who aren't white," the cook jumped in and proudly tried to demonstrate to the others that he went the furthest in geography class, by exclaiming "No, he's a sand nigger/camel jockey. It's obvious!" I never felt fear or anger.

In fact, by the end of that tour I was great friends with the person who pronounced me a "camel jockey," and I came to understand that his open racism was an honest expression of the reality of his upbringing and not a personal and empirically based hatred of me as a person. By the end of that trip that person told me that he was 14 years old the first time he ever saw a person of color and had no idea "what" he was seeing. Despite his reflexive reaction to me, he turned out to be a kind human being, who, once exposed to difference, was apologetic for his presumptions about different people, and we got along famously. The others remained assholes for reasons unrelated to racism.

Fast forward 20 years, and it's 2007, and I am beginning my job as a tenure-track law professor in Topeka, Kansas. My biracial three-year-old daughter and white wife join me on this journey. The experience of that child, the 2016 election, and the ease with which my opinions on things I was the most expert on were dismissed and given short shrift by colleagues and friends who adored me introduced me to another form of racism, way more harmful than the conscious racism I experienced on the boat.

It introduced me to the racism of people who genuinely supported anti-racism and genuinely believed they were anti-racist. People who became genuinely offended and hurt when you pointed out to them that they engaged in behavior that reflected and perpetuated racist societal structures. In other words, it introduced me to unconscious racism and the reality that an essential aspect of being human is constantly and without realizing it, reframing reality such that we are able to act completely inconsistently with our genuinely held beliefs while simultaneously remaining blissfully unaware we are acting inconsistently with them.

This book is an attempt to understand systemic racism and to shed some light on the more complex but difficult truths about American society and for that matter, all human societies. It uses contemporary examples to illustrate how the very things we consider good and hold moral, dear, and fundamental are products of the identical, unconscious cognitive reframing mechanisms that blind us to society's powerful and unforgiving systemic prejudices. This reality is difficult to acknowledge. Yet acknowledge and explain it is what I try to do. But explaining them involves delving into some humbling and disturbing aspects of human brain function and behavior.

Reading this book might initially make you uncomfortable and even defensive, but as the book explains, truth and discomfort are necessary waypoints on the path, *if such a path exists*, to actually achieving the society most residents of this unique and magnificent country genuinely desire.

And at the end of the day, it is important for me to make certain the reader knows this is a book written out of love for the United States, the country and its people who gave me opportunities that would not have been available to a person like me in any other society. But true love is honest.

CHAPTER 1

An Introduction to Reality Reframing Mechanisms

System Justification

System justification[1] is the reason humans can do things we consider cruel, immoral, evil, and inconsistent with our belief set, yet reframe those things in a way to convince ourselves we are acting consistently with our genuinely held belief set and within our moral compass.

If we consider our societies as systems, then systems tend to gravitate towards stability, and change is usually the opposite of stability. So, system justification results in a tendency to perpetuate the stability of the society we live in and to consider unnatural or immoral anything that produces structural changes or instability to society. In this way, system justification is thought to reduce uncertainty, threat, and social disruption, and in so doing, provides a sense of stability and order to our society.[2]

Ultimately, system justification results in humans defending, reinforcing, and justifying the status quo of societal structure because, as John Jost explains, this results in humans satisfying one of their basic needs, which is to live in and feel a sense of belonging in a society.[3]

My previous work on the legal profession and legal education explores how this unconscious cognitive reframing of information and actions operates in a way that makes the conclusions we consciously draw from them *feel* moral and good.[4] Despite the conscious conclusions we arrive at, the genesis of these conclusions is the result of the evolutionary reality that all humans process much of the information we receive unconsciously. This heuristic-based processing tends to overvalue information which reinforces the societal status quo and devalues information which is inconsistent with the societal status quo.[5] These heuristics are directed mostly by our biases.[6]

Bias should not be a polarizing word. It simply is an acknowledgement of human brain functioning and the creation of information-processing shortcuts without which human evolution would have proceeded much more slowly. As Dan Subotnik suggests, if bias didn't facilitate our speedy processing of information, we would still be cave-dwelling creatures,[7] or we may not even have survived as a species this long. Biases are simply information processing shortcuts that allow us to use prior knowledge and experience to inform the decisions we are making now without having to engage our slower and effortful conscious brain.[8] So before half of the readers roll their eyes at the mention of that polarizing word *bias*, it is important to remember that if you have a brain, you are biased.[9] The dilemma is that bias and prejudice, while the source of significant inequity, are also necessary features of all human societies.

As Pamela Fuller explains, "[B]ias is not inherently negative; rather, it is a natural part of the human condition, born of survival instincts and reinforced by experiences."[10] Russell McClain at Maryland's Carey School of Law uses a particularly informative example of how bias works. He suggests that if you are mowing your lawn and the grass is tall, and in your peripheral vision, you see something slither in the grass not too far away from you, you run away at full speed *immediately* because your brain uses unconscious bias to conclude *SNAKE!!!* long before you consciously process there is a snake in the grass. You would be speeding away from the spot long before your conscious brain proceeded along the following conscious reasoning path:

1. I am in tall grass.
2. I see a creature moving in an S-shaped pattern in the grass near to me.
3. Snakes live in grass and move in an S-shaped pattern.
4. Therefore, this thing moving next to me in an S-shaped pattern could be a snake.
5. Some snakes are venomous and dangerous.

6. As a result, I should move my left foot rapidly away from the snake, then move my right foot and repeat in quick succession until I am away from the danger as quickly as possible.

This demonstrates why Subotnik suggests that without bias, we would process information so slowly we would still be cave-dwelling creatures. You start running away from that potential snake long before your conscious processing involving steps one through six above occurs.

Another example of bias at work is when you make a left turn at a traffic light. When you approach that light in the left turn lane and observe a red arrow on the relevant traffic light you stop and when the light turns green you turn left. These left turns happen without you repeating the following conscious processing sequence every time you turn left at a light:

1. The light ahead of me turned green.
2. Therefore, I need to:
   a. Move this lever such that my left blinker is activated.
   b. Check to see if, despite the light, cross traffic has stopped.
   c. Remove my right foot from the broad pedal on the left.
   d. Move my right foot to the slimmer pedal on the right.
   e. Gently press down on the slimmer pedal until my vehicle moves forward in such a way that I don't hit the car in front of me.
   f. Turn the steering wheel to the left just enough to stay in the lane as I turn.
   g. Straighten out the steering wheel once the turn is completed.

That left turn happened without you consciously thinking about all the above steps. That left turn happened in that sequence because of bias. Daniel Kahneman, in his amazing book *Thinking, Fast and Slow*,[11] delves deeply into the different ways our brains process information, and *Scientific American* illustrates Kahneman's work as follows:

> To survive physically or psychologically, we sometimes need to react automatically to a speeding taxi as we step off the curb or to the subtle facial cues of an angry boss. That automatic mode of thinking, not under voluntary control, contrasts with

> the need to slow down and deliberately fiddle with pencil and paper when working through an algebra problem.[12]

It is important to glean from the above language that bias occurs "automatically."[13] Additionally, we have very little ability to modulate the conclusions we draw from these bias-driven heuristics because they are not under our "voluntary" control.[14] In contrast, our reasoning and calculating conscious brain operates much more slowly than these unconscious processing heuristics.[15]

Even though bias is essential to humanity's survival and evolutionary success,[16] according to Gulati, it results in differential judgments towards people based on how similar or dissimilar we perceive them to be.[17] Bias also leads people to believe that their own view of the world is more valid than the perspectives held by those who see it differently.[18] Employing unconscious processing heuristics to rapidly come to conclusions, rather than expending the cognitive effort required to engage rational and conscious processing mechanisms,[19] may sometimes result in erroneous conclusions and is the basis of otherism or discrimination. Of course, as noted above, our unconscious brain is an essential part of the human condition. This biased favoring of people we view as similar to us has been explored by Konrad Bocian and Bogdan Wojciszke.[20] Their study suggests that the more familiarity we feel with an individual, the higher the risk that we will be favorably biased when judging that person's behavior.[21]

These bias-driven heuristics also operate more globally at the societal level, facilitating system justification such that people, no matter their socioeconomic status, powerfully and unconsciously justify societal status quos.[22] Bias, or unconscious reframing mechanisms, leads individuals to conclude that status quo-buttressing information and actions, as well as those perceived as similar or part of "us," are powerfully moral and good, while change, difference, or "the other" are viewed as equally immoral and wrong. Hopefully, the empirical evidence in support of my assertion that, in America, white people still occupy the highest rungs on the socio-economic ladder,[23] makes this relatively uncontroversial.

And, exactly like the snake in the grass, your conscious mind is incapable—without massive effort, retraining, and motivation, as discussed in Chapters 10 and 11—of altering these feelings and conclusions. This is because biases are not subject to introspection and operate in such a way that you reach these conclusions automatically, without the power to consciously control the mechanisms behind them.[24] As I discuss later in this book, it is debatable whether American society is currently in a place where the retraining, effort, and motivation required to alter the heuristics is considered worthwhile.

Finally, these unconsciously arrived-at conclusions are incredibly powerful and are much more impactful than our conscious, deliberative conclusions because they are generated by the limbic brain. As a result, they are "nasty, brutish and short-sighted," in their operation, such that they override even our conscious value sets.[25] They are so powerful they even make it impossible for us to discern when we are acting outside of our own moral constructs or value sets,[26] leading us to engage in conduct that we ourselves would conclude was morally hypocritical if we were conscious of it.[27] Humans are capable of retaining a completely clear conscience and a firm belief in their own morality, even while they are simultaneously behaving completely inconsistently with their own moral beliefs.[28]

The Necessity of System Justification

Shannon and McCoy explain that for system justification—or the unconscious buttressing of societal status quos—to exist, there must also be unconscious support of the societal structure by disenfranchised or low socio-economic status (SES) members of society.[29] One purported fundamental tenet of American society is the belief that we live in a meritocratic society, where socioeconomic status is determined by individual work ethic, and, as a result, people get what they deserve.[30] As Shannon and McCoy explain,

> Americans adhere to a cultural worldview in which social rewards and status are assumed to reflect individual merit and hard work (Kluegel & Smith, 1986). This worldview is a central component of the American Dream and is reflected in the cultural stories of "Horatio Alger" and "The Little Engine that Could," which promote the belief that anyone can get ahead if they work hard enough and are talented enough. Although endorsement of this belief in a meritocracy varies at the indi-

> vidual level, it is so widely held that it has been termed America's dominant ideology.[31]

Conversely, meritocracy implies those who are poor or low-SES individuals are personally deficient and have failed to achieve because their work ethic is sub-optimal. Ultimately, an essential component of meritocracy is the belief that we live in a just world or belief in a just world (BJW).[32]

Why would the disenfranchised and poor unconsciously reinforce the notion that they deserve to be disenfranchised and poor? The alternative—that they live in an inequitable world with no merit-based rhyme or reason for why some are rich and others are poor—would lead to severe depression.[33] Instead, if the poor and disenfranchised unconsciously reframe reality to believe that there is a merit-based distinction to high- and low-SES, then they convince themselves there is a way out of their situation, one they have absolute control over: work hard and pull themselves up by the bootstraps.[34] In this way, meritocratic beliefs and BJW have a palliative effect, offering a tangible means of transitioning from a "have-not" to a "have."[35]

As will be discussed later in this book, we know we don't live in a meritocratic society, and we know the world is not just. Why, then, do we justify the system by unconsciously reframing our world to believe that it is just? Well, think about how much easier it is to shrug your shoulders and "meh" away things like starving Palestinian and African children, the cruelty of the caste system in India, the inequity of Kikuyu tribalism in Kenya, and the abject poverty in the Appalachians if you believe it is part of a merit-based plan and a universal justice structure or BJW where people get what they deserve.[36] The alternative is to constantly remind ourselves of the truth: that life is unfair, we have way less control than we believe, and people randomly and without empirical reasons, starve, suffer, and die.[37]

According to Sapolsky, the famed Stanford neurobiologist, we would all be depressed if we lacked this ability to unconsciously reframe our realities. He describes depression as the loss of the ability to reframe reality by rationalizing it away.[38] Sapolsky further argues that we need to continue fooling ourselves into believing that we live in a meritocratic society, even though rationalizing our society as a meritocracy is nonsensical.[39] The truth is that we live in a country that reinforces the illusion about the equality of economic potential for all people, while the reality is that over thirty percent of the nation's wealth is held by one percent of the population, and less than three percent of all wealth is held by the entire lower socioeconomic half of society.[40] He also explains that this reframed reality is so powerfully entrenched in our society that he discovered an advice column confidently suggesting that it isn't anyone's fault if they are born poor, but it is most certainly their fault if they die poor—adding that such individuals should be considered "'a wasted sperm'" if they die poor.[41]

The unconscious dishonesty and reframing associated with BJW are palliative, system justification-based, "cognitive re-evaluations of unjust events," that are essential for human existence because they help us cope with the massive injustice and suffering we observe every day.[42]

Because BJW reinforces the notion that people get what they deserve, BJW and meritocracy also facilitate victim blaming.[43] Ironically, low-SES members of society also rely on meritocracy and BJW to provide comforting justification for their lot in life by externalizing the reason for their poverty and disenfranchisement.[44] Meritocracy-based beliefs like BJW make injustice, poverty, and belonging to a lower-SES group seem inherently fair and just.[45] BJW also encourages lower-SES members to work especially hard because BJW reinforces the idea that they have some control over their lot in life.[46] This cognitive reframing and justifying of the system makes the disenfranchisement of the low-SES groups more comforting for them, as injustice and poverty are construed as more deserved, fair, and just in a meritocratic world. At the same time, BJW motivates members of low-SES groups to work harder because they believe they can meritocratically work their way out of their position.[47]

Ultimately, an erroneous belief in meritocracy and BJW is necessary for people to perceive the world as a predictable place where they have some control. This belief makes them feel safer, more positive, and able to manage their socioeconomic trajectory.[48] However, like all cognitively reframed fictions based on system justification, these beliefs also powerfully blind us to the nonsensical nature of the conclusions and principles we consider universal and unwavering truths. This leads to the polarizing and controversial premise discussed in Chapter 2: religion is the genesis of the belief in a just world.[49] However, religion—and, by extension, the belief in a just world—is illogical at best and nonsensical at worst.

Endnotes

1. A term coined by John Jost. John T. Jost, *A Theory of System Justification: Is There a Nonconscious Tendency to Defend, Bolster and Justify Aspects of the Societal Status Quo?*, Am. Psych. Ass'n (June 2017), https://perma.cc/LR7X-68MF.

2. *Id.*

3. *Id.*

4. *See* Rory D. Bahadur, *Law School Rankings and the Impossibility of Anti-Racism*, 53 St. Mary's L. J. 991 (2022).

5. *See id.*

6. *See id.*

7. Dan Subotnik, *Does Testing = Race Discrimination?: Ricci, the Bar Exam, the LSAT, and the Challenge to Learning*, 8 U. Mass. L. Rev. 332, 398 (2013).

8. NLI Staff, *Here's Why Having a Brain Means You Have Bias*, NeuroLeadership Inst. (July 22, 2020), https://neuroleadership.com/your-brain-at-work/unconscious-bias-in-brain.

9. *Id.*

10. Pamela Fuller, *The Nature of Bias*, Ass'n for Talent Dev. (Dec. 19, 2019), https://www.td.org/insights/the-nature-of-bias [https://perma.cc/28S8-3PHD]; Mary E. McLean & Linelle Campbell, *Implicit Bias Is Both Helpful and Harmful, So What Can We Do?*, EM Resident (June 11, 2020), https://www.emra.org/emresident/article/implicit-bias.

11. Daniel Kahneman, Thinking, Fast and Slow 415 (2011).

12. Daniel Kahneman, *Of 2 Minds: How Fast and Slow Thinking Shape Perception and Choice [Excerpt]*, SciAm (June 15, 2021), https://www.scientificamerican.com/article/kahneman-excerpt-thinking-fast-and-slow/.

13. *Id.*

14. *Id.*

15. *Id.*

16. *See* Bernard J. Luskin, *MRIs Reveal Unconscious Bias in the Brain*, Psych. Today (Apr. 7, 2016), https://www.psychologytoday.com/us/blog/the-media-psychology-effect/201604/mris-reveal-unconscious-bias-in-the-brain. This mirrors the idea, developed in psychologist Daniel Kahneman's book *Thinking, Fast and Slow*, that we have two systems of thinking: one that is fast, intuitive, and impressionistic (System 1), and one that is slow, deliberate, and systematic (System 2). System 1 is automatic and efficient, but it's in a hurry and prone to mistakes. It seeks to quickly identify patterns, a skill that has been key to human survival and evolution. But in doing so, it jumps to conclusions of causality based upon even the sketchiest of information and tries to interpret scant input by creating a narrative, however flawed it may be. System 2 thinking, on the other hand, seeks to test concepts and detect complexity and nuance.

17. NLI Staff, *supra* note 8.

18. *Id.*

19. *Id.*

20. *See generally* Konrad Bocian & Bogdan Wojciszke, *Self Interest Bias in Moral Judgments of Others' Actions*, 40 Personality & Soc. Psych. Bull. 898 (2014).

21. *Id.* Explaining that, "studies suggest that cherishing positive attitudes toward other individuals—because of cooperation, *similarity*, trust and otherwise laudable qualities—increases the risk of being biased and forming overly positive impressions of their behavior as serving the common interest of the perceiver and behavior perpetrators."

22. *See generally* John T. Jost, *A Quarter Century of System Justification Theory: Questions, Answers, Criticisms, and Societal Justifications*, 58 Brit. J. of Soc. Psych. 263 (Nov. 28, 2018), https://as.nyu.edu/content/dam/nyu-as/psychology/documents/facultypublications/johnjost/A%20Quarter%20Century%20of%20System%20Justification%20Theory.pdf; *see also* B. Keith Payne & C. Daryl Cameron, *Divided Minds, Divided Morals: How Implicit Social Cognition Underpins and Undermines Our Sense of Social Justice*, Uni. of N.C. at Chapel Hill 1, 21–22 (2010), https://bkpayne.web.unc.edu/wp-content/uploads/sites/7990/2015/02/PayneCameron2010.pdf.

23. *See* Darren L. Hutchinson, *Continually Reminded of Their Inferior Position: Social Dominance, Implicit Bias, Criminality, and Race*, 46 Wash. U. J. L. & Pol'y 23, 28 (2014).

24. *Understanding Implicit Bias*, Kirwan Inst. (May 29, 2012), https://kirwaninstitute.osu.edu/implicit-bias-module-series/module-1-understanding-implicit-bias [https://perma.cc/J9Y3-35F6].

> [T]he attitudes or stereotypes that affect our understanding, actions, and decisions in an unconscious manner. These biases, which encompass both favorable and unfavorable assessments, are activated involuntarily and without an individual's awareness or intentional control. Residing deep in the subconscious, these biases are different from known biases that individuals may choose to conceal for the purposes of social and/or political correctness.

25. B. Keith Payne & C. Daryl Cameron, Handbook of Implicit Social Cognition: Measurement, Theory, and Applications 445 (Bertram Gawronski & B. Keith Payne eds., 2010) ("Implicit reactions are often hierarchical, dividing the world into 'us' and 'them[]'.").

26. Daniel C. Batson, Elizabeth R. Thompson, Greg Seuferling, Heather Whitney & Jon A. Strongman, *Moral Hypocrisy: Appearing Moral to Oneself Without Being So*, 77 J. Personality & Soc. Psych. 525, 525–26 (1999).

27. *Id.*

28. *Id.*

29. Shannon K. McCoy, Joseph D. Wellman, Brandon Cosley, Laura Saslow & Elissa Epel, *Is the Belief in Meritocracy Palliative for Members of Low Status Groups? Evidence for a Benefit for Self-Esteem and Physical Health via Perceived Control*, 43 Eur. J. Soc. Psych. 1, 2 (2013) [hereinafter McCoy et al., *Meritocracy Palliative*].

30. Shannon K. McCoy & Brenda Major, *Priming Meritocracy and the Psychological Justification of Inequality*, 43 J. Experimental Soc. Psych. 341 (2007) [hereinafter McCoy & Major, *Priming Meritocracy*].

31. *Id.*

32. *See* Katherine Stroebe, Tom Postmes, Susanne Täuber, Alwin Stegeman & Melissa-Sue John, *Belief in a Just What? Demystifying Just World Beliefs by Distinguishing Sources of Justice*, PLOS ONE (Mar. 24, 2015), https://journals.plos.org/plosone/article?id=10.1371/journal.pone.0120145 [https://perma.cc/3W8T-ZTQX].

33. *Id.* at 2.

34. *See generally* McCoy et al., *Meritocracy Palliative*, *supra* note 29.

35. *Id.*

36. *See* Stroebe et al., *supra* note 32 (linking religious belief to belief in a just world).

> Lerner describes the manner in which he began thinking about the BJW concept when he saw people working with dying children or being confronted with the bad health and suffering of parts of the American population. How do people function normally under, and cope with, extreme suffering? Ac-

> cording to Lerner such injustices are particularly impactful because of people's fundamental need to see the world as a place in which good deeds are rewarded and bad deeds are punished. Responses to such threats are motivated by the need to uphold one's BJW: Individuals adapt their perceptions of injustice (or the reality at hand), for example by seeing unjust outcomes as caused by victims of injustice, rather than facing a potentially unjust world. This mechanism functions across many contexts (e.g., with respect to victims of AIDS, rape, robbery, cancer, discrimination). Building on this initial work, scales were developed to assess people's explicit beliefs about the world as just. This research on scale construction reveals that individual differences in levels of BJW influence, among others, people's goals in life, personal well-being, achievement behavior in schools, and responses to many types of personal and group disadvantage.

37. Kristin Wenzel, Simon Schindler & Marc-André Reinhard, *General Belief in a Just World Is Positively Associated with Dishonest Behavior*, 8 Frontiers Psych., (Oct. 10, 2017), https://www.ncbi.nlm.nih.gov/pmc/articles/PMC5641360 [https://perma.cc/6ZU4-WRL8] (discussing a narrowed examination of "the influence of people's dispositional general and personal BJW on (dis)honest behavior[]").

38. Robert M. Sapolsky, Determined: A Science of Life Without Free Will 387 (2023).

39. *Id.* at 401.

40. *Id.*

41. *Id.* (quoting Emmanuel A. Anderson, *It's Not Your Fault if You Are Born Poor, but It's Your Fault if You Die Poor*, Medium (Jan 21, 2020), https://medium.com/illumination-curated/its-not-your-fault-if-you-are-born-poor-but-it-s-your-fault-if-you-die-poor-36cf3d56da3f).

42. Kristin Wenzel et al., *supra* note 37.

43. *See* Stroebe et al., *supra* note 32.

44. *See generally* McCoy et al., *Meritocracy Palliative*, *supra* note 29 (connecting high-status and low-status groups by their shared beliefs in meritocracy and personal responsibility); McCoy & Major, *Priming Meritocracy*, *supra* note 30; Virginie Wiederkehr, Virginie Bonnot, Silvia Krauth-Gruber & Céline Darnon, *Belief in School Meritocracy as a System-Justifying Tool for Low Status Students*, 6 Frontiers Psych. 1, 1–2 (July 30, 2015); Ana Filipa Madeira, Rui Costa-Lopes, John F. Dovidio, Goncalo Freitas & Mafalda F. Mascarenhas, *Primes and Consequences: A Systematic Review of Meritocracy in Intergroup Relations*, 10 Frontiers Psych. 1, 1–2 (Sept. 19, 2019).

45. *Id.*

46. McCoy et al., *Meritocracy Palliative*, *supra* note 29, at 1–2.

47. *Id.*

48. *Id.*

49. *See* Stroebe et al., *supra* note 32.

> Religiosity has consistently correlated highly with the BJW. Indeed, attributing unjust and tragic outcomes in one's own and the life of others to God's will can be a way of coping with these negative life outcomes and of regaining feelings of personal control by attributing negative outcomes to God's will. In line with our idea that the perceived source of justice influences action tendencies, those who are religious experience more positive well-being/affect and engage in more prosocial behavior.

CHAPTER 2

The Illogic of Religion and Belief in a Just World

Sometime in the late 1100s, a young English boy is awoken in his village and told that his God requires him to ride to what is now Tel Aviv and kill Muslims. He, and thousands of other young men, made this journey and died on battlefields all over the Middle and Near East during what we call the Crusades. None of them has ever seen, nor can they be sure of the existence of, the deity in the sky. Yet their faith in the deity's existence and only that is enough to compel them to travel the globe to die by the thousands for the sake of this deity. This same faith continues to be responsible for, and to justify, wars even today.

Faith is powerful, but it is curious. Faith is the belief in that which cannot nor hasn't been proven. According to Hebrews 11:1, "[F]aith is assurance of things hoped for, a conviction of things not seen."[1] Let's be clear: if the deity in the sky were to pop its head out of the sky and speak in all languages to the entire world simultaneously and say in a loud booming voice, "I am real, and to provide proof to you, I will turn Alaska to sand for 24 hours and turn the Sahara to snow at the same time," and then were to proceed to do so, it is hard to imagine how faith-focused religions would survive.

This is because, for example, in Christianity, faith is essential for salvation. Therefore, if the existence of God is proven, Christianity might collapse because then the need for faith would evaporate as you would no longer be believing in that which cannot be proven. Thus, the very thing that separates the saved from the unsaved in Christianity—faith in an unproven deity—can only be sustained if the existence of a deity is never proven. Consequently, all our beliefs, morals, rules, and much of our societal structure and history relies on the belief in something which can only be sustained if its existence is never established.

Furthermore, each religion has a text or writing purporting to provide an understanding of the behaviors and belief sets that this unproven deity in the sky demands. In Islam, that book is the Quran, and in Christianity, for example, that book is the Bible. What often remains unsaid, due to the discomfort it causes, is that no one really knows what the alleged deity in the sky requires. Religious texts are written so vaguely that everyone who claims to believe and conform to their requirements is, in practice, selectively ignoring parts of the text and picking and choosing the parts that make sense to them.

Consider, for example, that in countries like Saudi Arabia and Afghanistan some interpret Islam as requiring women not to drive and to wear clothing that covers their entire body. Yet, the same book appears not to require those things in the more liberal Muslim nations like Turkey or Indonesia. Similarly, according to the Amish interpretation of the Bible, Amish people should not use technology, and women must dress in a certain way and generally not take part in decision-making. Nor should they hold leadership positions in the church. And this hierarchy is justified by the biblical text. By contrast the Quakers, Episcopalians, and United Church of Christ read the same Bible and see no restriction on the participation and leadership of women in the church or society.

Other examples of this selective interpretation abound in Christianity. Leviticus 15:19–23 unambiguously provides that a woman and anything she touches is unclean during her menstrual period and should not be touched or touch anything during that time.[2] Most modern Christian denominations do not abide by these teachings but rationalize that Jesus and his doctrine of inclusivity rendered this language from Leviticus inapplicable. Yet, because the deity in the sky has never popped its head out to tell us which is the correct interpretation, different religious sects ignore or apply these Old Testament purity laws. One thing is clear: despite not knowing the correct interpretation of these texts—or perhaps because no one knows—people remain convinced that their interpretation is the right one. Throughout history, people have believed so strongly in that which cannot be proven that they have killed, murdered, and subjugated people based on their beliefs.

Voltaire exclaimed, "There is no God but don't tell that to my servant lest he murder me at night."[3] This perfectly captures the role religion has played in the development of human society. It has served as the perfect tool for oppressing people and justifying hierarchies in human society. We can use other religions to demonstrate the same thing, but my focus on Christianity is because it is the religion of choice for most Westerners and the one which I was raised in.

Christianity and Slavery in America

Many people interpreted the Bible to condone slavery. People of African descent were thought to be fated for servitude and slavery based on the curse of Ham in Genesis. In case, like me, you are unsure what this refers to: it is the curse Noah placed on his grandson Canaan, decreeing that all his descendants would remain slaves forever because Noah was embarrassed that Noah's son Ham saw Noah drunk and naked. So, in this way, for centuries the slave trade was thought to be biblically prescribed. New Testament language found in Ephesians also commands slaves to obey their earthly masters with respect.

Of course, abolitionists read the same Bible and concluded that slavery was an abomination and inconsistent with the teachings of Christianity. They relied on verses like Galatians 3:28 and its suggestion that all people are the same to Christ, to suggest that Christianity did not support slavery but rather was based on egalitarianism and the equality of all people.

The bottom line is that many different people read the same religious text and justifiably reach exactly opposite conclusions. And because no deity has confirmed which interpretation is correct, we hate, enslave, subjugate, or kill the people who don't share our view and feel the certainty of God's approval in doing so. But more importantly, because the texts are subject to varying interpretations, those in power have always managed to convince a critical enough mass of people that the interpretation that makes the most sense is whatever interpretation perpetuates power hierarchies. Religion, therefore, is the basis of the reality that might is right, and the perfect example of this is the traditional oppression of women by religion.

Christianity and the Oppression of Women

One of my cousins, who is far brighter than I am, suggested that if men got pregnant, there would be anonymous drive-thru abortion clinics with the same frequency as McDonald's restaurants. And I agree.

Let's initially examine some biblical language that suggests women are inferior to men. First Corinthians 14:34–35 can be interpreted as limiting the role of women in public speaking and church leadership. That language is as follows: "Women should remain silent in the churches. They are not allowed to speak, but must be in submission, as the law says. If they want to inquire about something, they should ask their own husbands at home; for it is disgraceful for a woman to speak in the church."[4]

Then, in 1 Peter 3:1, the Bible provides this language used to justify the submissiveness of women to men, "Wives, in the same way submit yourselves to your own husbands so that, if any of them do not believe the word, they may be won over without words by the behavior of their wives."[5]

Similar language is found in Ephesians 5:22–24, which provides: "Wives, submit yourselves to your own husbands as you do to the Lord. For the husband is the head of the wife as Christ is the head of the church, his body, of which he is the Savior. Now as the church submits to Christ, so also wives should submit to their husbands in everything."[6] This language is still the basis of many Christian religious sects where the man is considered the head of the household.

Additionally, there is Timothy 2:11–15, which provides: "A woman should learn in quietness and full submission. I do not permit a woman to teach or to assume authority over a man; she must be quiet. For Adam was formed first, then Eve. And Adam was not the one deceived; it was the woman who was deceived and became a sinner."[7] This passage is the basis of women not holding leadership positions in church and the basis of some Christian sects' assumption that women are generally inferior to men.

More progressive Christians who espouse gender equality brush these verses off and justify ignoring them because Jesus was friends with Mary Magdalene and dealt with her respectfully. For them, this respectful interaction is enough to render all the other contrary textual provisions irrelevant and supports a gender equality biblical interpretation for some.

All I am trying to demonstrate here is that there is no right interpretation of the biblical texts, only an interpretation that individuals think is the right one. Despite this reality, much of Christianity's default position—and the derived societal realities of that position—involves historical oppression of women by men. Again, this is an example of interpreting religious texts to perpetuate a patriarchal society.

Because we are wired to reframe reality, we often choose to forget how much the oppression of women forms an integral part of the institutions we rely on and consider holy. One only has to research the witch hunts to realize that the Catholic Church conveniently changed its position on the existence of witches, tacitly supporting the *Malleus Maleficarum* and the torture and killing of thousands of women when men were dying in battle and women were becoming more socially powerful as they inherited the property of their deceased husbands.[8]

Our automatic reframing of reality also prevents us from confronting the systemic inequity of religion, and it is easier to single out and blame individuals. Just ask Harrison Butker, the Kansas City Chiefs kicker.

Harrison Butker: Don't Hate the Player but Instead Question the Game

In 2024, Harrison Butker delivered the commencement speech at an all-Catholic college in Atchison, Kansas. Butker, a Catholic, suggested that much of society's woes and people's unhappiness was based on nonconformance to the aforementioned Bible verses, which suggest female subservience to men, and which espouse the more traditional religious gender norms.

People were outraged. Social media exploded with angry people suggesting that the Chiefs dismiss him. But there was nary a voice suggesting that Butker was simply articulating the views of Catholicism. Similarly, no one challenged the legitimacy of Catholicism as an institution whose philosophy is expressly based on the inferiority of women.

Catholic theology relies heavily on the teachings of St. Augustine. Augustine believed that women were subordinate to men and that this subordination was necessary to maintain order in society.[9] But he came to that belief, and the belief that sex was a sin, only after living a very promiscuous life from his teens through his thirties and then feeling guilty about how much he enjoyed sex.[10]

He concluded that something so powerful could only be evil, and hence the notion that sex for pleasure is evil became an essential tenet of Catholicism.[11] But it is the reasoning Augustine employed in getting there that we often ignore. The limited role of women in Catholicism is not superficial; it is deeply rooted in Augustinian philosophy.

Augustine believed that it was Eve's (read as female) inferiority and lack of rationality that was responsible for her succumbing to temptation in the Garden of Eden. Therefore, it is Eve and sexual desire that is responsible for the fact that our current existence is not in a utopian garden.[12] Recall also, the biblical verse quoted above, "And Adam was not the one deceived; it was the woman who was deceived and became a sinner."[13]

According to Augustine, as he interpreted the teachings of Aristotle, the dominance of males over females has to do with active versus passive minds, and it is a biological necessity.[14] He thinks the male/female dominance is as natural and unavoidable as the dominance of masters over slaves and the people of Greece over "orientals."[15] Furthermore, he analogizes the dominance of men over women as no less normal a result than the dominance of the human species over animals.[16]

This dominance, according to Augustine, is the reason only men can become priests—because they are the only members of our species that can be Christ-like.[17] In his view, it is not simply a man-made rule that bars women from the priesthood; rather, their natural inferiority renders this an inevitable result.[18] Augustine, who adopted Aristotle's view, believed that women were defective beings who were incapable of imaging Christ, demonstrating excellence, or exercising sovereignty, and therefore are not capable of receiving the sacrament of priesthood.[19]

So, the next time we or someone we know expresses outrage at Butker or anyone expressing traditional Catholic views, know that we are cowards. Instead, we should be braver and address the express sexism of one of the world's most populous religions. However, for most of us, that is too heavy a lift. It is too disruptive to our social order, so we justify the system by hiding the reality of the scale of the problem, conveniently ignoring how fundamental to Catholicism Butker's views are.

Sexism and the perceived inferiority of women is an essential part of Catholic theology, yet many feminists remain Catholic and find ways to rationalize this inconsistency. To further understand how our minds hide inconsistencies and reality from us, consider that few people seem to question the continued existence of the Catholic Church. Is it not inconceivable that over 1 billion people—about 17% of the world's population—remain members of an institution that facilitated the rape of children for centuries and tried to cover it up from the top down by reassigning offending priests to different jurisdictions?[20]

Without the belief in the unproven deity in the sky, any institution operating on such sexist assumptions about women and engaging in child rape to this extent would cease to exist. Yet we find a way to justify the system. We are afraid to leave the sect because the same people who covered up child rape tell us that a piece of bread and a sip of wine are the body and blood of the son of the unproven deity. In this way, sexism survives, and its perpetuation is facilitated by people who are ostensibly antisexist but who just "meh" away the reality of the religion they support. Moreover, religion also reframes oppression as divine.

Reframing Oppression as Divine

When I was a child in Trinidad, our neighbors were an older couple of African descent. They believed, "God is something white people invented to keep Black people happy with their lot in life."

Consider, we celebrate the power of the genre of music known as the negro spiritual. We use it as an example of the strength and power of enslaved Africans. What we fail to do, because it would upset the stability of our current system, is acknowledge that it, and the Christian religion it is based on, made slavery seem divine even for the enslaved.

Somehow, we were able to convince people being treated worse than animals and whose children were sold like commodities, and whose lives involved brutal work till death, that their participation in this system ensured them eternal life. Not only did the belief in a yet unproven entity in the sky make the slavers feel what they were doing was just, but it also resulted in the enslaved Africans buying into the notion that their treatment was part of a divine plan. This plan meant the more you suffered on earth and the more cruelty you endured, the larger the reward in an unproven hereafter.[21] The opiate of the masses, indeed.

Dr. Everett McCorvey explains that the genre of music known as the Negro spiritual represents the resolve of enslaved Africans, who were so strong that they survived by singing these religious songs that told of heroes and triumphs even while they were suffering.[22] He reinforces the notion that, even though these songs were created during the darkest periods of American history, we should rightfully continue to celebrate them, and the reverence the entire world has for the genre is appropriate.[23] Despite their age, he suggests that these centuries-old songs need to be remembered and that we should continue to sing them as a celebration of the strength of the enslaved people.[24]

Is it too uncomfortable to acknowledge that perhaps, instead of celebrating, we should also be questioning the logic of a system that allowed enslaved people to buy into the notion that there was something good and holy to the brutality meted out to them? Shouldn't we be seriously questioning the sanity of a system that allowed people to believe that the more they suffered the more they would be rewarded in a place that no one has ever seen, nor will any living person ever see?

What religion did was to make the enslaved people easier to contain and manage. Christianity was a powerful management tool for the oppressed and brutalized slaves. And system justification played a huge part in perpetuating this belief in God, in the same way meritocracy beliefs play a part in maintaining societal order today. The brain of the slave had a choice. Their brains could either let the slave see the depressing reality that their experiences represented humanity's limitless capacity for evil and that they were going to live a life that had no real meaning beyond living and dying to make a white plantation owner richer—a life in which they and their children were sold, beaten, branded, had limbs amputated, and were powerless to stop it. Or, in the alternative, their brains could embrace the teachings of the drug of religion, allowing them to palliatively reframe this reality as a blessing and a necessary cog in the wheel of eternal salvation.

Nothing can be more powerful than this to remind us that the only truth that governs our existence is that might is right and that everything else we contrive in this world, including the ridiculous notion that the more we are brutalized the more we are blessed, is our brain's palliative attempt to disguise this reality. Distracting ourselves from the cruelty of reality is an unavoidably human condition.

Answered Prayers and Counted Blessings

According to the United Nations, 25,000 people starve to death every day in our world, and of that number, 10,000 or more are children. When we in the West say "Thank God" we have enough, or we count our blessings for the abundance that we have, we are again unconsciously reframing and hiding the truly cruel nature of our species. Implicit in "thanking God" for the fact that you are not starving is the assumption that the deity has chosen you to have food as part of its divine plan and has decided to let others starve.

This gratitude suggests that we as humans are powerless to change the divine plan, which involves thousands of starving children. And this powerlessness leads to acceptance. We remain grateful that we were not the ones chosen by the deity to starve. We justify our superiority and survival when we "thank God" because we are thanking the deity for favoring us over the ones who had to starve to death as part of the divine plan. Not only does this allow us to detach from the brutal reality that starvation is caused by human-controlled resource distribution for profit, but it also makes us rejoice and be grateful when this happens. We are the special, selected, and chosen ones the deity thinks should not starve, and no mere mortal can disrupt the divine plan.

Similarly, what does it mean when two people have relatives with cancer and both people pray, but only one relative survives? When the survivor's relative gives thanks to the theoretical deity, they are implicitly giving thanks that, as part of the divine plan, the deity chose to save their relative and not the relative of the other person.

Religion itself is also unavoidably discriminatory. Whatever version of the earthly/supernatural dynamic you decide is valid generally means that you have decided that others are invalid. For example, if you believe in the multiple gods of Hinduism and Greek mythology, then you have dismissed the monotheistic formulation of Christianity, Judaism, and Islam as wrong. Similarly, what gives any modern religious practitioner the certainty that the Aztecs and their worship of the sun was any less "correct" than the religious practices of the West today? What makes Mormons so certain of their story and book?

Imagining themselves as the tolerant liberals, some people rationalize that these formulations are not inconsistent because "God or Gods" simply used different messages to reach people in different demographics on Earth and that we are all God's children, or some similar cliché. But if you did that, you would be dismissing the viewpoints of the majority of humanity, who, throughout history and up to the present time, have believed that the differences in these stories were significant enough to justify the destruction of entire civilizations and societies. In essence, you would be saying the majority of humanity is wrong and you are right—without any empirical basis for this assumption other than that feeling of certainty in your heart.

The single most harmful aspect of religion is that it deftly stresses the importance of individual conduct. In doing so, it distracts us from the systemic reality of hierarchy and oppression, convincing us instead to look at individual behavior as a solution to inequity. If I have a good heart and genuinely believe I am doing good, I will improve the world—or so the reasoning goes. However, I suggest that when you have powerful moral justifications for a belief or action, it is a sure sign that system justification is at work. The more you believe in the innate "goodness" of your individual actions, the more powerfully those actions perpetuate inequities at the systemic level.

For example, in the context of systemic racism, Ijeoma Oluo beautifully explains that there will be no change to systemic injustice even if everyone in the United States feels only love, because individual feelings, morality, and behavior are largely irrelevant to systemic inequity.[25]

The power of religion, despite its illogic, can be explained by system justification and the palliative effect belief in a just world ("BJW") provides. As Katherine Stroebe explains:

> Religiosity has consistently correlated highly with the BJW. Indeed, attributing unjust and tragic outcomes in one's own and the life of others to God's will can be a way of coping with these negative life outcomes and of regaining feelings of personal control by attributing negative outcomes to God's will. In line with our idea that the perceived source of justice influ-

> ences action tendencies, those who are religious experience more positive well-being/affect and engage in more prosocial behavior.[26]

My unapologetic conclusion is, therefore, that no social movement which is religiously based can ever be effective at achieving systemic equality or antiracism. In this regard, Derrick Bell famously states:

> I have focused on the economic, political, and cultural dimensions of racism, suggesting its permanence because of the social stability it provides in a system that contains great disparities in income and wealth.... But I want to raise... the possibility of a deeper foundation growing out of an undeniable fact. Most racists are also Christians.[27]

The incoherent doctrines we frame as religion are the source of the belief in a just world, which serves as one of the central catalysts of system justification. To the many well-meaning and genuinely good people who are offended at my suggestion that their desire to do good by conforming to religion instead buttresses societal inequity, I apologize—but my argument is well documented by research.[28]

Endnotes

1. *Hebrews* 11:1–2 (American Standard).

2. *Leviticus* 15:19–23 (New International).

3. Yuval Noah Harari, Sapiens: A Brief History of Humankind 151 (2015) (quoting Voltaire).

4. Wikipedia, *Paul the Apostle and Women*, https://en.wikipedia.org/wiki/Paul_the_Apostle_and_women, quoting the New International Version (last visited Dec. 19, 2024).

5. 1 *Peter* 3:1 (New International).

6. *Ephesians* 5:22–24 (New International).

7. 1 *Timothy* 2:11–15 (New International).

8. *See* Rory Bahadur, *Individual Sovereignty, Freer Sex, and Diminished Privacy: How an Informed and Realistic Modern Sexual Morality Provides Salvation from Unjustified Shame*, 8 Elon L. Rev. 245 (2016).

9. *Id.*

10. *Id.*

11. *Id.*

12. Rosemary Radford Ruether, *Women in Creation, Fall and Redemption: The Classical Paradigm*, Scribd 1, https://www.scribd.com/document/343211699/Women-in-Creation-Fall-and-Redemption-The-Classical-Paradigm.

13. 1 *Timothy* 2:11–15 (New International).

14. Ruether, *supra* note 12, at 5.

15. *Id.*

16. *Id.*

17. Ruether, *supra* note 12, at 6.

18. *Id.*

19. *Id.*

20. Katie Zavadski, Topher Sanders, ProPublica & Nicole Hensley, *Dozens of Catholic Priests Credibly Accused of Abuse Found Work Abroad, Some with the Church's Blessing*, ProPublica and Houston Chronicle (Mar. 6, 2020), https://www.propublica.org/article/dozens-of-catholic-priests-credibly-accused-of-abuse-found-work-abroad-some-with-the-churchs-blessing (last visited Jan. 16. 2025).

21. Nathaniel Holmes Jr., *Redemptive Suffering and Christology in African American Christian Theology*, 4 Journal of the Black Catholic Theological Symposium 97, 108–09 (2010) explaining

> The idea was that God would bring about complete liberation in God's own time. Everything will eventually work out, maybe in this world, but if not, then the next world. God was preparing a "home in glory" for those who were faithful in their lives despite the horrible afflictions of existence. For much of Black America it was futile to expect good from American society and hope of rectifying their situations themselves because they were powerless. Only God had the power and God's will was seemingly that Blacks suffer in this life to receive greater rewards in the next.

22. National Association of Teachers of Singing, https://www.nats.org/History_of_American_Negro_Spiritual.html (last visited Dec. 19, 2024).

23. *Id.*

24. *Id.*

25. *See* Ijeoma Oluo, So You Want to Talk About Race 22 (2018) (explaining "We can get every person in America to feel nothing but love in their hearts, and if our systems aren't acknowledged and changed, it will bring negligible benefit to the lives of people of color.").

26. *See* Katherine Stroebe, Tom Postmes, Susanne Täuber, Alwin Stegeman & Melissa-Sue John, *Belief in a Just What? Demystifying Just World Beliefs by Distinguishing Sources of Justice*, PLOS One (Mar. 24, 2015), https://journals.plos.org/plosone/article?id=10.1371/journal.pone.0120145.

27. George H. Taylor, *Race, Religion, and Law: The Tension between Spirit and Its Institutionalization*, 6 Md. L.J. Race, Relig., Gender & Class 51 (2006) (quoting Derek Bell).

28. *See* Deborah L. Hall, David C. Matz & Wendy Wood, *Why Don't We Practice What We Preach? A Meta-Analytic Review of Religious Racism*, Personality & Soc. Psych. Rev. 135, 135 (2010); *see also See* John Chenault, *Western Christianity and the Origins of Antiblackness, Eurocentrism, and White Supremacy*, Univ. of Louisville 375 (2022), https://ir.library.louisville.edu/cgi/viewcontent.cgi?article=5140&context=etd (last visited Jan. 22, 2025).

CHAPTER 3

The "Meh Relegation" of Information

Alosha

The unconscious processing mechanisms of bias cause us to cognitively reframe reality such that we can perceive our inequitable society as a utopian meritocracy because our brains automatically amplify the effect of information that conforms to societal biases and relegates nonconforming information to the realm of the insignificant. This reality is commonly referred to as confirmation bias.

I find it best to illustrate this phenomenon by imagining that the brain is a person. When the brain receives information that is contrary to the belief set that supports our palliative and fictionalized utopia, it simply exclaims "Meh, whatever," shrugs its shoulders, forgets about the information, and proceeds to think about something else. One of my former law students' experiences perfectly captures how bias impacts human thinking.

In 2017, my blind student Alosha Moore, together with his guide dog Frosty, completed law school and earned a law degree. Alosha went on to pass the bar exam on the first try. After graduation, Alosha worked and continues to work for the United States Air Force as a contracting attorney. He also owns a ranch where he trains performance horses.

Alosha was born in Russia and spent the first seven years of his life in an orphanage in the city of Rostov-on-Don. Alosha was also born with glaucoma, and because of this, during his stay at the orphanage, it damaged the vision in his left eye and left him blind in his right eye. Currently, Alosha has no functioning vision in either eye.

At age eight, Alosha was adopted by an American family and began living in Wichita, Kansas. During his childhood, he recognized injustice and inequality, contradictory to the principles he was being taught in school, and this led him to pursue a career in law.

Shortly after graduating law school, Alosha was invited by a professional association to do a presentation for practicing lawyers as part of a disability continuing legal education program. At the end of his presentation, a member of the audience said to Alosha, "You are an excellent example of what this country represents. Anything is possible in the United States if you work hard. Look at where you started and despite being blind and your childhood hardships you worked hard and became successful."[1]

Undoubtedly, this statement resonates with us all and if we were present, we would have *felt* a deep and moving pride at the uniqueness of America and its meritocratic society. We would have *felt* the certainty of what appeared to be the unwavering and absolute truth that if you work hard in America, you will be successful. Alosha's response to the audience member would have brought us all back to reality.

Alosha responded by saying, "Thank you, but that is not accurate. Most people in my situation and with the handicap I have would find it impossible to become successful. I am the exception, but you are reframing me as the rule, because it is comforting. This way you avoid accepting or facing the real truth, that in this society it is damn near impossible to get ahead if you have a disability. I am the exception not the rule."[2]

Alosha and I have spoken often about the ease with which the audience member constructed and felt the truth of the meritocracy fiction he unconsciously reframed reality as. To us, it remains a classic example of system justification as a palliative mechanism. The audience member's brain, unconsciously and due to evolution, framed the facts into a narrative that conformed to the comfortable notion that we live in a just world and a good society. The cognitive load of constantly acknowledging that societal meritocracy is a myth, and rather that our reality involves gross, systemic, and sometimes random inequity, would be exhausting, depressing, and lead to social instability.

Remember, the audience member did not consciously reframe reality; his unconscious brain evolved to make him feel part of a stable and just society so he could sleep better at night rather than thinking about the intractable and painful reality of the world. We as a species can only create and maintain complex social structures we view as stable and just because we are constantly and unconsciously, evolutionarily wired to perceive events and reality in a manner that reinforces the validity of the societies we inhabit.

Just try now to think about the reality that most disabled people won't succeed in their endeavors despite their best efforts. That truth is hard to even acknowledge; our brains feel overwhelmed. We find ourselves, without trying, relegating that reality to a distant, hazy thought. This relegation of information that does not conform to your fictional reality to the level of insignificant is what I call the "meh relegation" of information due to system justification. In other words when you hear non-system-conforming information, the tendency is for your brain to shrug its shoulders and think, "Meh. Oh well," to blunt the impact of that information.

The established narratives around the efficacy of peaceful protest in bringing about societal reform are also an example of "meh relegation." Nowhere is this more evident than in the established—and false—narrative of the efficacy of Mahatma Gandhi in bringing about Indian Independence from England.

Gandhi

The British first landed in India in 1608 at the port of Surat. The initial landing was by representatives of the East India Company, who were interested in trading spices with the Indians. The East India Company had been authorized by the British Crown to establish factories and forts in the East Indies. A major turning point in the influence of the British East India Company on the Indian subcontinent occurred during the Battle of Plassey.[3]

During the Battle of Plassey, the British East India Company defeated the Nawab of Bengal, who was supported by the French. By 1772, the company had taken control of all of Bengal. This marked the beginning of the British expansion of control over vast swaths of India.[4]

The British East India Company controlled affairs in India until around 1857, when Indian soldiers employed by the company rebelled and killed the British officers in charge. This uprising led to the months-long siege of Delhi, during which the East India Company and loyal soldiers are estimated to have killed over 5,000 of the Indian mutineers.[5]

The rebellion led to the British government abolishing the East India Company and initiating direct British rule in India. This transition was formalized with the passage of the Government of India Act in 1858, which transferred power over Indian affairs from the East India Company to the Crown.[6] This marked the beginning of the British Raj, or the period of direct British rule of India, which lasted until Indian Independence in 1947.

From 1858 to 1947, there were numerous armed uprisings against British rule. While none were ultimately successful on their own, they collectively chipped away at British dominance in India. Gandhi is largely credited with achieving Indian Independence through peaceful means, but the truth is far more complex than this conveniently reframed reality.

Gandhi just happened to be the person involved in independence movements when Britain, devastated after World War II, no longer had the military capacity to maintain control over India as a territory. Seventeen years before India's post-World War II independence, Gandhi led the famous 1930 Salt March, protesting laws that prohibited Indians from selling or collecting salt from the country's salt flats.

That peaceful and powerfully symbolic protest resulted in the arrest of more than 60,000 Indians, including Gandhi himself, as well as the vicious beatings of thousands of other protestors.[7] Gandhi was released from prison in 1931, but to many Indians of the time, he was viewed as a white sympathizer whose sole goal was to appear to be morally superior by advocating for peaceful but ultimately ineffective protests.

Scholars suggest that Ghandi's approach delayed Indian Independence by suppressing the more radical Indian independence movements.[8] In fact, the notion that Gandhi's peaceful movement was the driving force behind Indian Independence is a fairy tale. By 1947, the British were no longer capable of governing India or their other colonies after the devastation they suffered during World War II. As Susmit Kumar points out, there was no Gandhi or even a Gandhi-like movement present when Britain granted independence to other colonies, such as Jordan, Palestine, Sri Lanka, Myanmar, Egypt, and Malaysia, during the same post-World War II period from 1946 to 1957.[9]

As Ramesh Chandra Majumdar points out, Indian Independence had nothing to do with Gandhi or his peaceful protest movement, which had already met with abject failure 14 years before India gained independence.[10] According to Susmit Kumar, the then British Prime Minister Clement Atlee also confirmed that Gandhi and his movement played no role in bringing about Indian Independence.[11]

Instead, we reframe the reality of the situation and support the palliative fiction that peaceful protest resulted in Indian Independence. As I wrote in a previous article:

> Gandhi is the way the British saved face when violent uprisings in the Indian colony for fifty years prior made it clear to the devastated, post-World War II, British that they could no longer control India. So instead, they deified a peace activist to pretend that their love of peace, friendliness, and civility led to Indian Independence.[12]

The power of this reframing of the truth, or "meh relegation" of information, should not be underestimated. It convinces oppressed people all over the world that peaceful protest is the solution to oppression, when the opposite is often true. Systemic power shifts rarely occur without violently disruptive events, such as the American War of Independence or the Civil War. Our cognitive reframings obscure this reality, and as a result, contribute to societal stability and the perpetuation of societal systems. We powerfully internalize and believe falsities that justify the systemic structure. As Jost would say, we engage in system justification, and in doing so, we do not experience any dissonance between reality and the palliative fictions that render our inequitable and cruel world tolerable.

Consider the discomfort and resistance you are experiencing when hearing these historical facts about the reality of Gandhi. Our minds are actively engaging in "meh relegation," dismissing reality to sustain the comforting fiction that allows us to feel good about ourselves as a species.

"Meh relegation" also makes you unable to accept that Gandhi was a racist misogynist[13] who detested the lower castes of Indian society,[14] and often invited his teenage grandniece to sleep naked in the same bed with him.[15]

But closer to home, and perhaps even more disturbing, is that we do the same thing when we celebrate Martin Luther King Jr., *Brown v. Board of Education*, and the civil rights movement.

The truth is that Martin Luther King Jr., for most of his life, was a disciple of Gandhi's methods, and his peaceful movement achieved nothing tangible.[16] White America celebrates him as a civil rights hero; however, his inefficacy ensures that his methods pose no threat to systemic structure. This celebration reinforces the notion that White Americans are such evolved and peace-loving creatures that peaceful protest alone was enough to convince them to change their stance on affording civil rights to Black Americans. Black America also celebrates him, but for different reasons. It is far more palliative to believe that his peaceful protests were effective because it obscures the reality that the civil rights achievements of the 1970s would not have materialized but for decades of violent, deadly, and disruptive struggle. Additionally, at the time, America needed to portray itself globally as a moral leader, and Jim Crow-era laws were inconsistent with this image.[17]

Even King's march from Selma to Montgomery is often misrepresented. There were multiple marches. The first took place on March 7, 1965, led by John Lewis and Hosea Williams.[18] During this march, when the protestors attempted to cross the Edmund Pettus Bridge in Selma, Alabama, they were beaten with batons and teargassed.[19] This event is now referred to as Bloody Sunday.[20] Two days later, King led approximately 1,500 Black and white marchers along the same path taken by the protestors led by John Lewis.[21] When they reached the bridge and were confronted by the police, King instructed the marchers to kneel in prayer and turn back.[22] We will never know if this march led by King was merely performative symbolism, but some of the marchers accused him of being a coward for deciding to turn the march around.[23]

Weeks later, on March 21, after a federal judge ruled the marches legal, King returned with the protection of soldiers and led a large march out of Selma to Montgomery.[24] There, he delivered his speech, where he stated that prejudice would not last long because, although change is slow, it eventually moves in the direction of justice.[25] This book demonstrates this is not true. Rather, the reality is that humans are an oppressive, violent, and conquering species, and our historical reality that "might is right" is the only true law of the universe. Yet, through "meh relegation" and the reframing of reality, we are palliatively convinced otherwise.

One white protestor who joined the march exemplifies the power of the euphoria and emotion in reframing reality when he explains: "Dr. King welcomed the multitude. The sound system was not great. We struggled to make out his words as his voice reverberated from the buildings lining the street. But his words filled our hearts like a call to worship at the shrine of equality and freedom."[26] Even though they struggled to make out his words, limbic brain emotional processing filled their hearts with the certainty of his efficacy.

This, of course, stands in stark contrast to the views of other Black civil rights leaders. For example, Malcolm X branded Martin Luther King Jr. as "Uncle Tom."[27] He stated:

> The white man supports Reverend Martin Luther King, subsidizes Reverend Martin Luther King, so that Reverend Martin Luther King can continue to teach the Negroes to be defenseless—that's what you mean by non-violent—be defenseless in the face of one of the most cruel beasts that has ever taken a people into captivity—that's this American white man.[28]

The truth is we will continue to celebrate him as one of the most important figures of the civil rights movement because our reframing of reality makes us feel happy and allows us to falsely recast ourselves as a peaceful and altruistic species governed by logic, love, civility, and common sense—even though a superficial examination of reality completely refutes this.

Our recreation of him makes white people feel comfortable and convinces Black and white people of the fiction that innate human goodness is the key to changing race relations and power dynamics. Toward the end of his life, when he realized this was not true[29] and said as much, he was killed. One year before his death, in his "Beyond Vietnam" speech, he admitted that civility and playing the good guy were not sufficient solutions to inequity and racial progress. He recognized the need for deep and systemic societal "restructuring."[30]

And even in the face of these truths I have written here, your brain conveniently minimizes the impact of this information so that you continue to exist in a comfortable world where there is no dissonance between your conception of reality and actual reality. This is the power of "meh relegation." You are engaging in meh relegating if you claim to support critical race theory being taught but reject my formulation of

MLK and the civil rights reality, because the father of critical race theory, Derek Bell, suggests I am correct.

According to Derrick Bell:

> [D]iscourse about race in America is mired in the sugarcoated myth that equality for blacks will be found just around the corner, as soon as the country completes its fitful but inevitably progressive journey toward enlightenment and justice. The myth is sweet but ultimately disabling and dangerous, he believes, because it denies to both blacks and whites understanding of a truth that is almost exactly the opposite: that racism is not a passing phase but a permanent feature of American life, and that the path is marked not by real progress but by occasional short-lived judicial or legislative victories that serve to obscure the underlying truth even more.[31]

Bell explained the civil rights movement and *Brown v. Board of Education* as a convenient convergence of white and Black interests, wherein African Americans were given a small crumb so the loaf of continued systemic racism could be baked. "In many countries, where U.S. prestige and leadership have been damaged by the fact of U.S. segregation. [*Brown v. Board of Education*] will come as a timely reassertion of the basic American principle that 'all men are created equal.'"[32] Furthermore, Bell suggests the decision offered reassurance to returning Black World War II soldiers, who were discriminated against and violently attacked in the South upon their return to America, that America was turning the page on this chapter of its history.[33]

The decision also reflected the realization that unless the South changed its image from a rural, segregated, plantation-style economy, it would be impossible to transition to the profitable Sunbelt tourism image.[34] This transition could only occur—and white landowners could only profit from it—if the South appeared to "end[] its struggle to remain divided by state-sponsored segregation."[35] Segregation was an impediment to the development of the South and the associated profits to white landowners.[36] Bell viewed the apparent success of the civil rights movement in this same vein.

I need to digress here because perpetuating the false narrative of civil rights and *Brown v. Board of Education* as an altruistic or moral shift in American attitudes towards race exemplifies how humans powerfully reframe reality for palliative reasons. Remember, in Chapter 1, I discussed how, for system justification to exist, even the socially disenfranchised or those with low socioeconomic status must buy into the palliative false narratives we create. Nowhere is this more evident than the fact that many Black scholars will be incensed when I suggest that *Brown* and the civil rights movement of the 1960s and 1970s were token rather than substantive achievements—achievements necessitated by America's need to convince the world it was worthy of being called the moral leader of the free world. Bell warned us about what we are seeing now: once those interests no longer converged, the country would creep back to its racially divisive norms.[37] This regression is evident in cases like *Students for Fair Admissions v. Harvard* (2023) and the current political climate in general.

However, African Americans—and Americans in general—feel compelled to reframe and celebrate this "crumb" as more than it is because doing so prevents an acknowledgment of the bleak truth. Celebrating *Brown* and the civil rights movement as monumental shifts in race relations shields us from recognizing that, in all societies, those in power establish the norms, and those norms persist despite demographic changes. Historically, the only thing that has changed those norms is tumultuous disruption that threatened the stability of the power dynamic. Disruptions like the Civil War. Disruptions of this magnitude are impossible now because no one wants widescale societal violence and because of the distribution of power and the militarization supporting white dominance.

So rather than face the depressive reality that there is nothing that can be done now to make any real change, we palliatively and unconsciously revise history such that what we end up celebrating when we celebrate *Brown* and the civil rights movement is how effectively we were manipulated by the *Brown* decision and the civil rights movement. But this reframing of history is not unconscious or palliative for many people who understand the truth of these events. Rather, it has become profitable. Consider the revenue generated from the countless books, films, and documentaries perpetuating these fictions about civil rights and Dr. Martin Luther King Jr. Not to mention licensing and intellectual property, and the national holidays, museums, and parks generate significant revenue as well. An example of the profitability of this reframing of reality is that the family of Martin Luther King Jr. recently charged

$800,000 for the use of his words in a memorial project on the National Mall that celebrates the life of Martin Luther King Jr.[38]

We need to realize that by celebrating the crumb, even though doing so is comforting and heartwarming and provides us with a sense of hope, what we are really doing is being sheep that are herded by the humanity of our unconscious minds. It makes us feel happy to perpetuate this myth that race relations have improved or that there was something altruistic about what happened in the sixties and seventies. The truth is that none of those beatings or protests would have amounted to anything unless white America stood to gain from the appearance of reduced racism.[39]

The fight against systemic inequity, therefore, is a fight against the weight of our evolutionary history and our very humanity. It is a fight against deeply embedded human instincts that bring us joy and motivate us to participate in a society that we reframe as favorable. Without these mechanisms at work, human societies would not be as stable as they are. The task cannot be comfortable. If it is comfortable, then it is our unconscious mind reframing reality so you never have to face the sheer magnitude of the task.

My point is that "meh relegation" is a universal, deeply embedded, and essential part of humanity. Unless we understand this, we will continually underestimate the magnitude of the task required to achieve greater racial equity. "Meh relegation" allows us to deeply believe one thing while the truth is glaringly the opposite of what we believe. More importantly, it allows us to act outside the parameters of our own sincerely held moral beliefs without realizing we are doing so.

For example, try to remember if you were incensed during the 2020 Super Bowl halftime show when J. Lo and Shakira performed in revealing outfits because you thought it demeaned women. If you were incensed, then try remembering whether you comfortably voted, in 2016, for the man who advocated, just four years earlier, for just grabbing "them by the pussy" *to be president of the United States*, even though that man oversaw the hiring of judges and government officials who would determine the rights of women. Your absolute unawareness of the inconsistency of those two positions is "meh relegation" at work.

Perhaps the uncomfortable truth is that in our patriarchal, white-dominated society, without even trying, you became angry at two minority women who were mere entertainers but accepted and justified the conduct of the majoritarian white male. And when I point this inconsistency out to you now, you simply shrug it off. Your brain does not even let you dive too deeply into the nature of the inconsistency because it would reveal that, despite you genuinely not being a racist or sexist person, you acted in a way that perpetuates a racist and sexist systemic structure—and you never even realized it. Instead of dwelling on this panic-inducing reality, you simply "meh relegated" and reframed his suggestion that sexual assault is permissible as "mere locker room talk," moving on to fill your brain with more comfortable things that don't rip the bandage from our comfortable illusion of the world. That is the palliative reality of "meh relegation." In Chapter 10, I explain in detail the cognitive science behind this phenomenon.

Endnotes

1. The statement is in quotation marks to set it off as the audience member's comment. The language in the quotes is an approximation of the statement because the exact words are lost to memory.

2. Similarly, this statement is also an approximation of the words actually spoken but they accurately convey the content of the statement.

3. WIKIPEDIA, *Battle of Plassey*, https://en.wikipedia.org/wiki/Battle_of_Plassey (last visited Dec. 26, 2024).

4. *Id.*

5. WIKIPEDIA, *Siege of Delhi*, https://en.wikipedia.org/wiki/Siege_of_Delhi (last visited Dec. 26, 2024).

6. Stanley A. Wolpert, *British Raj*, BRITANNICA (Nov. 21, 2024), https://www.britannica.com/event/British-raj.

7. History.com Editors, *Salt March*, HISTORY (June 10, 2010), https://www.history.com/topics/asian-history/salt-march.

8. SUSMIT KUMAR, MODERNIZATION OF ISLAM AND THE CREATION OF A MULTIPOLAR WORLD ORDER 17–21 (2008).

9. *Id.*

10. RAMESH CHANDRA MAJUMDAR, THREE PHASES OF INDIA'S STRUGGLE FOR FREEDOM 58–59 (1967).

11. Kumar, *supra* note 8, at 17–21.

12. Rory D. Bahadur, *Civility as Morally Justified Oppression*, TEX. J. ON C. L. & CIV. RTS. (forthcoming 2025); *The Forgotten Violence That Helped India Break Free from Colonial Rule*, THE CONVERSATION (Nov. 19, 2016, 10:45 AM), https://theconversation.com/the-forgotten-violence-that-helped-india-break-free-from-colonial-rule-57904; Kumar, *supra* note 8, at 17–21. In fact, Gandhi delayed Indian Independence. *See* SUSMIT KUMAR, RE-EVALUATING GANDHI: HOW HE DELAYED INDEPENDENCE AND MAINSTREAMED RADICAL ISLAM (2023).

13. Tanya A., *The Great Soul: Ghandi the Father of India, Ghandi the Misogynist, Gandhi the Racist*, CORNELL UNIVERSITY: CIW REPORTS, https://blogs.cornell.edu/issues/looking-at-dc/the-great-soul-gandhi-the-father-of-india-gandhi-the-misogynist-and-gandhi-the-racist/.

14. *Id.*

15. *Id.*

16. Ramin Jahanbegloo, *In Good Faith: America's Gandhi—Martin Luther King Jr.*, BOMBAY SARVODAYA MANDAL / GANDHI BOOK CENTRE (Dec. 18, 2017), https://www.mkgandhi.org/Associates%20&%20Disciples/american-gandhi-martin-luther-king-jr.php#:~:text=He%20became%20Gandhi's%20greatest%20disciple,place%20of%20justice%20in%20history.

17. Derrick A. Bell, Jr., *Brown v. Board of Education and the Interest-Convergence Dilemma*, 93 HARV. L. REV. 518 (1980).

18. Jeff Wallenfeldt, *Selma March*, BRITANNICA (Jan. 7, 2015), https://www.britannica.com/event/Selma-March.

19. *Id.*

20. *Id.*

21. NATIONAL ARCHIVES, *Selma Marches*, https://www.archives.gov/research/african-americans/vote/selma-marches (last visited Dec. 27, 2024).

22. *Id.*

23. History.com Editors, *Selma to Montgomery March*, HISTORY (Jan. 28, 2010), https://www.history.com/topics/black-history/selma-montgomery-march.

24. Jeff Wallenfeldt, *"We Shall Overcome": LBJ and the 1965 Voting Rights Act*, BRITANNICA (Jan. 7, 2015), https://www.britannica.com/event/Selma-March/We-Shall-Overcome-LBJ-and-the-1965-Voting-Rights-Act.

25. *Id.*

26. Bob Yuhnke, *Marching with King in Selma*, AMERICAN HERITAGE (2023), https://www.americanheritage.com/marching-king-selma.

27. Terry Gross, *Black Power Scholar Illustrates How MLK and Malcolm X Influenced Each Other*, NPR (Aug. 12, 2020, 12:39 PM ET), https://www.npr.org/2020/08/12/901632573/black-power-scholar-illustrates-how-mlk-and-malcolm-x-influenced-each-other.

28. TEACHING AMERICAN HISTORY, *A Summing Up: Louis Lomax Interviews Malcolm X*, (Mar. 8, 1964), https://teachingamericanhistory.org/document/a-summing-up-louis-lomax-interviews-malcolm-x/.

29. *See also* ALEX ZAMALIN, AGAINST CIVILITY: THE HIDDEN RACISM IN OUR OBSESSION WITH CIVILITY 85 (2021).

30. *See* Dr. Martin Luther King Jr., *Beyond Vietnam—A Time to Break Silence*, AMERICAN RHETORIC (April 4, 1967), https://www.americanrhetoric.com/speeches/mlkatimetobreaksilence.htm (last visited Dec. 28, 2024).

31. Linda Greenhouse, *The End of Racism, and Other Fables*, NY TIMES ARCHIVE, https://archive.nytimes.com/www.nytimes.com/books/00/06/04/specials/bell-well.html?scp=26& sq=end%2520of%2520tenure&st=cse [https://perma.cc/P8VV-3D2X].

32. Bell, *supra* note 17, at 524 (quoting Derrick Bell, *Racial Remediation: An Historical Perspective on Current Conditions*, 52 NOTRE DAME LAW 5, 12 (1976).

33. *Id.*

34. *Id.*

35. *Id.* at 525.

36. *See id*; *see also* History.com Editors, *Segregation in the United States*, HISTORY (Nov. 28, 2018), https://www.history.com/topics/black-history/segregation-united-states.

37. *See generally id.*

38. The Associated Press, *King Family Draws Fees from Memorial Project*, NBC NEWS (April 17, 2009, 2:20 PM CDT), https://www.nbcnews.com/id/wbna30267589. An example of the profitability of this reframing is that the family of Martin Luther King recently charged $800,000 for the use of his words in a memorial project on the National Mall that celebrates the life of Martin Luther King.

39. *See* Bell, *supra* note 17.

CHAPTER 4

Morality Isn't Real

Terrorism

The British governor general of the Caribbean Island of Montserrat from May 2004 to July 2007[1] was one of my former students.[2]

She explained that she only understood the uniqueness of the American passion for private property ownership, and the importance of that concept to Americans, when she became familiar with some of the details of the volcanic eruptions between 1995 and 2013 on the island which rendered large parts of the country uninhabitable and necessitated evacuations of certain regions of the country.[3] The Americans were the most reluctant to leave and had the strongest attachment to their property.

This American reverence for property ownership and its inclusion as part of the American dream is unsurprising, given the inclusion of the Takings Clause of the Fifth Amendment of the Constitution. The clause reiterates the importance of private property ownership to the essence of what it is to be American by providing, "Nor shall private property be taken for public use without just compensation."

In other words, the Constitution of the United States of America expressly provides that, when the government attempts to use privately owned land for the good of the public, the owner of that land must be compensated, regardless of how much the use of that land will benefit the public. Everyday occurrences of this include the use of private land on either side of a roadway to widen a highway as traffic begins to exceed the highway's capacity.

Contemporary illustrations of the sanctity of private property ownership include the many films and novels in which a landowner confidently commands someone—under threat of being shot to—"Get off my property," and the semi-humorous signs available for purchase everywhere that say the equivalent of "Trespassers will be shot." There is a moral certainty to the sanctity of private property ownership in America. But even this moral certainty is the product of cognitive fiction.

The Fifth Amendment and its recognition of the sanctity of private property ownership was ratified in 1791. In 1823, almost 32 years after the Fifth Amendment was ratified, the Supreme Court of the United States decided the case of *Johnson v. M'Intosh*, which held that American Indian ownership and transfer of land was invalid and unrecognizable in the United States because the American Indians were barbarians, defeated in battle, and that land obtained by conquest stripped the conquered of any rights to the land.

This disregard for American Indian ownership of land, despite the simultaneous reverence shown for white land ownership by the Fifth Amendment, was justified on principles that become clear after examining the Supreme Court's *Johnson* opinion. The opinion provides: "The right of discovery given by this commission, is confined to countries 'then unknown to all Christian people.'"[4]

Morality, therefore, involved a complete subjugation of anyone non-Christian, or in this context, non-white. As the opinion further states, non-white ownership of property was irrelevant. No other population mattered, so the settlers could pretend no one was on the land before they arrived because the land possessed by the Natives was "such remote, heathen, and barbarous lands, as were not actually possessed by any Christian prince or people."[5]

The court proclaims that even though brutal murder and genocide resulted in white land ownership, it was sustainable because:

> Conquest gives a title which the Courts of the conqueror cannot deny, whatever the private and speculative opinions of individuals may be, respecting the original justice of the claim which has been successfully asserted. The British government, which was then our government, and whose rights have

> passed to the United States, asserted title to all the lands occupied by Indians, within the chartered limits of the British colonies. It asserted also a limited sovereignty over them, and the exclusive right of extinguishing the title which occupancy gave to them.... It is not for the Courts of this country to question the validity of this title, or to sustain one which is incompatible with it.[6]

And the court goes on to state that even though, on some level, this reasoning is admittedly nonsensical and a pretense for displacing people, it is the right thing to do:

> However extravagant the pretension of converting the discovery of an inhabited country into conquest may appear; if the principle has been asserted in the first instance, and afterwards sustained; if a country has been acquired and held under it; if the property of the great mass of the community originates in it, it becomes the law of the land, and cannot be questioned. So, too, with respect to the concomitant principle, that the Indian inhabitants are to be considered merely as occupants, to be protected, indeed, while in peace, in the possession of their lands, but to be deemed incapable of transferring the absolute title to others. However this restriction may be opposed to [natural] right, and to the usages of civilized nations, yet, if it be indispensable to that system under which the country has been settled, and be adapted to the actual condition of the two people, it may, perhaps, be supported by reason, and certainly cannot be rejected by Courts of justice.[7]

So, one of the most fundamental tenets of American society, the sanctity of private land ownership and the absolute morality of the rights associated with private land ownership, only existed after white people had murdered the American Indians and taken their land. Before, when the land was occupied by American Indians, morality was irrelevant to the rights of the American Indians to the land. Once the land became owned by white people, the Fifth Amendment suddenly reaffirmed that an essential component of our governing system recognized the sanctity and inviolability of private landownership.

When the white landowners who ratified our Constitution claimed land as their own, suddenly widely accepted moral principles justified their use of deadly force to protect what was now "theirs." And deeply rooted, unquestionable fundamental principles of "justice" would support their use of deadly force to protect what was now inherently and morally theirs from people trying to take that land from them by using the very methods they used to take it from the American Indians.

Not only that, but these wealthy, white, land-owning ratifiers of the Constitution inserted a clause to ensure that even the government could not take the land from them without compensating them for it, even if the government was taking the land to benefit wide swaths of the public. In other words, if you use my land that I acquired by murderous acts of genocide, even if it is to help the public, you must pay me so that I maintain my resource-superior position.

Once white people became landowners in America, morality and justice morphed into whatever principles facilitated them retaining the land and preventing people from stripping them of the land in the very fashion they stripped others of the land. And they applied these allegedly universal moral principles to themselves as early as 1791 with the ratification of the Fifth Amendment, but as the *Johnson* case demonstrates, over thirty years after, these principles were deemed inapplicable when non-white ownership of land was at issue.

Given the American reverence for private land ownership, picture for a moment an unfortunate series of events whereby America's military shrank to the point of not being able to defend the homeland, and the rest of the planet decided to unify against the United States of America. And somehow the world decided that all the land that is now upstate New York State should be given to the descendants of the present-day Canadian Iroquois, who were forced to abandon their land and move north from what is now upstate New York after the American Revolution, when the losing British gave away their territory without consulting them.

Under threat of the use of force, imagine the world attempted to relocate every American who resided in upstate New York to other parts of the country and repopulated the land with the descendants of the Canadian Iroquois, whose ancestors once occupied the land. The Canadian Iroquois, with the backing of the world, then decided that they needed even more land and began, with the support of the world, using force to claim more land than they were given initially.

Given our passion for the sanctity of the rights associated with private land ownership, nothing would be more American than continued resistance and doing everything we could to evict those Canadian Iroquois and reclaim what is "ours." No amount of violence or terrorism would be out of the question.

This isn't hypothetical either. Terrorism is exactly what we employed when we wanted Native American land to become our land. We often conveniently forget the reality that:

> In addition to sexual abuse, the murder of Native women by U.S. soldiers and settlers was pervasive during the Indian Wars (1600–1900) and was part of the strategy of Indigenous extermination. Native women were singled out for slaughter because of their ability to sustain the tribes through childbearing.
>
> Military historian John Grenier explains that the "first way of war" in the United States included killing Native women and children and brutalizing other Native noncombatants. "Successive generations of Americans, both soldiers and civilians, made the killing of Indian men, women, and children a defining element of their first military tradition and thereby part of a shared American identity."[8]

And if this is what we employed when we were trying to take *their* land, even more violence would be tolerated when we were trying to recover land that was already established as *our* land. And it would include, just like in the American War of Independence, where the American fighters were outgunned, guerilla tactics like ambushes, hit-and-runs, and unconventional warfare. And we would be passionately certain of the morality of what we were doing. We would be considered freedom fighters.

Despite this, we Americans comfortably and unambiguously brand the Palestinians as evil terrorists, even though they are employing the very same American tactics described above while trying to recover from the world expelling them from their land in 1948 and giving their land to the Jewish settlers brutalized in the Holocaust, who were descendants of the Jewish people who left the Middle East generations prior. Yet, when we have historically deployed these tactics for the exact same reasons, we are proud American freedom fighters justified by the unextinguishable American thirst for justice, morality, and equity.

Nikki Haley, for example, understanding the predominant American sentiment towards Palestinians, wrote the genocidal message, "Finish Them," on an Israeli artillery shell, just two days after an Israeli air strike killed over 40 people, including children sheltering in tents.[9] She felt this would increase her chances of being elected.

It is the same reason seeing a picture of one Israeli hostage makes us all so sad, fearful, and sympathetic, but "Meh relegation" makes it impossible for most Americans to feel the same sympathy for the countless Palestinian children killed since 1947 and in the current post-October 7, 2023, war. It is because our brains are wired to minimize the humanity of those people we consider as "others" (Muslim and brown) that we don't question the labelling of Palestinians as barbarians.[10]

It is almost impossible for the American public to even acknowledge that, if we define terrorism as the use of threats that intimidate or coerce and violence for political purposes then the state of Israel was founded in part on terrorism as well. Remember, as part of the formation of the Israeli state, the Jewish militias, including the Irgun and the LHI, planted bombs in bus stops to kill women and children.[11]

Here are more truths about the formation of the state of Israel that system justification and bias make it uncomfortable to acknowledge:

1. In June of 1948, once the Israeli government had used force to threaten and scare Arabs from their land and decided not to allow them to return, they considered the property the Arabs had abandoned as loot.[12]
2. A year later they began systematically destroying the abandoned Arab villages and divided up the property among returning Jewish settlers.[13]
3. But during the war and immediately after, Israel also actively depopulated more than 400 villages and towns that Palestinians were living in when the Western world "gave" Israel the land the Palestinians lived on.[14]

According to Jewish scholars like Benny Morris—who is a former history professor at Ben-Gurion University, a fierce supporter of the state of Israel, and was an Israeli paratrooper—these Israeli actions were unquestionably ethnic cleansing.[15] According to Morris, however, this ethnic cleansing and genocide was "justified."[16]

Nothing should make the meaninglessness of morality patent than the fact that we reframe the conduct of a people engaging in the very same conduct we proudly consider "Murican" when it involved our westward expansion as so immoral and unjustifiable that a politician gains momentum by saying we should kill them all. And to make matters even more uncomfortable and destabilizing, how is Ukraine's struggle morally different from that of the Palestinians?

The discomfort and paralysis we feel when trying to fully acknowledge the extreme complexity of the Israel/Palestine situation is why bias and system justification exist. Think of how much relief and reduced cognitive tension we experience when our human brains unconsciously reframe the situation so that, even though it is unjustified, we end up in Nikki Haley's comfortable moral position of "meh just kill them all."

Despite the intractable parallels when we compare Ukraine and Palestine, most Americans feel empathy for Ukrainians and none for the Palestinians. Meh relegation, bias, and system justification relieve us of the cognitive dissonance of having to consciously wrestle with inconsistent parallels. Rather, our unconscious limbic brain relegates the inconsistencies, allowing us to feel morally sure about our unsupported distinctions. Without this bias mechanism, humans would be paralyzed with the complexity of everything in our world and unable to move forward with policy decisions at the speed we do. Progress would be so slow because if we carefully and consciously think about our world, very few actions seem right or wrong. Instead, bias simply brings us to a conclusion we feel is right. Once we reach these places of certainty, we can move forward as a species because it feels as though we are moving in a coherent direction. This is the reason humans have evolved so rapidly compared to other animals. Without this speedy processing, we would indeed still be cave-dwelling creatures.[17]

This need to frame our positions and beliefs as coherent or as based in something larger, like morality, prevents us from seeing even the glaring inconsistencies in our positions. For example, then-Democratic presidential nominee Kamala Harris suggested that forcing Ukraine to give up parts of its sovereign territory was not a proposal for peace but rather it was surrender.[18] And neither she, nor the media, appears to see any inconsistency between that statement and the call for a two-state solution in the Middle East, even though that solution validates Palestinians being forced to surrender at least half of their territory and making 700,000 people landless refugees in what was, until the stroke of a British pen and ensuing conflict, their homes.

Just try to consciously figure out why it is a crime for a starving individual to steal the jewelry of a wealthy person to feed their children, but it is not a crime when a pharmaceutical CEO prices a lifesaving drug at a price that results in 10,000 people dying because they can't afford it. Well, we "meh" away reality, and it becomes easy to answer the question with the bias-contrived fiction that we live in a meritocracy and a just world and people get what they deserve. So, the individual who stole the jewelry must be a worthless human, and the CEO deserves what he has because he worked for it.

COVID Lockdowns

On March 24, 2020, I sent a letter to some colleagues and some family members fiercely arguing that the COVID lockdowns were yet another example of something that felt right because they benefitted the powerful and harmed the lower-SES individuals in society. Because it maintained the societal hierarchy it felt moral.

The responses ranged from "you're a psychopath who doesn't care for people," to "you are probably right, but you should not say this right now as so many people will be angry with you." People on the left of the political middle felt absolutely certain that lockdowns were the moral, humane, and civilized thing to do.

During the lockdowns, highly educated people like law professors (I am one of them) were able to sit at home behind a computer screen and continue to earn a living. I was even able to make more than I normally did because schools from different parts of the country asked me to teach in their programs via Zoom, and I did. I would suggest the same was true for most well-educated, white-collar workers; they could work remotely without losing income.

By contrast, my oldest daughter and her husband, both in their 20s, had just moved to Omaha, Nebraska, with my two-year-old granddaughter in early 2020. They moved there because her husband, who was a bartender and worked other various positions in the restaurant industry, accepted a job as a restaurant manager with a national chain. Neither of them had a college degree.

Just as they arrived in Nebraska, COVID resulted in the shutting down of the restaurant he had moved there to manage, and now, away from home, with no family support in terms of childcare, they found themselves dealing with the expense of moving, a young child to take care of, and suddenly half of their previous income. They were at risk of losing it all, including losing health insurance for my young granddaughter. Their situation mirrored the reality of job and income loss suffered by 22 million Americans by April 2020.[19]

The lockdowns felt moral because supposedly we were protecting the vulnerable in society. But we could substitute the word "vulnerable" for "socio-economically advanced" or "elderly." In this case, the elderly were mostly retired and so had already had a lifetime of earning and were perhaps more socially influential than young people just entering the labor market.

The job loss was greatest in the leisure and hospitality industries, or industries that involve people coming in close contact with each other. Think waiters, bartenders, and hotel workers such as cleaners, receptionists, and so on. Now try to imagine who these people were. The picture that emerges for waiters and bartenders is one of young people working, perhaps to finish college or high school, or older people with limited education or potential for employment in other fields.

In terms of hotel cleaners, my mind, admittedly perhaps because of bias, paints a picture of an immigrant mother working two jobs to make ends meet. The people that the lockdowns harmed were the very people who could not afford to miss work. The people the lockdowns protected were high-income earners who could continue to earn money from home.

Morality during COVID therefore involved asking the youngest, most financially vulnerable, healthiest and *least at-risk people to develop serious COVID* to stop working completely to protect the elderly and the wealthy. In 2020, I suggested that if the shutdown went on long enough for the wealthy and more powerful in society—most of whom were able to work remotely—to run out of savings and reserves, we would see these then pro-shutdown folks beginning to adopt a different viewpoint akin to, "The economy and the entire country's economic well-being is too important to shut things down just because some people will die.

Life must go on and death will eventually happen to all of us." Once these people began suffering the mental and fiscal impacts of the lockdowns, the moral absolute that was being echoed by this crowd about human life versus the economy, would be revealed for what it was: a shallow statement that was easy to utter when their resource availability was so high they didn't have to fight for food to keep their families alive. And I was correct. Today the COVID-19 requirements are identical to the guidelines for the flu.[20]

Additionally, there was also never any real evidence that the lockdowns would work. And they did not work.[21] Rather, they were performative attempts at political favor that preyed on the emotion and panic associated with the limbic brain-driven "we have to do something, even if it doesn't make sense" approach we as humans involuntarily experience when the comforting illusion of our control over the natural world is shattered. Consider the absolute stupidity of the dining rules that mandated that you wear a mask in route to your table from the entrance of a crowded restaurant, but you were free to remove the mask during the entire time you were at the table dining. The vector was a microscopic airborne virus! Likewise, I marveled at the incredulity of constant crowds in the liquor stores which were deemed essential services during the pandemic, while restaurants, coffee shops, and groceries were either shuttered or permitted to operate at a fraction of their capacity.

The lockdowns felt moral because they justified the system by benefiting the powerful and harming the powerless. According to the IMF, COVID resulted in a global recession which caused extreme poverty for 120 million people.[22] Simultaneously, the wealth of global billionaires increased faster than at any previously observed time. In 2020, for example, they experienced an increase in net worth of $3.6 trillion and raised their share of global household wealth to 3.5%.[23]

Every policy choice we make as a species, and every choice we made during the COVID pandemic, was a choice about which segment of society should bear the burden of the pandemic. And again, what seemed moral was to let the poor and politically powerless, who would be devastated by even slight reductions in their income, become even poorer and more powerless. And this calculus did not even include the impact of isolation and stay-at-home orders on the millions of Americans with a depressive or mental health disorder.

It likely would have been illuminating to poll the people advocating for stricter shutdowns and arguing that morality makes economic destitution irrelevant whenever loss of life is at stake, to determine what percentage of those people were financially situated such that they would not have lost their ability to keep a roof over their heads and feed their families if they missed even a single paycheck.

Nowhere is the irrationality of COVID morality more evident than the left's boycott of Florida because they disagreed with Governor DeSantis' decision not to lockdown Florida during the pandemic and what they considered his anti-immigrant and sexist policies and his opposition to LGBTQ+ freedoms. Many of my wealthy, liberal friends remain, to this day, genuinely outraged and refuse to visit or vacation in Florida because they view Governor DeSantis' policies as oppressive and immoral. Yet their actions cause harm to the very people they think it is immoral to harm, and again, because of "meh information relegation," their unjustified moral certainty is unassailable.

Consider that over 300,000 people migrated to Florida from other states in the period April 2020 to April 2021.[24] Presumably, this number included hospitality and restaurant workers from states that, unlike Florida, were enforcing lockdowns, because between April 2020 and April 2021 Florida added 302,000 jobs in hospitality and leisure, which represented a 42.7% growth rate increase in these jobs in the state.[25] The people moving there were probably people like my daughter, her husband, and my granddaughter who could have become homeless because of the lockdowns in their states.

When we examine the demographics of the hospitality industry, it turns out that the left's moral outrage is counterproductive. Consider that immigrants make up 36% of the people employed as building and maintenance workers,[26] and that 27% of hotel workers are immigrants.[27] Seventy-eight percent of hospitality employees work multiple jobs,[28] and 60% of the people who have multiple jobs are women.[29] Finally, more than 16% of retail workers identify as LGBTQ compared to just 10% in the rest of the workforce.[30]

Even though DeSantis is unquestionably racist, sexist, and xenophobic, your huge liberal moral sacrifice (sarcasm present) to vacation in Europe instead of Florida doesn't hurt DeSantis or wealthy Florida, but it hurts the very class of people you insist you are defending by boycotting Florida. But once your limbic brain harnesses mood and emotion and makes you *feel* good about your performative sacrifice, your erroneous conviction is unwavering. "Meh relegation," indeed.

There was never any evidence that lockdowns would help, but we as humans basked in the palliative comfort of the illusion that we were doing something moral. And the lockdowns did not work. Countries like the Cayman Islands and China, which enforced strict lockdowns, experienced the surges in infection rates after the lockdowns that other countries experienced earlier. We killed the global economy and ensured that the poor became poorer and the rich richer for *nothing* except a baseless and indefinable concept called morality. We reframed reality so that even when our moral decisions were actually harming the most vulnerable in our society and perpetuating inequities that most people consider immoral, we were unable to see this.

Putting a Price on Human Life

Another popular and mindless retort to anti-lockdown proponents during COVID was, "Who cares about money when you can't put a price on human life?" My Jamaican ancestors, who watched their children being sold by plantation owners, would wonder how the fuck a person with a brain could say something so stupid.

But of course, it is palliative to believe in our own goodness and the justness of our species, so we reframe reality yet again and confidently utter this refrain that we consider essential to our morality, even though it is absolute bullshit. We put a price on human life all the time. Just ask an actuary what their job entails. Or ask a compensation expert in a wrongful death trial what their role is. My research assistant, who, at the time of this writing had just participated in her first wrongful death trial, commented, "I don't think may people understand that putting a price on human life is a common practice in everyday life." But we also put a price on human life in other, more conveniently invisible ways as well.

When a pharmaceutical company is allowed to price a drug such that thousands of people die each year from lack of access to that drug, we are putting a price on human life. When you claim to be pro-life because you disagree that a woman should have the right to choose, or you object to a teenager electing to have an abortion so that she can have the same opportunities at success that all males her age have, you claim we can't put a price on human life. But you are conveniently glossing over the fact that your pro-life absolutism allows you to remain fiercely opposed to universal healthcare, the lack of which puts a price on human life because the lack of universal healthcare kills almost 68,000 Americans a year.[31] And our healthcare system is the way it is because too many people make ridiculous amounts of money from the system. Consider these findings from a 2023 study:

1. "As millions of American families face bankruptcy and financial ruin because of the outrageously high cost of health care, the CEOs of 300 major health care companies collectively made $4.5 billion in total compensation in 2021."[32]
2. "While one out of four Americans cannot afford the life-saving medicine their doctors prescribe, last year ten of the top pharmaceutical companies in the United States made over $112 billion in profits, and the top 50 executives in these companies made a combined $1.5 billion in total compensation."[33]
3. "The seven major health insurance companies in America made over $69 billion in profits last year—up 287 percent since 2012."[34]

Remember, universal health care means, according to those who object to it, "My taxes shouldn't have to go to ensure that a lazy bum gets healthcare." And this moral reasoning and inconsistency ties back into the fact that our unjustified belief in a just world, or BJW, blinds us to the inconsistent and nonsensical nature of morality.

Human Sexuality

Today, in most of the Western world, monogamy is considered normal.[35] But for most of human history, monogamy was not the norm.[36] It is considered normative only because of the influence of religion. As Timothey Reing points out, "[T]here is nothing in the English-American social structure which has had more influence upon present patterns of sexual behavior than the religious backgrounds of that culture."[37]

There is no greater influence on contemporary sexuality than St. Augustine, and the idea of monogamy as good or essentially human is Augustinian in its genesis. But as I mentioned in Chapter 2, St. Augustine was a promiscuous individual and was likely a sex addict.[38] He had a mistress for more than 10 years[39] with whom he had a child, and when they separated, he took another mistress because he needed to continue to satisfy his sexual desires.[40] Augustine's view on sexuality and promiscuity as evil when it occurred outside the purpose of procreation was his way of dealing with his guilt at the power of sexual desire.[41]

St. Augustine believed that the forbidden fruit in Genesis was sex.[42] Further, he associated the pain of childbearing as punishment for sex.[43] He was so overwhelmed by sexual desire and his conclusion that sex was the greatest bodily pleasure that he thought that nothing this powerful, over which control was difficult, could be a good thing. And some interpretations of his work suggest that even sex during marriage outside of the purpose of procreation was evil.[44]

St. Augustine is responsible, then, for the traditional view of sex in the Western world. And as Martha Chamallas explains, these involved moral double standards that resulted in the subordination of women.[45] For example:

> the traditional view of sex coexisted peacefully with the double standard of sexual morality. Under the double standard, men were expected to be sexually active before marriage and on occasion to engage in casual extra-marital sex. Women were ordinarily denied such freedom and were subjected to harsh social penalties if they exerted sexual independence. One serious threat a woman could face in a society that embraced this double standard was to be labeled "immoral" and ineligible for the respectable roles of wife and mother.[46]

Beyond Christianity, this sexual double standard exists globally. Consider the dress codes of modesty and chastity for women in Islam while boys are sold into homosexual sexual slavery in Afghanistan,[47] and the established sexual trade involving Arab tourists buying underage girls in Egypt as sex slaves.[48] Additionally, consider the genital mutilations of females to prevent women from experiencing sexual pleasure in Africa, the Middle East, and Southeast Asia. Equality Now explains this genital mutilation is "largely rooted in the desire to control women's sexuality and bodily autonomy."[49] My own view is that the level of male insecurity in a society is directly proportional to the levels of control men exert over women, but that isn't scientific.

While monogamy has useful social results, therapists have known for years it is not natural or the norm. According to the *Psychotherapy Networker*:

1. Half of married women have "have at least one lover after they're married and under the age of 40;"
2. 55% of married men and 65% of married women admit to having been unfaithful.[50]

The data related to the use of dating apps and apps for affairs on the internet also sheds some light on the false normativity of monogamy. Consider that Tinder had 75 million users in 2023. In Europe, the users are almost 50% male and 50% female.[51] And 65.3% of Tinder users are in a relationship or married.[52] And there are 4 billion swipes per day on Tinder.[53] Either all these people are immoral, or we are finally seeing the reality of human sexuality in the democratized information age. Because the internet is revealing the reality of human sexuality, Millennials are not conforming to stereotypes about monogamy, and as far as sexuality is concerned, they consider themselves the "Don't Judge Generation."[54]

In fact, the reality is that adultery is a worldwide phenomenon, and this is so even in the places where adultery is punishable by death.[55] Unknown to most people is that adultery laws have their origins in barbarian laws, which considered the woman to be the property of men. As Mischler explains:

> While early prohibitions of adultery were "concerned with power, not with religion," as Christianity spread, sexual conduct took on a moral dimension. In the eighth and ninth centuries, "adultery became a sin as well as a wrong against the husband." During the Norman reforms of the twelfth century, the criminal law became more developed with the state "co-optation of private vengeance" for most crimes. Adultery, however, was not viewed as a crime against the state, but rather as an ecclesiastical offense. Because church remedies were insufficient, Norman law, explicitly or implicitly, allowed an offended husband to act on his own behalf despite the church's jurisdiction. "The state, having failed to provide an

> adequate remedy, did not punish the cuckold's vengeance, and thus institutionalized it through permission."[56]

The laws preventing adultery and fornication are concerned with preserving a patriarchal order where the only acceptable expression of female sexuality is in a monogamous marriage.[57] But the concept of monogamous marriages arose in an era when one partner in the marriage would likely be dead within a decade of marriage.[58]

More and more research suggests that monogamy is a way to control women.[59] But because our morality tends to gravitate towards preserving a patriarchy, we must "meh relegate" the reality that women very likely find it more difficult to be monogamous than men do.[60] And I ask you to do some research on the difference between the male and female refractory periods. If you are an insecure male, you most certainly will end up touting the morality and normativity of monogamy.

The bottom line is that the availability of information today via the internet has reduced the monopolistic power those with access to mass media had over the narrative of what is and isn't normal human sexuality and what is and isn't sexually moral. Dr. Alfred Kinsey concluded long ago that what humans considered deviant sexual behavior was actually normal human sexuality, and what we considered normal was a shame-based fiction.[61] This fiction was perpetuated by the moral majority's monopoly over the media and information dissemination. Now, with the internet, we understand the reality of humanity and morality.

Morality is simply the selective and unconscious processing of information such that we experience no sting of conscience when we act inconsistently with our belief set, and it simultaneously produces in us a superiority complex about our benevolence and pro-sociality, even as we engage in unspeakable cruelty and oppression.

And nowhere is this unconscious processing and reframing more apparent than in the discourse about race in America.

Endnotes

1. Wikipedia, *Deborah Barnes-Jones*, https://en.wikipedia.org/wiki/Deborah_Barnes-Jones#:~:text=In%202004%20Barnes%2DJones%20was,post%20until%206%20July%202007 (last visited May 16, 2025).

2. *The Diplomat: From the British Diplomatic Service to Washburn Law*, 53 Washburn Lawyer 16–17 (2016), available at https://wordpress.almabaseapp.com/wp-content/uploads/sites/56/2024/07/Lawyer-Spring-2016.pdf (explaining

> One person who's made her feel particularly at home is Professor Rory Bahadur. Hailing from Trinidad, Bahadur actually has family in Montserrat—business owners who were friends to Barnes Jones during her stay. If that weren't coincidental enough, he's also been heavily involved in Washburn Law's ongoing work with Free University of Tbilisi in Georgia.

3. Wikipedia, *Soufrière Hills*, https://en.wikipedia.org/wiki/Soufri%C3%A8re_Hills#:~:text=The%20Soufri%C3%A8re%20Hills%20(%2F%CB%88s,last%20eruption%20was%20in%202013 (last visited May 16, 2025).

4. Johnson v. M'Intosh, 21 U.S. 543, 576 (1823).

5. *Id.* at 577.

6. *Id.* at 588–89.

7. *Id.* at 591–92.

8. Robin Whyatt, *Violence Against Native Women Has Colonial Roots*, The Progressive Magazine (Mar. 2, 2023, 9:35 AM), https://progressive.org/magazine/violence-against-native-women-has-colonial-roots-whyatt/#:~:text=Native%20women%20were%20singled%20out,and%20brutalizing%20other%20Native%20noncombatants.

9. Moustafa Bayoumi, *Why Is Nikki Haley Scrawling Genocidal Messages on Israeli Bombs?*, The Guardian (May 29, 2024), https://www.theguardian.com/commentisfree/article/2024/may/29/why-is-nikki-haley-scrawling-genocidal-messages-on-israeli-bombs.

10. *See* Rob Copeland, *Warning of 'Grave' Errors, Powerful Donors Push Universities on Hamas*, NYTimes (Oct. 15, 2023), https://www.nytimes.com/2023/10/15/business/harvard-upenn-hamas-israel-students-donors.html.

11. Benny Morris, The Birth of the Palestinian Refugee Problem Revisited 80 (Charles Trip et al. eds., 2nd ed. 2004).

> And the IZL and LHI also committed more discriminating atrocities.... [For example], a squad of IZL or LHI gunmen on 10 February 1948 stopped an Arab truck carrying workers near Petah Tikva, took off the passengers, and killed eight and wounded 11 (apparently after robbing them). Another ten Arabs, one of them a woman, were reportedly murdered ('probably') by IZL gunmen, in early February in a grove, where they apparently worked, near Abu al Fadl ('Arab al Satariyya), west of Ramle.

12. *Id.*

13. *See id.*

14. *See id.*

15. *Id.* at 589. Morris explains:

> [T]here was nothing ambiguous about Israeli policy, from summer 1948, toward those [Palestinians] who had been displaced and had become refugees, and toward those who were yet to be displaced, in future operations: generally plied with resolution and often, with brutality, the policy was to prevent a

> refugee return at all costs. And, if somehow, refugees succeeded in infiltrating back, they were routinely rounded up and expelled. In this sense, it may fairly be said that all 700,000 or so who ended up as refugees were compulsorily displaced or 'expelled.'

16. Ari Shavit, *Benny Morris on Ethnic Cleansing*, 26 New Left Rev. 35, 42 (Mar.–Apr. 2004). Morris explains:

> There are circumstances in history that justify ethnic cleansing. I know that this term is completely negative in the discourse of the 21st century, but when the choice is between ethnic cleansing and genocide—the annihilation of your people—I prefer ethnic cleansing....
>
> That was the situation. That is what Zionism faced. A Jewish state would not have come into being without the uprooting of 700,000 Palestinians. Therefore, it was necessary to uproot them. There was no choice but to expel that population. It was necessary to cleanse the hinter land and cleanse the border areas and cleanse the main roads. It was necessary to cleanse the villages from which our convoys and our settlements were fired on.

17. Dan Subotnik, *Does Testing = Race Discrimination?: Ricci, the Bar Exam, the LSAT, and the Challenge to Learning*, 8 U. Mass. L. Rev. 332, 398 (2013).

18. DW, *Ukraine: Kamala Harris slams Ukraine 'surrender' proposal* (Sept. 27, 2024), https://www.dw.com/en/ukraine-kamala-harris-slams-ukraine-surrender-proposal/live-70329113 (last visited Jan 7, 2025).

19. Center on Budget and Policy Priorities, *Chart Book: Tracking the Recovery from the Pandemic Recession* (Apr. 3, 2024), https://www.cbpp.org/research/economy/tracking-the-recovery-from-the-pandemic-recession#:~:text=Total%20nonfarm%20employment%20fell%20by,a%20decade%20of%20job%20growth (last visited Jan. 7, 2025).

20. Youri Benadjaoud, *CDC Releases New Guidance Ending 5-Day Isolation Period for Recovering COVID-19 Patients*, ABCNews (Mar. 1, 2024, 4:31 PM), https://abcnews.go.com/Health/cdc-drops-5-day-isolation-period-recovering-covid/story?id=107725198.

21. Moshe Yanoskiy & Yehoshua Socol, *Are Lockdowns Effective in Managing Pandemics?*, Int'l J. Evn't Rsch. & Pub. Health 1, 9 (Jul. 29, 2022), https://www.ncbi.nlm.nih.gov/pmc/articles/PMC9368251/.

> While our understanding of viral transmission mechanisms leads to the assumption that lockdowns may be an effective pandemic management tool, this assumption cannot be supported by the evidence-based analysis of the present COVID-19 pandemic, as well as of the 1918–1920 H1N1 influenza type-A pandemic (the Spanish Flu) and numerous less-severe pandemics in the past. The price tag of lockdowns in terms of public health is high: we estimate that, even if somewhat effective in preventing death caused by infection, lockdowns may claim 20 times more life years than they save. It is suggested therefore that a thorough cost-benefit analysis should be performed before imposing any lockdown in the future.

22. Francisco H. G. Ferreira, *Inequality in the Time of COVID-19*, International Monetary Fund (Summer 2021), https://www.imf.org/external/pubs/ft/fandd/2021/06/inequality-and-covid-19-ferreira.htm (last visited Jan. 7, 2025).

23. Tami Luhby, *As Millions Fell into Poverty During the Pandemic, Billionaires' Wealth Soared*, CNN Business (Dec. 7, 2021, 7:05 AM), https://www.cnn.com/2021/12/07/business/global-wealth-income-gap/index.html.

24. Julia Manchester, *How the Pandemic Turned Florida Red*, The Hill (May 16, 2023, 6:00 AM), https://thehill.com/policy/healthcare/3999734-how-the-pandemic-turned-florida-red/.

25. Sarah Oulman, *Local Businesses Struggle to Find Workers to Enter Hospitality Industry*, Daily Commercial (Jun. 8, 2021, 3:28 PM), https://www.dailycommercial.com/story/news/local/2021/06/08/floridas-hospitality-industry-struggles-keep-up-demand/7582369002/.

26. Arloc Sherman, Danilo Trisi, Chad Stone, Shelby Gonzales & Sharon Parrott, *Immigrants Contribute Greatly to U.S. Economy, Despite Administration's "Public Charge" Rule Rationale*, Center on Budget and Policy Priorities (Aug. 15, 2019), https://www.cbpp.org/research/immigrants-contribute-greatly-to-us-economy-despite-administrations-public-charge-rule (last visited Jan. 7, 2025).

27. *Id.*

28. Zachary Russell, *More Workers Relying on Multiple Jobs to Get By*, Chain Store Age (Jan. 1, 2024), https://chainstoreage.com/report-more-workers-relying-multiple-jobs-get#:~:text=The%20majority%20of%20individuals%20holding,industry%20as%20a%20second%20job.

29. Gili Malinsky, *60% of People Who Work Multiple Hourly Jobs Are Women: 'They Will Do What They Have to Do'*, CNBC (Apr. 5, 2024), https://www.cnbc.com/2024/03/19/60-percent-of-those-holding-multiple-hourly-jobs-are-women.html.

30. United for Respect, *Pride in Retail*, https://united4respect.org/pride-retail/ (last visited Jan. 7, 2025).

31. Bernie Sanders, *Medicare for All Fact 2023 Sheet*, Office Of U.S. Senator Bernie Sanders (2023), https://www.sanders.senate.gov/wp-content/uploads/Fact-Sheet_Medicare-for-All-2023.pdf.

32. *Id.*

33. *Id.*

34. *Id.*

35. Joseph Henrich, Robert Boyd & Peter J. Richerson, *The Puzzle of Monogamous Marriage*, 367 Phil. Trans. Soc. B. 657 (2012), https://www.ncbi.nlm.nih.gov/pmc/articles/PMC3260845/. Explaining: "[t]oday, however, with absolute wealth gaps greater than any seen in human history, monogamous marriage is both normative and legally enforced in most of the world's highly developed countries."

36. *Id.* "Approximately 85 per cent of societies in the anthropological record permit men to marry multiple wives."

37. Timothy W. Reinig, *Sin, Stigma & Society: A Critique of Morality and Values in Democratic Law and Policy*, 38 Buff. L. Rev. 859, 872–73 (1990).

38. David S. Wisener, *Sexcapades with St. Augustine*, David S. Wisener (Nov. 15, 2014), https://davidswisener.com/2014/11/15/sexcapades-with-st-augustine/.

39. Frank A. James III, *Augustine's Sex-Life Change: From Profligate to Celibate*, Christian History Institute (1987), https://christianhistoryinstitute.org/magazine/article/augustines-sex-life-from-profligate-to-celibate#:~:text=After%20a%20year%20of%20promiscuity,for%20more%20than%20a%20decade.

40. Stephen Greenblatt, *How St. Augustine Invented Sex*, The New Yorker (Jun. 12, 2017), https://www.newyorker.com/magazine/2017/06/19/how-st-augustine-invented-sex.

41. Wijngaards Institute For Catholic Research, *St Augustine on sexuality*, https://www.thebodyissacred.org/origin-st-augustine-sexuality-sin-sex-pleasure/ (last visited Jan. 7, 2025).

42. Charles Phillips, Another Look at Sex: The Biblical Perspective 41–44 (1994).

43. *Id.*

44. Greenblatt, *supra* note 40.

45. 42 Martha Chamallas, *Consent, Equality, and the Legal Control of Sexual Conduct*, 61 S. Cal. L. Rev. 777, 787–89 (1987). The subordination of wives meant that the only legitimate environment for sex was destined to be controlled by men. Although men as well as women could feel trapped by a traditional marriage, women typically had more to lose from divorce than men. Women were less likely to remarry and were far more vulnerable to poverty if they had no support from a man.

46. *Id.*

47. *FRONTLINE: The Dancing Boys of Afghanistan* (PBS television broadcast, Apr. 20, 2010).

48. Daily Mail Reporter, *Sordid Trade in the 'Summer Brides': Arab Tourists Are 'Buying Underage Egyptian Sex Slaves' to Serve Them for Just a Few Months*, DailyMail (July 15, 2012, 5:10 EST), https://www.dailymail.co.uk/news/article-2173796/Rich-Arab-tourists-buying-age-brides-Egypt-just-summer-3-200.html.

49. Equality Now, *Female Genital Mutilation (FGM)*, https://equalitynow.org/female-genital-mutilation/#:~:text=It%20is%20largely%20rooted%20in,male%E2%80%9D%20or%20%E2%80%9Cunclean.%E2%80%9D (last visited Jan. 7, 2025).

50. Tammy Nelson, *The New Monogamy: How Far Should We Go?*, Psychotherapy Networker (July 7, 2010), https://www.psychotherapynetworker.org/article/new-monogamy/?srsltid=AfmBOorYo1drpvJ_SLk-QWlb3YRtNggPQVxchNVPwS94-YpToRws5Vvd.

51. Mansoor Iqbal, *Tinder Revenue and Usage Statistics (2024)*, Business of Apps (Oct. 8, 2024), https://www.businessofapps.com/data/tinder-statistics/.

52. Brooke Kato, *Most Tinder Users Are in Relationships or Married: 'Game of Deception'*, New York Post (July 14, 2023), https://nypost.com/2023/07/14/majority-of-tinder-users-are-in-relationships-or-married-survey/.

53. Ben Bailey, *Tinder Statistics 2025: All You Need to Know About the Dating App!*, Roast (Updated Jan. 1, 2025), https://roast.dating/blog/tinder-statistics.

54. Cathy Lynn Grossman, *Millennials Are the 'Don't Judge Generation' on Sexual Morality: Survey*, Religion News Serv. (Mar. 27, 2015), http://www.religionnews.com/2015/03/27/millennials-dont-judge-generation-sexual-morality-survey/.

55. Linda Fitts Mischler, *Personal Morals Masquerading as Professional Ethics: Regulations Banning Sex Between Domestic Relations Attorneys and Their Clients*, 23 Harv. Women's L.J. 1, 21–22 (2000).

56. *Id.* at 28.

57. *Id.* at 24.

58. Tammy Nelson, *The New Monogamy: How Far Should We Go?*, Psychotherapy Networker (July 7, 2010), https://www.psychotherapynetworker.org/article/new-monogamy/?srsltid=AfmBOorYo1drpvJ_SLk-QWlb3YRtNggPQVxchNVPwS94-YpToRws5Vvd.

59. Ali Ziegler, Jes L. Matsick, Amy C. Moors, Jennifer D. Rubin & Terri D. Conley, *Does Monogamy Harm Women? Deconstructing Monogamy with a Feminist Lens*, 22 J. Für Psychologie 1–18 (2014).

60. Justin Lehmiller Ph.D., *Monogamy May Be Even More Difficult for Women Than It Is for Men*, Vice (Sept. 9, 2018, 12:00 PM), https://www.vice.com/en/article/monogamy-may-be-even-more-difficult-for-women-than-it-is-for-men/.

61. Lawrence S. Kubie, M.D., *Psychiatric Implications of the Kinsey Report*, 10 Psychosomatic Med.: J. of Behavioral Med 95–106 (March 1948).

CHAPTER 5

Unconscious Racism

Even though I focus on unconscious racism in this book, I do not discount the impact of deliberate and conscious racism and the significant role it played and continues to play in shaping American society. However, I ignore it in this book for two reasons. The first is you can't fix stupid, and even if you can, I don't want to spend my precious brief time on earth engaging with idiots who believe skin color validly determines hierarchy. They are beyond the scope of this work.

The second reason is that over 70% of white Americans now genuinely believe racial discrimination is problematic.[1] Therefore, I prefer to focus on teaching this significant majority of white people how, even though they genuinely believe they are antiracist, they perpetuate systemic racism unconsciously. I would say accidentally, but that word seems a little too generous given what I have to say in this section of the book. The following are examples of the racist realities in our society that we fail to recognize because of the same palliative, cognitive reframing, or "meh" relegation of information this book has already discussed in other contexts.

Poland and Refugees

In 2022, at the height of the Russian invasion of Ukraine, Poland took in 100,000 Ukrainian refugees per day. Western news entities celebrated the generosity and kindness of the Polish people.[2] Poles felt a deep and genuine solidarity with the Ukrainian refugees, which the world recognized and celebrated as the quintessentially moral, human, and natural obligation to help their fellow humans in their hour of need.[3] For example, University of Warsaw Sociologist Przemyslaw Sadura describes the Polish welcoming of Ukrainian refugees as *feeling* "like a festival of solidarity, a reflex."[4] Polish border towns also suggested that they did not need donations because they had abundant supplies of everything they needed for the refugees.[5] Today, over 1 million Ukrainian refugees live in Poland, unsure of when or if they might return home.

However, in November of 2021, when approximately 3,000 to 4,000 Syrian refugees whose country had also been destroyed by Russia tried to enter Poland from Belarus, the Polish response was the polar opposite of what the response to the Ukrainians was.

In November of 2021, in freezing conditions, these migrants, who were invited to Belarus, tried to cross into Poland to seek asylum. The migrants included children. When they tried to enter Poland, they were forcibly repelled by the Polish army with teargas and water cannons.[6] Poland sent 12,000 troops to the border region and reinforced the border with barbed wire.[7] The migrants ended up stranded between Belarus and Poland and some froze to death.[8]

A CBS News senior correspondent in Kyiv justified the difference in treatment by suggesting that the Ukrainians were *civilized* in contrast to the refugees from the Middle East:

> This isn't a place, with all due respect, like Iraq or Afghanistan that has seen conflict raging for decades. This is a relatively civilised, relatively European—I have to choose those words carefully, too—city where you wouldn't expect that, or hope that it's going to happen.[9]

Similarly, news organizations broadcast Ukrainians making Molotov cocktails and went into detail about how the use of grated Styrofoam helped the devices stick better to cars.[10] One social media user correctly observed that if this was being "done by Palestinians, Afghanistan or other nations resisting occupation, it would be terrorism," but when Europeans are doing it is reframed as "resistance."[11] Another social media commentator captured the hypocrisy perfectly in his statement that "It would be great to see just a little of that enthusiasm for the legitimacy of armed resistance extend to people who are not white."[12] Claudia Webb, a British MP, also captured the dissonance in the treatment of people based on color as follows: "The sorrow & despair we all feel for Ukraine should be identical to the sorrow & despair we feel for Yemen, Palestine & Syria."[13]

But we don't *feel* the same, and we *can't* feel the same without confronting the fact that the distinctions and rules we draw to justify our actions, and the very structure of our society, are incoherent and empirically baseless. Instead of acknowledging that, we reframe reality into a series of empirically unsustainable paradigms such as civility[14] to prevent us from confronting the hypocrisy of our own morality. Meh relegation at is finest. Where was the Western media's in-depth coverage of the contrast between Syrian and Ukrainian refugees by Poland? It was non-existent because we could not consciously see and develop this narrative without feeling uncomfortable about our own society. We "meh relegated" the information to the realm of the insignificant.

In a previous article, I demonstrated how the illusion of civility allows us to feel comfortable with our hypocrisy and inequitable treatment of people based on race:

> For example, in 1819 after massacre and genocide to get their land, Congress decided to "civilize" the First Peoples by "[assigning religious denominations] to specific tribes. While encouraging the tribes to convert, the hired missionaries also urge[d] them to adopt white styles of dress, housing, and farming." System justification prevents us from recoiling at the patent irony and dissonance that the people who behaved in the most uncivilized and barbaric fashion, engaged in ethnic cleansing to dominate another culture and obtain their land, suggested that civility meant adopting the same religion that rendered the obscenity of civility invisible.[15]

Similarly, in *Against Civility: The Hidden Racism in Our Obsession with Civility*, Alex Zamalin suggests that an overemphasis on "civility" suppresses minority voices and perpetuates systemic racism.[16] Zamalin contends that calls for civility are often nothing more than ensuring that we give priority to the comfort of the powerful at the expense of the injustice of inequity. This prioritization dissuades protest, dissent, and change.[17] Ultimately, according to Zamalin, civility is an effective tool for preserving the status quo while simultaneously dissuading and silencing frank and open debate about the need for racial justice.[18]

And to loop back to Chapter 2, about religion, part of the effectiveness and stability of the baseless civility distinction is that civility has its roots in the divine, and according to Theresa Johnson, this theory of divine origin necessarily implies some people are naturally civil, while others are not.[19] Civility is a convenient concept that masks what may be the only true norm of human behavior: might is right. And in America, might is white. I intend to back up that controversial statement.

But first, it is necessary to define whiteness. "Whiteness and white racialized identity refer to the way that white people, their customs, culture, and beliefs operate as the standard by which all other groups are compared."[20] The rest of this chapter examines many of the things clearly proving white privilege to be true that we constantly "meh relegate" into irrelevance.

World War II as White Privilege

Even though we love to pretend that the Greatest Generation got involved in the war to do the ethical and morally correct rescue of the Jews from the Holocaust, that aim was a late development close to the end of the war. We got involved in the war when Japan bombed Pearl Harbor, and we only declared war against Japan, and initially did not declare war against Germany, even though the Holocaust was occurring. Rather, two days after we declared war on Japan, Germany declared war on the U.S., and then we reciprocated with a declaration of our own against Germany.[21] Before that, America was largely unconcerned with the Holocaust and the murder of the Jewish people. For example, in 1938, *Time* magazine named Hitler as its "Man of the Year," and the story only tangentially mentioned the murder of the Jewish people; when it did, it mentioned this atrocity only as one of number of other atrocities committed against other people by the Nazis.[22]

Perhaps this was because, up until World War II, American Jews viewed themselves as a distinct race with a unique connection to their religion and culture, and white America also viewed Jewish Americans as a different race.[23] White America considered the Jews as an insular group that kept to themselves, did not intermarry, and lived in distinct Jewish neighborhoods.[24] At the highest levels of government, anti-Jewish sentiment was patent. Kennedy and Lindbergh, for example, suggested that American Jews seeking greater American involvement in the Holocaust were merely trying to push America to war.[25] Scholars suggest that antisemitism was the motivation for Congress not increasing the established immigration quota to allow 20,000 Jewish children into the country in 1939.[26]

In fact, even though the declaration of war against Germany was made in 1941, we were still turning away Jewish refugees by the thousands in 1942.[27] And before that, in 1939 we did not allow the passengers of the vessel *St. Louis* into America when the ship docked in Miami.[28] The vessel was transporting over 900 European Jews fleeing the Holocaust and seeking asylum.[29] About 25% of those passengers who were not allowed to land in America were subsequently murdered by the Germans in the Holocaust when they were forced to return to Europe.[30] And as late as April 1939, 83% of Americans opposed any legislation to change immigration laws to facilitate Jewish resettlement in America.[31]

By 1944, however, President Roosevelt created the War Refugee Board, though by then five years had passed before the U.S. finally designated the European Jews as refugees and the Holocaust as an example of genocide.[32] Only then did saving the Jewish people become official U.S. policy. At the time the War Refugee Board was formed, antisemitism and the associated tropes led most Americans to believe that the Jewish people brought the Holocaust on themselves.[33] How this government agency was able to reframe American public opinion so that the public eventually viewed the Jewish people as innocent victims of murder and tyranny—deserving of American help—is an example of the power of whiteness or white privilege.

In 1944, the War Refugee Board issued the following official U.S. government statement describing the Jewish people as "innocent victims":

> [H]undreds of thousands of Jews ... are now threatened with annihilation as Hitler's forces descend more heavily upon

> these lands. That these innocent people, who have already survived a decade of Hitler's fury, should perish on the very eve of triumph over the barbarism which their persecution symbolizes, would be a major tragedy.[34]

The shift in the political will that the War Refugee Board facilitated was multifaceted, but one essential component of that shift was fueled by the massive, government-level efforts to change the discourse by using the media to flood the public with stories about the suffering of the Jewish people.[35] Additionally, the War Refugee Board began using the term "extermination camp" instead of "concentration camp."[36] The War Refugee Board generated publicity about what was happening at the camps through extensive publication of eyewitness reports and made sure to suggest to publishers that books about the Holocaust be considered for book-of-the month type designations.[37]

At the same time, activist groups such as the Bergson Group took out full-page ads in major newspapers, graphically demonstrating the suffering and horrors experienced by the Jewish people.[38] This group, led by Hillel Kook (aka Peter Bergson), who was a Palestinian Jew,[39] also arranged with others the production of a Broadway play highlighting the plight of the Jewish people titled *We Will Never Die*.[40] The play debuted in March of 1943, with audience numbers in excess of 40,000, and was also staged in five other large North American cities.[41]

But the most effective method to alter public opinion occurred in November 1944, when the War Refugee Board released eyewitness accounts of the atrocities at the Auschwitz and Birkenau camps to all the major newspapers, accompanied by a War Refugee Board letter describing the camps as "German Extermination Camps" and containing the following statement: "It is a fact beyond denial that the Germans have deliberately and systemically murdered millions of innocent civilians—Jews and Christians alike—all over Europe [and] the Board has every reason to believe that these reports present a true picture of the frightful happenings in these camps.[42]"

Most of the larger newspapers and at least 70 smaller ones carried the story generated by the War Refugee Board, and the War Refugee Board was thrilled with the reaction of the public and the change in sentiment towards the Jews they had achieved.[43] Just a week after the reports were first published, over 75% of Americans agreed that the Germans had murdered people in concentration camps. According to Goldstein, by the end of World War II, the Jews had become part of the American white mainstream, and this was in large part due to the efforts of the War Refugee Board.[44] This inclusion of the Jewish people in the white mainstream was the reason the War Refugee Board's campaign resulted in the *moral outrage* among the American public at the fact that America was not doing more to rescue the Jews. Today, most American Jews identify as white.[45]

This moral outrage would never have existed if the vast majority of the European Jews were people of color instead of Ashkenazi Jews, who present as phenotypically white and which the American population could feel a kinship with and empathy for. Two things make this clear.

The War Refugee Board represents the only time America has ever "founded a government agency to save the lives of non-Americans being murdered by a wartime enemy."[46] It is undeniable that since World War II, we have had ample opportunities to save millions of people of color whose governments are committing mass atrocities against their own people, but we have never done so in a single instance. We have not, nor will we ever, threaten military force to save the Uyghurs in China, even though we suspect that over a million people have been forced into internment, tortured, and sterilized. We will never help the Rohingya in Myanmar, despite concrete proof of mass killings, sexual violence, and forced removal. We will never help the Tigray in Ethiopia even though thousands of civilians have been killed and millions are refugees because of the violence. Similarly, there will be no American rescue or offer of refugee status to the non-Arab citizens of Darfur or the Yazidis in Iraq and Syria. Additionally, there was no U.S. involvement in Rwanda in 1994, where almost a million Tutsis and Hutus were killed in 100 days.

The second, and more viscerally painful, truth is personal to me. You will recall in the introduction, I mentioned that my Jamaican maternal grandmother's last name was Dryden. Her first cousin Charles Dryden (Uncle Charlie, as my mother and her siblings knew him), fought against the Germans as a Tuskegee Airman and authored the book *A-Train: Memoirs of a Tuskegee Airman*. In his book he, like others, documented the fact that the white American GIs treated the German prisoners of war better than they treated African American soldiers who participated in the fight to liberate the Jews.[47] He recalls visiting a base in South Carolina after the war, where German POWs were allowed to enter "the

'White' side of the post exchange cafeteria and WE COULD NOT!"[48] Similarly, Black soldiers were made to eat in the kitchen while white Nazi prisoners of war were served their meals in the main dining halls.[49] Black soldiers were deliberately humiliated by the white soldiers and were, for example, made to dump the feces of the army camp, including the feces of the white POWs.[50] Additionally, Black soldiers were required to squeeze into the crowded coach compartments of trains, while the Nazi prisoners of war, sitting in the spacious compartments with their white guards, laughed at the Black soldiers.[51]

In the book, even after desegregation, Dryden, an American soldier, remained uncertain and nervous about how they would be treated. This man who fought for the United States found himself asking, "could I get in the PX barber shop without worrying about having my hair chopped up, at the least, or my throat cut, at the worst?" All because he was not white.[52]

Even as we felt morally compelled to rescue the phenotypically white European Holocaust victims, we were simultaneously blind to the situation of our own Black citizens, whom we had brutally and cruelly enslaved for centuries. Citizens whom we had branded like cattle, amputated limbs from when they tried to escape, sold the children of, and considered property, and to whom we had effectively denied the right to vote until 1966, when the Supreme Court decided *Harper v. Virginia Board of Elections*.[53] At this same time, America was still operating Native boarding schools, ripping apart Native families, and denying them their basic human rights. Justice Neil Gorsuch, in *Haaland v. Bracken*,[54] describes these Native boarding schools as a deliberate attempt to forcibly remove Native children from their families and to educate them in the European tradition so that they would forget and abandon their culture. The project of disappearing the American Indian could be achieved through cultural genocide by creating "an existential threat to the continued vitality of the Tribes."[55]

This country was outraged at the suffering of the Jews because the Jews were white, and it treated Nazi POWs better than Black servicemen who fought to liberate the Jews because those POWs were white. *That is white privilege.* The term does not imply that individual white people have not suffered or experienced hardship. To interpret the term as suggesting that it implies all white people have it easy, or that it means no white person has experienced poverty, destitution, and a hellish existence, is a deliberate and unforgivable choice to replace reality with fake outrage. One drive through Appalachia makes this interpretation asinine.

But every single white person in America has benefited from this reality because they are perceived as more "normal," given the benefit of the doubt, and empathized with more than people of color in the same situation.[56] Even as we were celebrating the morality of our efforts and liberating white people who had been subject to German cruelty for nine years, we treated the Black soldiers who fought alongside us to liberate the Holocaust victims with disdain, even though, at that time, Black people had been subjected to our own unspeakable cruelty and oppression for 300 years.

Perhaps the most important part of this narrative is that the U.S. government engaged in a multifaceted, government-level campaign to change American sentiment towards the Jewish people. The government launched a massive information dissemination strategy to try to reduce antisemitism, such that it eventually became politically expedient to resettle the Jewish people. I suggest that there has never been an equivalent government public relations effort for African Americans, who were enslaved for centuries, though emancipated by the time the War Refugee Board was in full swing, or for Native Americans, whose families were being separated by boarding schools and child welfare systems that removed children from the home and placed them with white families for adoption up until the 1970s.[57] Furthermore, because of unconscious biases and the cognitive mechanisms examined in Chapter 10, I am not sure that such an effort could engender the same level of empathy and compassion among white Americans for dark-skinned people.

If we think of white privilege in this way, it becomes less of a divisive term and more of a reality of our social structure—one that, like all societies, seeks to perpetuate itself and buttress the status quo through the unconscious processing mechanisms mentioned in Chapter 2. Built into the revulsion white people have for the term "white privilege" is the erroneous belief that every individual, regardless of race, has equal opportunity for success in America. Hopefully, the discussion in this chapter has already proven that belief set to be false. But if you aren't convinced, read on.

The Inequity of the GI Bill

The systemic inequity continued after the Greatest Generation returned from World War II with the GI Bill. The GI Bill, or Servicemen's Readjustment Act, was federal legislation passed in June of 1944.[58] The bill was a response to the poor support we provided soldiers returning from World War I. Among other things, the bill provided veterans educational benefits, and the federal government paid for college and vocational schooling for returning veterans.[59] The bill also ensured the availability of low-interest loans to returning veterans so they could purchase homes, farms, and open businesses.[60]

Between 1945 to 1956, at least half of the veterans who served in World War II took advantage of the GI Bill, resulting in 2.2 million veterans going to college, 3.5 million going to technical or vocational school, and 700,000 taking instruction in agriculture.[61] The GI Bill was also responsible for the fact that the number of Americans with college degrees increased from 200,000 before the war to almost 500,000 after the war.[62]

We readily accept that the GI Bill allowed more people access to higher education and homeownership and that it created America's robust middle class after World War II.[63] We also view the GI Bill as an expression of how much we deservedly revere and respect the men and women who choose to put their lives on the line for America's security.[64] It is widely regarded as one of the most important socio-economic pieces of legislation in American history[65] because, by 1947, half of America's college students were veterans, and the GI Bill was responsible for the United States prospering post-World War II rather than experiencing a post-war recession.[66] To try to quantify the massive impact of the bill, consider that the bill was responsible for the funding the education of "of 22,000 dentists, 67,000 doctors, 91,000 scientists, 238,000 teachers, 240,000 accountants, and 450,000 engineers, as well as three Supreme Court justices, three presidents, a dozen senators, 14 Nobel Prize winners, and two dozen Pulitzer Prize winners."[67]

But it is hard to hear another truth—that the GI Bill was also the most effective tool for the exacerbation of the massive post-war, race-based discrepancy in wealth in America.[68] The GI Bill was originally envisioned to be administered federally, but Southern senators, most notably John Rankin of Mississippi, insisted that the individual states should administer the bill instead.[69] Rankin was an "unrepentant segregationist" who was against interracial marriage and had previously suggested the enactment of federal law mandating the confinement and deportation of everyone with Japanese ancestry during World War II. He did not think white and Black veterans should get the same benefits.[70]

Black veterans were denied benefits officially and unofficially. Officially, some were denied benefits because they had not been discharged honorably, when the reality was that Black veterans were "not honorably discharged" via a special discharge known as the "blue discharge," which was disproportionately given to homosexual and Black veterans. Between 1941 and 1945, over 22% of the blue discharges went to Black soldiers, even though they made up less than 7% of the Army.[71] This official policy resulted in nearly 25% of Black American veterans of World War II being denied benefits under the GI Bill, which prevented benefits to any one not honorably discharged.[72] The racism involved in this reality is exemplified by the blue discharge issued to African American veteran Nelson Henry Jr., who was discharged because he was deemed to have traits of character that were undesirable.[73] The blue discharge was an unspecific discharge, akin to an administrative discharge, that provided broad discretion in its utilization.

But unofficial methods were employed to prevent Black veterans from receiving benefits. Black veterans were intimidated when crowds hurled rocks at them as they attempted to move into a housing development in Chicago. And in Indianapolis, for example, vocational training programs claimed that, because the necessary equipment was available only to white students, Blacks were not able to learn trades such as plumbing and electricity.[74]

The bill was also administered to perpetuate racial inequity. For example, when the original GI Bill ended in 1956, over 8 million veterans had been educated or trained, and a total of 33 billion dollars had been given out for over 4 million home mortgages. These benefits, however, went disproportionately to white veterans, creating steep increases in college education and wealth for whites. Most Black veterans, however, were excluded from receiving these benefits, and as a result, the GI Bill exacerbated an already preexisting gap in wealth and education between Blacks and whites.[75]

For example, in Mississippi in 1947, there were a total of over 3,000 mortgages supported by the GI Bill, but only 13 of these mortgages were issued to Black veterans,[76] even though Mississippi's population at the time was 45% Black.[77] This disparity was not unique to the South but was observed nationwide.[78] In the New York and New Jersey suburbs, for example, over 67,000 GI Bill mortgages were issued, but fewer than 100 of these were issued to non-white veterans.[79]

The decision by Senator Rankin to deliberately disenfranchise Black veterans is an example of overt or conscious racism. It is a deliberate decision to treat a person differently based on their skin color. Our inability to internalize and accept the truth of the GI Bill, because it causes dissonance with our comforting, flag-waving, apple-pie-eating, fairy tale of American meritocracy, individualism, and equality, is how unconscious racism takes hold. We "meh relegate" to the realm of insignificance the uncomfortable information that causes us to reexamine everything we hold true and dear.

It is more comforting to pretend that every individual, regardless of color, has the same opportunity in America rather than face the truth that massive and powerful, government-level systems buttress the disparities in socioeconomic status based on race that originated in slavery. Whether those systems are express, like Jim Crow, or implicit and hard to stomach, like the untold reality of the GI Bill's administration and redlining, the effect is the same: the systemic perpetuation of inequality based on race. This is systemic racism.

And if you refer to Chapter 2 and reexamine Alosha's response to the audience member, you will know the error of trying to disprove systemic racism by pointing out that some Black individuals are wealthy and successful. Because of the cognitive reframing already discussed at length in this book, we normalize the exception and fail to see the true magnitude of systemic hierarchies.

And this is where the religion discussion in Chapter 2 again becomes relevant, because religion tends to focus only on the behavior of individuals and, in so doing, perpetuates the myth that individual reform and behavior are the keys to resolving inequity. However, religion's focus on individual behavior and reform significantly buttresses systemic inequity by diverting attention away from the need for systemic reform.

According to Robin DiAngelo, the typical argument genuinely antiracist, well-meaning white people make in support of individualism can be summarized as follows:

> My race has not made a difference in my life, so why do we have to talk about race as if it mattered? It is talking about race as if it mattered that divides us. I don't see myself as a member of a racial group; you shouldn't see me that way either. In fact, by saying that my group membership matters, you are generalizing. Generalizing discounts my individuality; unless you know me, you can't profess to know anything about my life and all of the ways I am unique relative to any one else. Further, as an individual I am objective and view others as individuals and not as members of racial groups. For example, if I were hiring I would hire the best person for the job no matter what their race was. Racism will disappear when we all see each other as individuals. In fact, it has disappeared because I already see everyone as individuals—it's just misguided people such as yourself who refuse to see everyone as an individual and thus keep racism alive.[80]

In her research, DiAngelo then lists eight specific ways in which the discourse of individualism distracts us from the reality of systemic racism. I will explore two of them here. She suggests that individualism hides the reality that individuals have different access to resources for success depending on whether they are perceived as white or as a non-white person.[81] Hopefully, the discussion of World War II and the GI Bill above demonstrate that people do have different access to resources based on their race. She also suggests that the discourse on individualism hides the unique accumulation of generational wealth white people were able to amass.[82] She explains that individualism masks the reality that the country was founded on slavery and that, even after slavery, we deliberately excluded people of color from wealth-generating opportunities—for example, through legislation that denied people of color access to FHA loans through the 1960s.[83] In this regard, she also points out that these exclusionary mechanisms continue through today via "illegal but common practices such as higher mortgage rates, more difficulty getting loans, real estate agents steering them away from 'good' neighborhoods, discrimination in hiring, and unequal school funding."[84]

Hopefully, this reveals the illegitimacy of the frequently posited "I didn't own slaves so I didn't benefit from racism" argument[85] and reinforces my claim in Chapter 2 that religion, with its focus on individual conduct, can never be the mechanism by which systemic reform is achieved.

This discussion of World War II and the GI Bill provides a nice segue into examining how systemic racism rears its ugly head when a Black athlete kneels during the playing of the national anthem. Our unconscious minds prefer to create comfortable, yet stupid and simple, fictions that determine the worth of a person by whether he chooses to stand or sing, rather than engage in the painful examination of history and reality required for an informed viewpoint.

Kneeling Athletes

The American national anthem was written by a slave owner at a time when he still owned slaves, and the third verse of the song we chose as our anthem glorifies the recapture of escaped slaves.[86] Here is the third verse of the song chosen as the United States' national anthem in its entirety:

> No refuge could save the hireling & slave/
> From the terror of flight or the gloom of the grave:/
> And the star-spangled banner in triumph doth wave/
> O'er the land of the free & the home of the brave.[87]

Yes, it's a lot more comfortable to "meh relegate" this truth and replace the complex, uncomfortable thoughts it generates with the simple, comfortable, yet asinine, "He's kneeling therefore he hates America."

Additionally, the author of the song aggressively prosecuted the founders of the anti-slavery movement and was close to the president at the time, Andrew Jackson, who was also a slave owner. Does none of this really matter to us? Or are we choosing to pretend that the anthem and its origin are unassailable, that America is a pure and perfect nation, and even demonizing me for writing the truth?

Admittedly, for all humans, regardless of race, it is simpler to reinforce societal status quos by reformulating reality. However, if this is what we decide to do in the face of uncomfortable truth, then perhaps we should not label ourselves as antiracist. Know that no matter what neutral image we convincingly conjure up of ourselves, we are facilitating racism, regardless of how good and kind we genuinely believe we are.

America is the greatest nation on earth, but that cannot justify stupidity and the refusal to understand and examine the complex dynamic of race relations in this country. Ultimately, if your attitude to Black and white athletes protesting *racial* inequity by kneeling remains unchanged after reading and understanding these harsh truths, is your racism really still unconscious? And if you hate Megan Rapinoe, it isn't because she is kneeling, but because she demonstrates that some white people are willing to face the uncomfortable truths of this great nation's past rather than hide behind fairy tales.

As Aaron Skubby eloquently explains, the story we say is the story of America contradicts the truth behind the founding of America.[88] We tend to recreate the falsity that fortunes and wealth was amassed by pure individual effort, while the truth is that systemic inequity and widespread racism facilitated the wealth of white people, built on the labor of slaves and the dehumanizing and legally sanctioned subordination of people of color.[89]

Crackheads versus Opioid Victims

If I asked you to describe a "crackhead," most likely you would think of a Black man or woman in the inner city, and you would further impute some defect in character to them as the reason they made the conscious and voluntary decision to smoke crack. In this way, they are to blame for the unfortunate results of their poor decision-making and values.

The National Institute of Health confirms that society generally perceives

> the crack user based on the user's virtual image, disregarding his/her real image, i.e., it does not see him/her as a singular person, with a life history, feelings, desires, learning, gains and losses. A stigmatizing identity of marginals, bums and violent persons predominates, creating the idea of non-citizens, without a social place, the ones who should be excluded.[90]

The ease with which we dehumanize and criminalize crack addicts is because the crack epidemic has been framed as an urban Black issue.[91] While crack cocaine was perceived as a Black drug, powdered cocaine was considered the drug of the white Hollywood elite—the drug the cool kids used. As a result, until 2010, people convicted of crack cocaine possession received a sentence that was 100 times longer than people arrested for the same amount of powdered cocaine.[92] After 2010, the disparity in sentencing time is 18:1, but there still is a disparity. There was never a valid scientific reason justifying the harsher sentences for crack possession as compared to powdered cocaine addiction, other than systemic racism. Because they are generally perceived as white, powdered cocaine "users" are framed as successful rich dudes blowing off steam, but "crackheads" are "associated with irresponsible practices, unrestricted pleasure, delinquency and the confrontation of socially accepted habits and customs."[93] Observe how even the way we refer to the people suffering from the disease of addiction differs based on the racial identity of the users. Powder cocaine addicts are "users," whereas crack cocaine addicts are "crackheads," suggesting that their entire identity is subsumed by their addiction.

But when white children started getting addicted to opioids by taking their parents' pain pills, our framing of addiction no longer involved individual delinquents doing something irresponsible because of innate character and personality flaws, as it was framed for crack addiction. Instead, addiction was reframed as a public health emergency—a disease affecting our good and innocent American children. As the Equal Justice Initiative points out, "when white people started getting addicted and dying from opioids, the narrative shifted. Those abusing heroin and prescription painkillers were routinely depicted in the media as sympathetic victims."[94]

The response to crack addiction, because it was perceived as a Black issue, was to criminalize and incarcerate. Congress "dedicated three-quarters of $1.7 billion in federal funds to law enforcement and incarceration [and] in 1988, Congress provided hundreds of millions more for police and prisons, and made crack the only drug for which simple possession was a federal crime."[95] By contrast, in response to opioid addiction, "three-quarters of the $7.4 billion Congress allotted in 2018 to fight the opioid epidemic went to research, treatment, and prevention rather than police and prisons."[96]

Not only did the federal government get involved in reframing opioid addicts as victims, but over 2,000 lawsuits have been filed by state attorneys general against pharmaceutical companies for their role in the opioid crisis.[97] Apparently, sympathy and help is the default response when white people get addicted, but mass incarceration, individual blame, character assassination, and criminal punishment is the response when the addiction is perceived as Black.[98]

Welfare versus Farm Subsidy

Both programs are government-funded entitlement programs designed to ensure the welfare of the recipients. When you hear "farm subsidy," does your brain rush off to a place where you see hardworking, salt-of-the-earth people ploughing fields in overalls, and you taste apple pie and hear the song "America the Beautiful" playing in your head? When you hear the word "welfare," do you recoil and feel resentment of lazy Black inner-city women, getting pregnant repeatedly and milking the system as "Welfare Queens"? If this is true, it is because most farm owners are white, and Ronald Reagan was able to convince you that the anomalous case of one Black woman in Chicago was typical of welfare.[99]

Josh Levin points out that Ronald Reagan was able to convince an entire swath of voters that Black people were serially and routinely abusing welfare on a massive scale by highlighting the actions of one Black woman in Chicago.[100]

> Linda Taylor, the haughty thief who drove her Cadillac to the public aid office, was the embodiment of a pernicious stereotype. With her story, Reagan marked millions of America's poorest people as potential scoundrels and fostered the belief that welfare fraud was a nationwide epidemic that needed to be stamped out. This image of grand and rampant welfare fraud allowed Reagan to sell voters on his cuts to public assistance spending. The "welfare queen" became a convenient villain, a [*black*] woman everyone could hate. She was a lazy black con artist, unashamed of cadging the money that honest folks worked so hard to earn.[101]

By now, I don't have to explain how system justification and unconscious bias make it so easy for the criminal actions of this unique woman to be so powerfully superimposed on all Black people, even though the reality is that welfare recipients are mostly white.

According to the *HuffPost*:

> The numbers reflect a significant overestimation of the number of black Americans benefiting from the largest programs. Medicaid had more than 70 million beneficiaries in 2016, of whom 43 percent were white, 18 percent black, and 30 percent Hispanic. Of 43 million food stamp recipients that year, 36.2 percent were white, 25.6 percent black, 17.2 percent Hispanic and 15.5 percent unknown.[102]

And why, even after I point out this is an example of unconscious racism, aren't you going to be able to shake the false stereotype when it is time to cast votes? It's the same reason Donald Trump has convinced you that immigrants are criminals. Even after reading Chapter 7 and learning that the notion of immigrant criminality as being different from white criminality is false, it will still be near impossible to let this false assertion go. "Meh. Whatever," right? It's easier to be comfortable than to delve into the reality of our world.

While both farm subsidies and welfare are government financial aid, the recipients are different. Welfare is typically described as assistance to families in need or the poor and is designed to help people meet basic needs such as housing and food. Farm subsidies, on the other hand, are government financial aid to the agricultural sector or farmers. Since farm subsidies began in the 1930s New Deal environment, they were provided to large-scale farming operations, which have always been predominantly white. Even though the truth about farm subsidies is that they are a joke—

> wealthy growers are paid even in good years, and may receive drought aid when there's no drought. It's become so bizarre that some homeowners lucky enough to have bought land that once grew rice now have subsidized lawns. Fortunes have been paid to Fortune 500 companies and even gentlemen farmers like David Rockefeller. Thus even House Speaker Boehner call[ed] the bill a "slush fund[.]"[103]

The truth is, we view this entitlement program favorably because it benefits what traditionally has been a rural and white group. Farmland ownership is a predominantly white reality, and African Americans rarely received land from homesteading.[104] To be clear, African Americans have received land through allotment processes, such as in Oklahoma, but farming has always been a predominantly white endeavor. Ultimately, while both farm subsidies and aid to families with children are a form of social welfare program, we only refer to one of them negatively as *government welfare*.

We have powerfully favorable feelings for farm subsidies because they preserve white wealth and perpetuate the concentration of land ownership among whites. When we discuss welfare, however, racist language and branding of the program as favoring inner-city Black people is the dominant discourse, but no one even thinks or cares that farm subsidies benefit almost exclusively large white agrarian interests.

Government aid is favorable and acceptable when it perpetuates the disparity in land ownership and wealth between white people and African Americans, a disparity that has its genesis in slavery. But government aid is viscerally disfavored when it is perceived as trying to make up for 246 years of slavery (1619–1865), followed by almost a century of Jim Crow, which even prevented access to higher education for many non-white people.

And this welfare/farm subsidy debate touches on another aspect of our perception that is particularly vile. System justification and firmly entrenched unconscious racism is the reason why you feel such visceral anger and scream, "No one should get special treatment in America," at the thought of one Black student getting into college via an affirmative action program, but simply "meh relegate" and find unimpactful the fact, that "43 percent of white students admitted to Harvard University were recruited athletes, legacy students, children of faculty and staff, or on the dean's interest list—applicants whose parents or relatives have donated to Harvard."[105] It gets worse: 75% of the white students admitted in this fashion would have been rejected if they were *not* athletes, legacy students, children of faculty and staff, or children or relatives of donors.[106]

To understand why systemic racism is hard to remedy, one must first understand that acknowledging it causes significant and uncomfortable dissonance because it challenges a comfortable, reframed, and simplistic fairy tale that humans are evolutionarily wired to substitute for reality. Acknowledging the truth is uncomfortable because, throughout history, humans have maintained societal stability by communally buying into false narratives at the societal level. No less than the very basic and core evolutionary mechanisms that have enabled humans to progress by maintaining stable and unified societies are what makes it almost impossible for you to accept the truths described so far in this book.

Celebrating White Criminality

> Pick a crime, any crime, and Western media has probably made a movie/TV series/play/etc. with a white person that romanticizes the criminal activity. No matter what, a white person can do whatever terrible crimes and still have a TV/movie fanbase that loves them.
>
> When you see black or brown people committing crimes on screen, you are to see them [as] thugs and criminal masterminds and people to be beat down.[107]

NASCAR is associated with patriotism in a way that few other sports are.[108] In fact, NASCAR fans identify patriotism as the single most important value they express.[109] NASCAR is also a celebration of white criminality, showcasing the competence and skill of the drivers who needed fast cars to outrun the law when they were transporting bootleg liquor during Prohibition.[110] Many of the early NASCAR drivers were the actual bootleggers who drove to evade the law during Prohibition.[111]

Pirate captains are also celebrated in our culture. We adore these predominantly white seafarers who brutally murdered, plundered, and raped their way into very special places in our hearts and minds. Disney World even has a ride themed after pirates. Similarly, we romanticize figures like Billy the Kid, Jesse James, Bonnie and Clyde, Italian gangsters, and even more recently, psychopaths like Charles Manson. Similarly, Luigi Mangione, who murdered the CEO of United Healthcare, was viewed favorably by almost 39% of people aged 18–29 as of this writing.[112]

But the same cannot be true of celebrating Black or non-white criminality. Consider, for example, the recent opinion of Kali Fontanilla,[113] who harshly criticized the rapper Common for reframing Black violence as heroic resistance, much like society has comfortably done for examples of white criminality mentioned above. Fontanilla's article, titled "The Costs of Romanticizing Criminals in the Black Community," is unapologetic and blistering in its critique, arguing that this kind of hypocrisy in the Black community is harmful.

Ironically, her forceful critique does not acknowledge that this identical reframing of white criminality is an essential aspect of white superiority and the reason for the disparately harsher sentencing of Black people in our country. Cognitive reframing is also the reason she feels so viscerally repulsed by Common's recasting of Black violence.

System justification creates ironic results like this. Consider that, even though most of the brutal and genocidal atrocities in American history have been committed by whites, we romanticize away that reality, transforming white criminals into heroes while reinforcing the case that Black people and minorities should be feared and must alter their behavior for the well-being of society. The problem is that we are incapable of discerning what society truly is because our unconscious minds construct a version of society that we erroneously believe we are observing with our conscious minds.

Unconscious Racism Is Exhausting for People of Color

In the introduction to this book, I mentioned that my first encounter with unconscious racism occurred when I moved to Kansas in 2007. However, the truth is that unconscious racism introduced itself to me a year earlier. Because it usually masquerades as benevolence and morality, I did not recognize it at the time.

In 2004, I was working as a pseudo-faculty member at my alma-mater, St. Thomas University School of Law in Miami, Florida. Although I was not a member of the tenure-track faculty, I had been hired by the Dean, Bob Butterworth, to come back and work with students who were struggling academically. My programing generated a significant level of engagement, and students perceived it as useful. Upwards of fifty students would voluntarily attend these academic support sessions on Saturday mornings to receive supplemental instruction on how to read cases and prepare for examinations, and so on.

Given the high student engagement I was generating, the dean, after suggestions from another professor at the institution, Stephen (Steve) Plass, took the liberty of allowing me to teach the doctrinal courses of

Torts and Admiralty and Maritime Law. I was voted First Year Professor of the Year each year I taught at St. Thomas University.

Steve was a Guyanese-born law professor of African descent. I encountered Steve on my second day of class as a law student when he walked into my Contracts class and proceeded to scare the shit out of the entire class. What we initially thought was rage or disdain for the class was his way of modeling excellence and messaging clearly that he thought we were also capable of excellence, and he expected it from us. What was initially fear very quickly became motivation to work as hard to prepare for class as Steve did.

The other thing Steve's presence in front of the class did for me was let me see a man of color excelling as a master of his craft in the legal profession. I instantly saw in Steve my own potential for success. As I got to know him better, I realized he was one of the brightest people I would ever come to know. He embraced the complexity of our existence, and his academic writing reflected his capacity for analyzing incredibly complex problems.

At the time, I did not understand that Steve knew that as a man of color, from a non-traditional background for legal educators, my potential for success in the legal education field was limited unless he took actions to ensure what he thought was my excellence was impossible to ignore. Hence his suggestion to the dean that I get experience in the doctrinal classroom to establish a record of excellence as an instructor. And to be clear, Steve was always unapologetic about the fact that he would not have helped me in this regard if he did not think I had the work ethic and intellectual capacity to succeed in the field.

Steve also insisted that no matter how busy I was, I must try to write a law review article every year I taught at St. Thomas, even though the position did not support research and writing. I can hear him say clearly and forcefully in our West Indian dialect, "Man yuh jes have to write."

In 2006, after two years of academic support and teaching in the classroom, and a publication on some abstract aspect of maritime jurisdiction ready to go, I signed up for what is typically referred to in legal academia as the "meat market." That was the common name for the centralized procedure for law school hiring. Anyone interested in landing a tenure-track position in legal academia would submit a standardized form, outlining their qualifications for the job, published papers, experience teaching, and preferred classes to teach. Every law school looking for candidates would conduct targeted searches of this database, select candidates they were interested in interviewing, and contact these candidates to schedule a 30-minute interview at the "meat market."

In 2006, as in every year until COVID, the meat market consisted of a two-day span where every law school interested in interviewing a candidate rented an interview room at the Wardman Park Marriott in Washington, D.C. During this two-day span, the schools would interview candidates they were interested in meeting for 30 minutes. Candidates would have to go from room to room, sometimes back-to-back, depending on how many schools were interested in interviewing them. After the meat market, when participants returned to their respective institutions and homes, the interviewing institutions would make decisions on which, if any, of the candidates they interviewed would be invited to a call back interview at the interested institution.

Just before I departed for Washington, D.C., to participate in what I think were eight or nine initial interviews over the two-day period, a senior white male professor at the law school I attended and was now working at approached me in the corridor outside my office and said, "I hope you are not expecting too much from the meat market. In fact, the experience may be a bit traumatic for you because you have neither the pedigree nor background to be an effective law professor." He also said something which I no longer remember perfectly, but it was the equivalent of, "You have not had exposure to the scholarly literature you would need to be effective."

In my ignorance and unconscious acceptance of my own inferiority that I now understand is a product of system justification, I was actually grateful that this man had taken the time to be real with me. I mentioned this to Steve, explaining to him that I now had realistic expectations for the interview process.

Steve became more enraged than I can describe. His words as I remember them were:

> These fuckers!!!!!! Never underestimate the depth of racism in this fucking country. You graduated first in your class, you're one of the best students we've ever had here, your teaching evaluations are excellent and way better than most of the people here, you are writing even though you have no support for writing. And this even though you are a foreigner who didn't

> have close to the privilege these fuckers were born with. You are going to be a fucking law professor and don't let any of these fuckers stop you.

I went to the meat market and received multiple call back interviews, including the call back from the school I am still at and love. When that school offered me a tenure-track position teaching the subjects I wanted to teach, I called Steve and said that I was told to let St. Thomas University know if I received a tenure-track offer. His words as best as I can remember were:

> When will you learn? Why are you so eager to come back to a place where they couldn't offer you a tenure-track position until another place recognized your worth? Go to Kansas and work your ass off. If they say you need two articles for tenure you make sure you do four or six. Make it impossible for them to deny you tenure. As a man of color in this country, you will soon learn the reality that faculty politics and friendships on the faculty are not things you can depend on. You have to work harder and accomplish more than anyone else just to get the same level of recognition. Don't take it personally, it is just the way it is. You shouldn't have to but that is the way it is. And take comfort in the knowledge that at some point if you work hard and excel above and beyond what is required no amount of racism can prevent you from success.

By the end of 2013, the year in which I was granted tenure at Washburn, after six years of being there, I was voted Professor of the Year twice, had amazing teaching evaluations, and had produced five law review articles, even though the requirement for tenure was just two. Throughout all those years and up to the present, Steve remained a supporter of my success. He read and critiqued every single law review article I wrote before I submitted it, and over the years we chatted often about my research and my interest in exploring and exposing systemic racism.

Recently, I read a tribute to Steve at a celebration of his life. Steve passed away in 2024, and in our conversation only weeks before, he shared with me that for the first time in his life, he felt that no matter how hard he worked or how much he excelled, he could not overcome the oppressive religious nationalism that he was fighting against. This man, who always told me—and believed—that excellence was a way around the limits of systemic oppression, reached a point where he realized this was no longer always true. His passing is one of the most important reasons this book needs to be read.

It's possible the white male professor who took it upon himself to warn me about my slim chance of success at the meat market was likely trying to benevolently help me prepare for the disappointment he was certain I would experience. Remember this as you get defensive and angry in Chapter 8, where I explain why intention and culpability are irrelevant to unconscious racism, and that we often feel powerless because the reality is that individuals who mean well or genuinely believe they are anti racist have no impact on systemic racism.

Endnotes

1. David Scharfenberg, *Here Come the White People—A New Antiracist Movement Takes Flight*, Boston Globe (June 12, 2020, 3:30 AM), https://www.bostonglobe.com/2020/06/12/opinion/white-anti-racist-movement-has-arrived/.

2. Anastasia Lapatina, *Here at the Polish-Ukrainian Boarder, I See Nothing but Humanity Towards Refugees*, The Guardian (Mar. 9, 2022, 9:52 EST), https://www.theguardian.com/commentisfree/2022/mar/06/polish-ukrainian-border-humanity-refugees. The author, speaking as a Ukrainian refugee, states:

> Most importantly, I was surprised by the generosity of Poles themselves. Since the war began, thousands have gone above and beyond to help in any possible way—hosting Ukrainians in their apartments, driving them to places, or simply giving them money to cover basic needs. Restaurants and stores around the country give Ukrainians discounts, while any services—including the train I took—are provided for free.

3. Magdalena Gwozdz-Pallokat, *Poland Rolls Out Welcome Mat for Ukrainians*, DW (Mar. 4, 2022), https://www.dw.com/en/in-u-turn-on-migrant-policy-poland-rolls-out-welcome-mat-for-ukrainians/a-61019601.

4. Deutsche Welle, *In U-Turn on Migrant Policy, Poland Rolls Out Welcome Mat for Ukrainians*, TaiwanNews (Mar. 4, 2022), https://www.taiwannews.com.tw/news/4462596.

5. *Id.*

6. BBC, *Poland Border Crisis: Migrants Tear-Gassed Trying to Cross from Belarus* (Nov. 16, 2021), https://www.bbc.com/news/world-europe-59302919 (last visited Jan. 9, 2025).

7. BBC, *Poland Blocks Hundreds of Migrants at Belarus Border* (Nov. 8, 2021), https://www.bbc.com/news/world-europe-59206685 (last visited Jan. 9, 2025).

8. *Id.*

9. Al Jazeera Staff, *'Double Standards': Western Coverage of Ukraine War Criticised*, Aljazeera (Feb. 27, 2022), https://www.aljazeera.com/news/2022/2/27/western-media-coverage-ukraine-russia-invasion-criticism.

10. *Id.*

11. *Id.*

12. *Id.*

13. *Id.*

14. *See generally* Rory D. Bahadur, *Civility as Morally Justified Oppression*, 30 Tex. J. on C.L. & C.R. 89 (2025); *see also* Alex Zamalin, Against Civility: The Hidden Racism in Our Obsession with Civility 3–5 (2021).

15. Rory D. Bahadur, *Civility as Morally Justified Oppression*, 30 Tex. J. on C.L. & C.R. 89 (2025) (citing Native Voices, *1819: Congress pays missionaries to 'civilize' American Indians, Timeline*, https://www.nlm.nih.gov/nativevoices/timeline/266.html (last visited Dec. 21, 2023).

16. *See generally* Zamalin, *supra* note 14.

17. *Id.*

18. *Id.*

19. Karen Grigsby Bates, *When Civility Is Used as a Cudgel Against People of Color*, NPR (Mar. 14, 2019, 5:04 AM), https://www.npr.org/sections/codeswitch/2019/03/14/700897826/when-civility-is-used-as-a-cudgel-against-people-of-color.

20. https://guides.libraries.uc.edu/racialjusticeresources/whiteness.

21. Andy Barr, *Hayworth: WWII 'Never Declared'*, POLITICO (May 24, 2010), https://www.politico.com/story/2010/05/hayworth-wwii-never-declared-037701#:~:text=We%20never%20formally%20declared%20war,before%20the%20onset%20of%20hostilities.

22. Susan Welch, *American Opinion Toward the Jews During the Nazi Era: Results from Quota Sample Polling During the 1930s and 1940s*, 95 Soc. Sci. Quarterly 615, 617–18 (2014).

23. William B. Anderson, *Production of Discourses to Counter Prevailing Attitudes and Stereotypes: How the War Refugee Board Developed a World War II Public Relations Campaign*, 23 Am. Const. J. 1, 3 (2021) (quoting Stemper, 1966).

24. *Id.*

25. Welch, *supra* note 22, at 618.

26. *Id.* at 18.

27. Daniel A. Gross, *The U.S. Government Turned Away Thousands of Jewish Refugees, Fearing That They Were Nazi Spies*, Smithsonian Magazine (Nov. 18, 2015), https://www.smithsonianmag.com/history/us-government-turned-away-thousands-jewish-refugees-fearing-they-were-nazi-spies-180957324/.

28. *Id.*

29. *Id.*

30. *Id.*

31. Anderson, *supra* note 23.

32. Rebecca Erbelding, *The War Refugee Board*, The National WWII Museum (Apr. 1, 2022), https://www.nationalww2museum.org/war/articles/war-refugee-board.

33. Anderson, *supra* note 23, at 4.

34. *Id.* at 6 (quoting Roosevelt, 1944).

35. *Id.* at 7.

36. *Id.* at 7–8.

37. *Id.*

38. The David S. Wyman Institute for Holocaust Studies, *Bergson Group*, https://enc.wymaninstitute.org/?p=127 (last visited Jan. 9, 2025), explaining:

> During 1943–1944, the Bergsonites placed more than two hundred advertisements in newspapers around the country, with headlines such as "How Well Are You Sleeping? Is There Something You Could Have Done to Save Millions of Innocent People from Torture and Death?" and "Time Races Death: What Are We Waiting For?" The ads attracted significant attention. On one occasion, the First Lady told Bergson that President Roosevelt complained that one of the ads was "hitting below the belt." Bergson replied that he was "very happy to hear that he is reading it and that it affects him."

39. Wikipedia, *Hillel Kook*, https://en.wikipedia.org/wiki/Hillel_Kook (last visited Jan. 9, 2025).

40. History Unfolded: US Newspapers and the Holocaust, "*We Will Never Die*", https://newspapers.ushmm.org/events/we-will-never-die.

41. *Id.*

42. Anderson, *supra* note 23, at 8. Perhaps interest convergence was also at work here. Hitler targeted Catholics along with Jews, and the U.S. government perhaps used his targeting of some Christians as an interest convergence tool to get Americans to see Hitler as a threat to American life, particularly to American Christianity.

43. Anderson, *supra* note 23, at 8.

44. Eric L. Goldstein, The Price of Whiteness: Jews, Race, and American Identity 1 (Princeton University Press, 2019).

45. Pew Research Center, *Jewish Americans in 2020: 9. Race, Ethnicity, heritage and immigration among U.S. Jews* (May 11, 2021), https://www.pewresearch.org/religion/2021/05/11/race-ethnicity-heritage-and-immigration-among-u-s-jews/ (last visited Jan. 9, 2025).

46. Anderson, *supra* note 23, at 2 (citing to Erbelding, 2018).

47. Matthew Taub, *'Are We Not American Soldiers?' When the U.S. Military Treated German POWs Better Than Black Troops*, TIME (July 28, 2020, 9:30 AM), https://time.com/5872361/wwii-german-pows-civil-rights/.

48. *Id.*

49. *Id.*

50. *Id.*

51. *Id.*

52. Charles W. Dryden, A-Train: Memoirs of a Tuskegee Airman 245 (2002).

53. Harper v. Virginia State Bd. of Elections, 383 U.S. 663 (1966).

54. Haaland v. Bracken, 599 U.S. 255 (2023).

55. *See id.* at 288, 297; *see also id.* at 300 explaining:

> Upon the children's arrival, the boarding schools would often seek to strip them of nearly every aspect of their identity. The schools would take away their Indian names and give them English ones. The schools would cut their hair—a point of shame in many native communities—and confiscate their traditional clothes. Administrators delighted in the process, describing the "metamorphosis [a]s wonderful," and professing that, in the main, "the little savage seems quite proud of his appearance." After intake, the schools frequently prohibited children from speaking their native language or engaging in customary cultural or religious practices. Nor could children freely associate with members of their own Tribe. Schools would organize dorms by the "[s]ize of cadets, and not their tribal relations," so as to further "br[eak] up tribal associations."

56. National Museum of African American History & Culture, *supra* note 20.

57. In *Haaland* Justice Gorsuch explains that "the mass removal of Indian children from their families [was still occurring] during the 1950s, 1960s, and 1970s." Haaland, 599 U.S. at 288, 297.

58. National Archives, https://www.archives.gov/milestone-documents/servicemens-readjustment-act#:~:text=Signed%20into%20law%20by%20President,WWII%20and%20later%20military%20conflicts (last visited Jan. 9, 2025).

59. *Id.*

60. Chandler Hansen, *The GI Bill and World War II's Farming Veterans*, MorningAgClips (Nov. 11, 2022), https://www.morningagclips.com/the-gi-bill-and-world-war-iis-farming-veterans/#:~:text=For%20farming%20veterans%2C%20the%20GI,their%20farming%20knowledge%20and%20practices.

61. Khan Academy, *The GI Bill*, https://www.khanacademy.org/humanities/us-history/postwarera/postwar-era/a/the-gi-bill (last visited Jan. 9, 2025).

62. James T. Patterson, Grand Expectations: The United States, 1945–1971 68 (New York: Oxford University Press, 1996).

63. Craig Coleman, *Celebrate 80 Years of the G.I. Bill: What Have You Achieved with Yours?*, VANews (June 21, 2024), https://news.va.gov/132445/celebrate-80-years-of-the

-g-i-bill/#:~:text=let%20them%20down.%E2%80%9D-,The%20G.I.,also%20had%20 important%20social%20impact (last visited Jan. 9, 2025).

64. The bill is reflective of the idea that America owes its veterans and soldiers, that make the sacrifice to go to war for this country, at the very least an education on return. Ryan Katz, *The History of the GI Bill*, APMReports (Sept. 3, 2015), https://www.apmreports.org/episode/2015/09/03/the-history-of-the-gi-bill.

65. Centre for Public Impact, *The US' GI Bill: The "New Deal for Veterans"* (Sept. 2, 2019), https://centreforpublicimpact.org/public-impact-fundamentals/the-us-gi-bill-the-new-deal-for-veterans/ (last visited Jan. 9, 2025).

66. Katz, *supra* note 64.

67. *Id.*

68. Blakemore, *supra* note 28.

69. *Id.*

70. Meredith Hindley, *How the GI Bill Became Law in Spite of Some Veterans' Groups*, National Endowment for the Humanities (July/August 2014), https://www.neh.gov/humanities/2014/julyaugust/feature/how-the-gi-bill-became-law-in-spite-some-veterans-groups; Blakemore, *supra* note 28.

71. Rachel A. Petrik, *The Blue Ticket Discharge: A Color That Has Stained the Lives of WWII-Era Veterans for Over 75 Years*, M-Vets (May 17, 2019), https://mvets.law.gmu.edu/2019/05/17/the-blue-ticket-discharge-a-color-that-has-stained-the-lives-of-wwii-era-veterans-for-over-75-years/.

72. *Id.*

73. *Id.*

74. *Id.*

75. Blakemore, *supra* note 28.

76. *Id.*

77. Wilson F. "Bill" Minor, *Six Decades of Watching Mississippi—Starting in 1947*, NiemanReports (Oct. 13, 2011), https://niemanreports.org/six-decades-of-watching-mississippi-starting-in-1947/.

78. *Id.*

79. *Id.*

80. Robin J. DiAngelo, *Why Can't We All Just Be Individuals?: Countering the Discourse of Individualism in Anti-Racist Education*, 6 InterActions UCLA J. of Educ. & Info. Stud. (2010), https://escholarship.org/uc/item/5fm4h8wm.

81. *Id.* Di Angelo explaining: "Insistence on seeing everyone as an individual and ignoring the significance of group membership denies the reality that not all individuals have the same access to resources based on whether they are perceived as white or a person of color."

82. *Id.*

83. *Id.*

84. *Id.* "Through illegal but common practices such as higher mortgage rates, more difficulty getting loans, real estate agents steering them away from 'good' neighborhoods, discrimination in hiring, and unequal school funding."

85. *Id.*

86. Jamie Stiehm, *'The Star-Spangled Banner's' Racist Lyrics Reflect Its Slave Owner Author, Francis Scott Key*, ANDSCAPE (Sept. 6, 2018), https://theundefeated.com/features/the-star-spangled-banners-racist-lyrics-reflect-its-slaveowner-author-francis-scott-key.

87. *Id.*

88. Aaron Skubby, *American Stories: How Narratives of Individualism Uphold Whiteness in the Post Civil-Rights Era*, Denison Student Scholarship 1, 21 (2021).

89. *Id.* Explaining:

> The American story contradicts the story of America. The American story is one of rugged individualism, where people pave their own paths and build their own success as singular entities. But the story of America is one in which law, practices, and institutions have been designed to uphold whiteness and institutionalized racism.

90. Nathália Duarte Bard, Beatriz Antunes, Cristine Moraes Roos, Agnes Olschowsky & Leandro Barbosa de Pinho, *Stigma and Prejudice: The Experience of Crack Users*, 24 Rev. Latino-Americana de Enfermagem (2016).

91. Andrew Goulian, Marie Jauffret-Roustide, Sayon Dambèlè, Rajvir Singh & Robert E. Fullilove III, *A Cultural and Political Difference: Comparing the Racial and Social Framing of Population Crack Cocaine Use Between the United States and France*, 19 Harm Reduction J. 1–2 (2022), https://harmreductionjournal.biomedcentral.com/articles/10.1186/s12954-022-00625-5.

92. Tonya Mosley, *Why the Crack Epidemic Hit Black Communities 'First and Worst'*, NPR (July 13, 2023, 11:49 AM), https://www.npr.org/2023/07/13/1186778651/crack-cocaine-epidemic-when-crack-was-king-donovan-x-ramsey.

93. Bard et al., *supra* note 90.

94. Equal Justice Initiative, *Racial Double Standard in Drug Laws Exists Today* (Dec 9, 2019), https://eji.org/news/racial-double-standard-in-drug-laws-persists-today/ (last visited Jan. 9, 2025).

95. *Id.*

96. *Id.*

97. National Association of Attorneys General, *Opioids: Oklahoma Trial against Johnson & Johnson*, https://www.naag.org/issues/opioids/#:~:text=In%202019%2C%20Oklahoma's%20lawsuit%20against,lawsuits%20filed%20around%20the%20nation. (last visited Jan. 9, 2025).

98. "Perceived" being the operative word because the truth is "crack cocaine use did not differ significantly for African Americans or Hispanic Americans as compared to white Americans." Marsha Lillie-Blanton, James C. Anthony & Charles R. Schuster, *Probing the Meaning of Racial/Ethnic Group Comparisons in Crack Cocaine Smoking*, J. of the Am. Med. Ass'n 993–97 (1993).

99. Josh Levin, *The Welfare Queen*, Slate (Dec. 19, 2013, 12:41 AM), https://www.slate.com/articles/news_and_politics/history/2013/12/linda_taylor_welfare_queen_ronald_reagan_made_her_a_notorious_american_villain.html.

100. *Id.*

101. *Id.*

102. Arthur Delaney & Ariel Edwards-Levy, *Americans Are Mistaken About Who Gets Welfare*, HuffPost (Feb. 5, 2018, 12:50 PM), https://www.huffpost.com/entry/americans-welfare-perceptions-survey_n_5a7880cde4b0d3df1d13f60b.

103. Deborah White, *What Are U.S. Farm Subsidies?*, ThoughtCo. (May 29, 2020), https://www.thoughtco.com/us-farm-subsidies-3325162.

104. *See* Keri Leigh Merritt, *Land and the Roots of African-American Poverty*, aeon (Mar. 11, 2016), https://aeon.co/ideas/land-and-the-roots-of-african-american-poverty.

105. Daniella Silva, *Study on Harvard Finds 43 Percent of White Students Are Legacy, Athletes, Related to Donors or Staff*, NBC News (Sept. 30, 2019, 12:04 PM), https://www.nbcnews.com/news/us-news/study-harvard-finds-43-percent-white-students-are-legacy-athletes-n1060361.

106. *Id.*

107. *Writing with Color: The Glorification of White Crime*, Tumblr (Jan. 4, 2017), https://writingwithcolor.tumblr.com/post/155404601965/the-glorification-of-white-crime.

108. Kimberly Elsbach, *NASCAR Fans Identify with Patriotism, Southern Tradition*, UCDavis (June 25, 2020), https://gsm.ucdavis.edu/news/nascar-fans-identify-patriotism-southern-tradition#:~:text=Elsbach%20found%20in%20her%20studies,of%20the%20national%20anthem%2C%20a.

109. *Id.*

110. John M. Jennings, *Prohibition Bootleggers: How Outrunning Cops Led to NASCAR's Creation*, JohnMJennings (Oct. 18, 2023), https://johnmjennings.com/nascars-prohibition-roots/#:~:text=The%20National%20Association%20for%20Stock,evading%20authorities%20while%20transporting%20moonshine.

111. *Id.*

112. Elad Vaida, *Almost 40 Percent of College-Age Americans View Suspected CEO-Assassin Favorably*, Campus Reform (Dec. 20, 2024), https://www.campusreform.org/article/almost-40-percent-college-age-americans-view-suspected-ceo-assassin-favorably-/27161.

113. Kali Fontanilla, *The Costs of Romanticizing Criminals in the Black Community*, Capital Research Center (Mar. 28, 2023), https://capitalresearch.org/article/the-costs-of-romanticizing-criminals-in-the-black-community/.

CHAPTER 6

CRT Bans as Conscious, Government-Level Racism

Critical race theory ("CRT") was originally developed as a legal academic framework by scholars such as Derrick Bell, Kimberlé Crenshaw, and Richard Delgado to name a few.[1] It emerged from Derrick Bell's convergence theory, which suggests that Black people only achieve victories in the fight against racism when those victories also benefit white people.[2] For example, Bell framed the *Brown v. Board of Education* decision as a case where the benefits to Black people were merely a byproduct of a coincidental alignment with white interests. At the time of the decision, America was striving to assert itself as a moral world leader in the post-World War II era, and the segregation of schools was inconsistent with this assertion.[3]

This entire book so far has explained and provided examples of how we continuously obscure reality, as Bell describes above. Hopefully, you are at least unsettled and thinking. This unconscious racism that I describe is an essential element of CRT, and its necessity to all the mechanisms described in this book so far was memorialized by CRT scholar Charles R. Lawrence III. Consider that, in his 1987 article, Lawrence describes the white moderate who is "not explicitly racist [but] only accidentally so."[4]

Kimberlé Crenshaw, a recognized critical race theorist, also recognizes what she calls white retrenchment—the reality that whenever Black and white interests converge, such that according to Bell, Black people achieve some progress in racial equality, there is a corresponding clawing back or retrenchment by whites to erase those gains.[5] Much like

I will describe here, she believes the backlash against critical race theory is an example of this retrenchment.[6]

In Chapter 3, I also framed the developments since the *Brown* decision and the civil rights movement in this way. Crenshaw points out that CRT has been around for decades, but people are only interested in it now because conservative right-wing politicians claim it is a radical and subversive movement.[7] Exactly as I suggest in this chapter about the intentions of those in favor of anti CRT legislation, Crenshaw argues that CRT is now a problem only because a "highly mobilized coalition" of right-wing politicians, with the money to achieve their goals, has made it a problem.[8]

Despite the often nauseating and exclusionary academic discourse about CRT that renders it inaccessible to the layperson, ultimately, it is nothing more than

> [T]he recognition that if people are unaware of the policies, politics, and practices that created segregated housing markets, the criminal injustice system, gaping wealth, health disparities, and more, they will default to understanding these conditions as natural, neutral, just there, leaving efforts to redress them to appear to be preferential.[9]

And the aim of CRT bans is to try to ensure that we remain unaware, so we experience visceral revulsion toward attempts to even acknowledge, much less address, the systemic inequities I have described in this book, particularly in Chapter 5. CRT bans remind us that, although much racism is unconscious, powerful members of society are consciously and deliberately pursuing the racist agenda to buttress and make permanent the unconscious racism that is deeply embedded in our society.

The deeply embedded nature of racism is illustrated by the ease with which a sexist, racist, and xenophobic political candidate can gain unwavering political support simply by saying things we *know* are untrue—such as claims that immigrants are mostly criminals or that they are eating cats and dogs in Ohio. This chapter attempts to demonstrate that this outcome is not accidental but is possible because phenomenally brilliant individuals on the Trump team understand how the human mind works and are astonishingly adept at weaponizing unconscious cognitive pathways and biases.

Without this weaponization of unconscious processing, the blatant hypocrisy of CRT bans would be obvious. Consider, for example, that on September 25, 2024, Rep. Clay Higgins, a Republican Congressman from Louisiana, posted on X:

> These Haitians are wild. Eating pets, vudu, nastiest country in the western hemisphere, cults, slapstick gangsters.... But damned if they don't feel all sophisticated now, filing charges against our President and VP. All these thugs better get their mind right and their ass out of our country before January 20th[.][10]

After he deleted the false tweet, he stated:

> I can put up another controversial post tomorrow if you want me to. I mean, we do have freedom of speech. *I'll say what I want*.... It's not a big deal to me. It's like something stuck to the bottom of my boot. Just scrape it off and move on with my life.[11]

He is unwavering in his belief that the constitutional guarantee of free speech entitles him to say whatever he wants, even if it is controversial and, like his tweet above, false, divisive, incredibly painful to immigrants, and causes people to feel hurt and anxious. People experience indescribable fear and anxiety at the prospect of the power of the United States government being deployed against them for non-criminal behavior.

As this book will explain more clearly in Chapter 10, because Clay Higgins is a white male, systemic inequity and "meh relegation" prevent most people from finding it incredulous that he can be so certain about the right to free speech regardless of how offensive the speech is while simultaneously representing Louisiana, a state where the government justified the banning of CRT in schools by suggesting "divisive concepts are antithetical to America's founding ideals of liberty, justice, equality, opportunity and unity."[12] One can only assume he neglected to clarify that he meant free speech protects anything, including statements that make people of color and immigrants ashamed and hurt, but it doesn't protect statements that make white people feel uneasy.[13]

The incredibly brilliant members of the team supporting now-President Trump absolutely understand that an effective way to mitigate implicit biases is by exposure to multicultural perspectives that run counter to establish societal stereotypes.[14] Just like me, anyone with an internet connection can discover the importance of multicultural perspectives in reducing implicit bias. So, it's safe to assume that well-resourced individuals like Ron DeSantis and the governors of states supporting critical race theory bans also know this. We can also assume people like Laura Ingraham, Sean Hannity, and Tucker Carlson are aware of this as well. Furthermore, we can assume that perhaps the most politically astute (I reluctantly mean brilliant) person ever on any political campaign, Kellyanne Conway, is also aware of this reality. Critical race theory is nothing more than a multicultural perspective on history.

Yet these are examples of the influential white politicians and public figures in support of bans to teaching critical race theory. Critical race theory, when stripped of the distracting emotional fuel surrounding it, is simply a perspective of American history developed by brilliant legal scholars of color to unapologetically document the role racism and the oppression of minorities have played—and continue to play—in the structure of American law and society.[15] Everything you have read here in this book so far is critical race theory. And while you may have had your feelings hurt and your fundamental assumptions challenged while reading, everything you have read so far is the truth. In America—even the version of America created through the cognitive reframing of reality—the government sponsored silencing of truth should *never* be appropriate, especially given the sanctity of the First Amendment.

Likewise, CRT involves a true multicultural perspective of history, based on rigorous academic work and research. Social science research confirms that exposure to multicultural perspectives significantly reduces intergroup bias.[16] CRT, therefore, is essential to mitigating implicit bias and dismantling the illusions this book demonstrates we create—illusions that lead us to become certain about the morality of our systemically racist social reality.

Because this is widely known, we can assume that all the powerful public figures and politicians opposing the teaching of CRT perspectives must also know that CRT bans perpetuate the biases that render systemic racism invisible at best and appear powerfully moral at worst. Their aim in banning CRT, therefore, is to prevent any change to the current structure of American society and to sustain the invisibility of systemic inequity. By banning the teaching of CRT, these powerful individuals are brilliantly and deliberately harnessing the power of bias and system justification to convince us of the immorality of the very narratives we *must* hear to mitigate the invisible societal inequities caused by bias and system justification.

This desperate, white supremacist effort to preserve the status quo is not surprising. As early as 2005, Edward Rubin at Vanderbilt Law School predicted that individuals supporting CRT bans and seeking to preserve the traditional societal hierarchies would, as a "last-ditch" effort, resort to morality as a tool in their arsenal.[17] This is especially powerful because, as I have already demonstrated in Chapter 4, morality is nothing more than the sense of certainty we feel about whatever belief system maintains societal hierarchies.

And by advocating for the banning of CRT and manufacturing moral panic over it because it hurts the feelings of some members of society,[18] they are tapping into a powerful force to prevent social reform. Consider the overwhelming power of the illusory concept we call morality.

> Exit polls conducted after the 2004 election revealed that "moral values" was the single most important issue that determined people's votes. The country was still recovering from the most deadly foreign attack it had ever sustained and fighting a war that had already claimed over a thousand lives and cost over one hundred billion dollars; the economy was faltering; the national debt skyrocketing; public education in disarray; Social Security heading toward collapse and health care in a widely acknowledged state of crisis. *But something called "moral values" managed to trump all these issues as the leading source of concern.*[19]

So, CRT bans are deliberate and brilliantly manipulative weapons that harness our powerful and essentially human unconscious tendencies to resist social change by making us feel it is immoral to hear the truths necessary to catalyze social change. I have provided many examples of this in Chapters 4 and 5.

However, the hypocrisy of this strategy and its incompatibility with the fundamental and uniquely beautiful American value of free speech is easy to expose. Hopefully, after reading this chapter, it becomes obvious to you.[20]

Conservative politicians who support CRT bans are notoriously loud about how harmful cancel culture is.[21] Cancel culture is generally defined as "the practice or tendency of engaging in mass canceling as a way of expressing disapproval and exerting social pressure."[22] These same conservative politicians also purport to be rabid defenders of truth and the right to free speech,[23] as well as fierce advocates for limiting the role of government.[24] However, these same legislators adamantly support CRT legislative bans, which involve asking the *government to get involved* in the *cancellation, disapproval,* and the *silencing of truthful speech* about race in America simply because it makes white people uncomfortable.

As *Time* magazine explains:

> A paradox lies at this largely conservative campaign against CRT. If you slice through the rhetoric, it rests on a view of free speech that the political right, until now, stridently and correctly rejected: That speech can and should be curtailed because it makes some people feel uncomfortable or threatened.[25]

CRT bans *are* violative of the First Amendment. First, consider that they are content-based restrictions, which are presumptively unconstitutional—subject to legal nuances that may not matter to the average reader. Furthermore, they directly violate the fundamental justification of free speech: the marketplace of ideas. In 1964, the United States Supreme Court, in *NY Times v. Sullivan*, beautifully articulated the unique American tolerance for speech in terms that underscore how fundamental this principle is to America's status as the home of the free. As an immigrant, I still tear up when I read the words of this opinion, as they remind me of the privilege I experience everyday as a naturalized American citizen. Nothing quite captures the American belief in freedom and the principles our men and women have laid down their lives for as effectively as these words describing the sanctity of free speech in our nation:

> The First Amendment, said Judge Learned Hand, 'presupposes that right conclusions are more likely to be gathered out of a multitude of tongues, than through any kind of authoritative selection. *To many this is, and always will be, folly; but we have staked upon it our all.*'
>
> [T]hat public discussion is a political duty; and that this should be a fundamental principle of the American government. They recognized the risks to which all human institutions are subject. But they knew that order cannot be secured

> merely through fear of punishment for its infraction; that it is hazardous to discourage thought, hope and imagination; that fear breeds repression; that repression breeds hate; that hate menaces stable government; that the path of safety lies in the opportunity to discuss freely supposed grievances and proposed remedies; and that the fitting remedy for evil counsels is good ones. Believing in the power of reason as applied through public discussion, they eschewed silence coerced by law—the argument of force in its worst form. Recognizing the occasional tyrannies of governing majorities, they amended the Constitution so that free speech and assembly should be guaranteed.[26]

The passage above emphasizes America as unique in the world because of free speech and that on this concept of free speech we have "*staked our all*" even though to the rest of the world "*this is, and always will be folly*." We should all be alarmed at the ease with which conservative legislators have been able to tap into the political will to ban true speech because it hurts some white people's feelings. These bans are so fundamentally un-American that we should be repulsed by them. They make a mockery of what makes this nation unique in the world. The widespread support for CRT bans should be a clear demonstration of the ease with which we can do things so fundamentally opposite to our genuine belief set and not even realize it—the ease of our moral hypocrisy, as I explained in Chapter 1.

Banning CRT in schools is especially perverse because the Supreme Court has also noted freedom of speech in the American classroom is especially important for the First Amendment and that our very future depends on it. Consider the language from *Keyishian v. Board of Regents of University of State of NY*:

> The vigilant protection of constitutional freedoms is nowhere more vital than in the community of American schools. The classroom is peculiarly the 'marketplace of ideas.' The Nation's future depends upon leaders trained through wide exposure to that robust exchange of ideas which discovers truth 'out of a multitude of tongues, (rather) than through any kind of authoritative selection.'[27]

We, as Americans, regardless of political leaning, must all face the frightening reality that banning exposure to CRT is a decision to jettison the core principles that make America unique among the world's nations. And we should be terrified at our comfort with government-level decisions to abandon these uniquely American principles simply because we find the truth uncomfortable. But we aren't, because we are evolutionarily wired to not recognize our moral hypocrisy, allowing us to remain comfortable with the world.

In addition to the principled reasons just discussed for opposing CRT bans, the cognitive science is clear: bans on CRT prevent us from reducing intergroup prejudices. One of the constant themes of this book so far has been the palliative effect of unconscious reframing. As mentioned before in Chapter 5, when discussing kneeling athletes, there is great comfort in simplifying the world so that our decisions seem right and certain. This desire to simplify situations and feel certain of our decision-making is called the need for cognitive closure, or NFCC.[28]

Stereotyping or over simplifying out-groups or people who are different allows us to achieve cognitive closure by creating firm answers to questions about those people who are different. The cognitive science is clear: cognitive dissonance, or uncertainty, is uncomfortable, and our unconscious processing heuristics have evolved to reduce this and provide us with cognitive closure.[29]

Consider the discomfort you experience when you just can't decide even something simple, like the best color to paint your kitchen. If you try to take in every valid opinion and reason for choosing a certain color—such as whether it matches the living room, whether a darker color would make it standout, whether a lighter color would make it seem dirtier than it is, whether you want it to be the focal point of your house, whether it's an open concept or separate kitchen, whether your significant other suggests a certain color is calming, or whether the color needs to compliment the backsplash, etc.—you end up feeling overwhelmed, restless, and uncomfortable. Often it's easier to drown out all the valid and differing opinions and just say, "Fuck it I'm painting it red just because." Simply making the decision is comforting. Sometimes you just need to decide, even though there's no right choice if you actively consider all the factors that are impacted by the decision. This is the need for cognitive closure. Because of this innate human need for cognitive closure, our brains are wired to accept any firm answer, even an inaccurate one, rather than experience uncertainty, confusion, and the resulting cognitive dissonance.[30]

As I explain below, exposure to multicultural perspectives, even those that do not involve interpersonal contact between different groups, reduces intergroup discrimination and bias. Additionally, it increases receptiveness to different perspectives because it ultimately reduces our need for cognitive closure and makes us more comfortable with the complexity of reality.[31]

When we are exposed to multicultural perspectives and encounter situations that contradict our stereotypes, it disrupts our unconscious heuristic decision-making processes because the observed reality does not align with the predictions of the heuristic.[32] This failure of the unconscious processing heuristic triggers the automatic engaging of our conscious processing and reasoning mind, which seeks to discern why the heuristic failed and resulted in unexpected outcomes.[33] When this happens, additional information is integrated into our heuristic, increasing our uncertainty.[34] To reduce that uncertainty, we must add new information to our unconscious processing mechanisms.[35]

Repeated exposure to multicultural experiences that cause us to experience a result different than we expected based on our preexisting stereotypes, itself engages a cyclic decrease in stereotyping.[36]

Basically,

> With each new cultural experience, people become exposed to more information—including behaviors, values, and norms—that is distinct from, inconsistent with, and even contradictory to their internalized representations of the related cultural group. As multicultural experiences accumulate, existing scripts and knowledge structures no longer provide guidance on how to act nor do they afford a sense of predictability. The accuracy of preconceived notions in terms of how well they describe the entire group is called into question.[37]

The process is called epistemic unfreezing,[38] and it has been recognized in cognitive science literature as one of the most important and influential mechanisms for reducing intergroup prejudice. Not only does it reduce racism, prejudice, and stereotyping, but it also has the additional benefit of making people more open about their prejudices.

It reduces the need for cognitive closure—the comfort we experience from feeling certain about something, even if we are wrong.[39]

In this way, we become increasingly comfortable seeking out information that might not align with our stereotypes or prejudices. Cognitive science research describes this as becoming "habitually motivated by a lower need for closure as a way of making sense of the world."[40] It might be akin to exercise—the fitter we get, the fitter we are able to become.

The importance of CRT as a multicultural perspective is that, once individuals begin seeking out opportunities to stretch their hypotheses and become more comfortable with less NFCC and greater uncertainty, the knowledge gained about one group they held prejudices against can transfer to other groups unrelated to the original multicultural perspectives.[41] Epistemic unfreezing involving one group that a person held prejudices and stereotypes about makes them aware and comfortable with the idea that similarly simplistic and stereotyped knowledge about other groups may also be incorrect. As a result, they actively seek out opportunities to stretch their understanding of other groups, thereby broadly reducing intergroup bias.[42]

Make no mistake, the legislators, politicians, and public figures opposing CRT are largely white, predominantly male individuals who know that society's current structure—and our comfort with it—is sustained by blatant falsities and erroneous assumptions masquerading as entrenched American moral principles to which the population is deeply tied.

They also know all too well that exposure to multicultural perspectives is the most effective way to correct the implicit biases and system justification that prevent us from seeing beyond the powerful fictions our unconscious minds create—fictions that cause us to perceive gross injustice and inequity as moral and egalitarian. The bans on CRT are, therefore, deliberate efforts to reduce societal exposure to these multicultural perspectives, thereby preserving the apparent impeachability of the hierarchy embedded in the current status quo—a status quo that the white proponents of the CRT bans have benefited from for generations.

If, after reading this book, we are comfortable living in a fictitious but inequitable reality created by our unconscious mind to make society seem just, fair, and moral—even though systemic structures ensure it isn't—then we should not protest the CRT bans. However, if we choose not to protest the bans, even after this new knowledge, then, like the legislators banning CRT, we would be engaging in the deliberate perpetuation of an unjust systemic structure. At least after making that decision, we can no longer hide behind the contrived reality of our created illusion. And this is America, so we are *free* to do that.

But if we truly love this country and our patriotism compels us to ensure the reality of American society reflects the stated American values of truth, equality, freedom, free speech, and the notion that all of us are equal, then CRT is an indispensable tool for achieving that goal. Based on everything this book has covered, it should be no surprise that critical race scholars see CRT "as a way to help the United States live up to its own ideals."[43]

Supporting CRT bans, then, is a deliberate refusal to even permit our brains to be burdened by an opposing narrative which we know to be the truth. Such is the brutal power of the quintessentially human need to feel comfortable in our own minds through what I have described throughout this book as unconscious cognitive reframing or the "meh relegation of information" due to implicit bias and system justification.

Endnotes

1. Mohammed Elnaiem, *What Is Critical Race Theory?*, JSTOR Daily (Sept. 2, 2021), https://daily.jstor.org/what-is-critical-race-theory/.

2. *See* Derick Bell, *Brown v. Board of Education and the Interest-Convergence Dilemma*, 93 Harv. L. Rev. 518 (1980).

3. *Id.* at 522.

4. Elnaiem, *supra* note 1.

5. Kimberlé Williams Creshaw, *Race Reform and Retrenchment: Transformation and Legitimation in Antidiscrimination Law*, 101 Harv. L. Rev. 1331, 1333–34 (1988).

6. Elnaiem, *supra* note 1.

7. Jacey Fortin, *Critical Race Theory: A Brief History*, NYTimes (Nov. 8, 2021), https://www.nytimes.com/article/what-is-critical-race-theory.html.

8. *Id.*

9. Kimberlé Creshaw, *The Manufactured Moral Panic over Critical Race Theory*, Open Society Foundations (Mar. 2, 2023), https://www.opensocietyfoundations.org/voices/the-manufactured-moral-panic-over-critical-race-theory.

10. Simon J. Levien, *Rep. Clay Higgins Posts, Then Deletes, Racist Comments About Haitians*, NYTimes (Sept. 25, 2024), https://www.nytimes.com/2024/09/25/us/politics/clay-higgins-haitians-springfield-ohio.html.

11. Annie Grayer, *GOP Rep. Clay Higgins Deletes Post Calling Haitian Migrants 'Thugs,' Telling Them to Get 'Their A** Out of Our Country'*, CNN (Sept. 25, 2024), https://www.cnn.com/2024/09/25/politics/clay-higgins-deletes-post-haitian-migrants/index.html.

12. Keymonte Avery & Bonnie Bolden, *Louisiana Gov. Jeff Landry Signs Order to Ban Critical Race Theory in Schools, Duplicates Existing Law*, Louisiana First News (Aug. 27, 2024), https://www.brproud.com/news/louisiana-news/louisiana-gov-jeff-landry-signs-order-to-ban-critical-race-theory-in-schools-duplicates-existing-law/.

13. Some might say this is not anomalous because the First Amendment has a long history of protecting the speech of the powerful despite the harms that speech inflicts on the powerless. *See, e.g.*, Citizens United v. Federal Election Commission, 588 U.S. 310 (2010) (Suggesting that powerful corporate interests have a fairly unrestricted right to spend money on independent political campaigns. In this way, wealthy individuals can monopolize the messages related to political debate by simply outspending and therefore drowning out the message of the less wealthy and powerful in society.).

14. *See* Melody M Chao, Franki Y.H. Kung & Donna Jingdan Yao, *Understanding the divergent effects of multicultural exposure*, 47 Int'l J. of Intercultural Relations 78–88 (2015).

15. Derek Bell, Kimberlé Crenshaw, and Richard Delgado are generally thought to be the founders of critical race theory.

16. Carmit T. Tadmor, Ying-yi Hong, Melody M. Chao, Fon Wiruchnipawan & Wei Wang, *Multicultural Experiences Reduce Intergroup Bias Through Epistemic Unfreezing*, 103 J. of Personality & Soc. Psych. 750, 751 (2021).

17. *See* Edward L. Rubin, *Sex, Politics, and Morality*, 47 Wm. & Mary L. Rev. 1 (2005).

18. Crenshaw, *supra* note 9.

19. Rubin, *supra* note 17, at 1–2; italics mine.

20. Again, some might legitimately argue that my description of free speech above is a utopian fantasy, as those in power have always deemed certain speech as dangerous and

sought to ban it. For example, consider the efforts to suppress speech in the 1950s McCarthy era. Similarly, note the absence of speech from those in power in the U.S. regarding the genocide of brown civilians in the Middle East, which I describe in Chapter 4. Furthermore, academics and others who have spoken out have been punished by those in power, suggesting that free speech is also a part of the myths and the hierarchy-reinforcing structures I have been describing in this book. The reality is that the First Amendment does not prohibit markets or individuals from marginalizing or punishing speech; it prohibits only the government from punishing speech.

21. *See, e.g.*, Kalli Holloway, *The Great Hypocrisy of Right-Wingers Claiming 'Cancel Culture'*, The Nation. (Mar. 19, 2021), https://www.thenation.com/article/society/republicans-cancel-culture-kaepernick/.

22. Educators4SC, *Teaching about Cancel Culture* (March 19, 2025), https://educators4sc.org/teaching-about-cancel-culture/?hsa_ver=3&hsa_grp=126863228775&hsa_src=g&hsa_cam=14427637196&hsa_net=adwords&hsa_kw=define%20cancel%20culture&hsa_ad=541880686956&gad_source=1&hsa_tgt=kwd-1118979004523&utm_campaign&hsa_mt=b&hsa_acc=2755491261 (last visited Jan. 13, 2025).

23. Adam Liptak, *How Conservatives Weaponized the First Amendment*, NYTimes (Jun. 30, 2018), https://www.nytimes.com/2018/06/30/us/politics/first-amendment-conservatives-supreme-court.html.

24. Ronnie Janoff-Bulman, *The Myth of Limited Government*, Yale University Press (Apr. 28, 2023), https://yalebooks.yale.edu/2023/04/28/the-myth-of-limited-government%EF%BF%BC/.

25. Aziz Huq, *The Conservative Case Against Banning Critical Race Theory*, Time (Jul. 13, 2021), https://time.com/6079716/conservative-case-against-banning-critical-race-theory/.

26. New York Times Co. v. Sullivan, 376 U.S. 254, 270 (1964), italics mine. The second paragraph quotes Justice Brandeis, in his concurring opinion in *Whitney v. California* (1927).

27. Keyishian v. Bd. of Regents of the Univ. of the State of N.Y., 385 U.S. 589, 603 (1967).

28. Tadmor et al., *supra* note 16, at 751.

29. *Id.* at 752.

30. *Id.*

31. *Id.*

32. *Id.*

33. *Id.*

34. *Id.*

35. *Id.*

36. *Id.* at 752–53.

37. *Id.* at 753.

38. *Id.* at 759.

39. *Id.* at 753.

40. *Id.*

41. *Id.*

42. *Id.* at 767.

43. Fortin, *supra* note 7.

CHAPTER 7

Reframing Immigration

The Myth of Immigrant Criminality

How many times have we been livid at immigrants because a teenager was killed by fentanyl? How many times have we felt a deep sense of agreement and anger when a politician says the equivalent of, "We have to shut down the border because illegal immigrants are bringing fentanyl across and killing our kids"? It makes you angry at those "bad hombres." The problem is that the statement is not true. As difficult as it is to accept, these are the relevant facts about fentanyl smuggling:

- Over 90 percent of fentanyl seizures occur at legal crossing points or interior vehicle checkpoints, not on illegal migration routes, so U.S. citizens (who are subject to less scrutiny) when crossing legally are the best smugglers.
- In 2021, U.S. citizens were 86.3 percent of convicted fentanyl drug traffickers—ten times greater than convictions of illegal immigrants for the same offense.
- Just 0.02 percent of the people arrested by Border Patrol for crossing illegally possessed any fentanyl whatsoever.
- Annual deaths from fentanyl nearly doubled from 2019 to 2021 after the government banned most travel (and asylum).[1]

Again, we might easily and powerfully buy into a false, racist, and xenophobic narrative because that narrative blames people unlike the "us." Even though, *of course,* we aren't racist, and we *genuinely* believe racism is abhorrent. By now, we should realize the irrelevance of our honest and genuine moral belief about racism. Otherism, unconscious bias, and narratives that justify the existence of an "us" and a "them," and giving more value to the statements of people who we think of as "us" will result in the truth being so disruptive to our need for cognitive closure that it stands no chance against the more comfortable fiction regarding fentanyl smuggling.

There, even though we genuinely believe we are not racist, we just perpetuated systemic racism. But we should not think of ourselves as "bad" or culpable for this. Remember, we are unconsciously "meh"ing these realities about fentanyl trafficking into "the insignificant data zone" because immigrants are conceived of as "those brown others" rather than as "the white us," to whom we give way more credibility—even when what they say is a complete and utter lie. The narrative that those evil, dog-eating immigrants are responsible for the majority of fentanyl deaths is much more comfortable than the truth, which is that most of the fentanyl deaths are caused by "good, white, American citizens" who the customs officers are less likely to be suspicious of as they return to America via legal and established border crossings.

This truth is so impossible to receive that when J.D. Vance restated this narrative during the 2024 vice-presidential debate, Tim Walz, the candidate from the supposedly more pro-immigration Democratic party, did not even try to dispel it emphatically. Instead, he only mentioned it wasn't true that undocumented children were used as drug mules, focusing instead on the need for tighter border control and the fact that then-candidate Donald Trump ensured Republican senators would not vote for a bill that beefed up border security.[2] Emphasizing the truth would have been fatal to Walz's political ambitions because the untruths associating immigrant criminality with fentanyl are so absolute, due to the comfort provided by this narrative being consistent with our implicit biases and systemic racism. The vast majority of conservative-leaning voters would have deemed Walz "insane" if he spoke the truth—a truth that was so unbelievable to them at that point.

As I discussed in Chapter 6, the reality of human existence is that humans give more credibility to people they consider similar to themselves. Consider why this is evolutionarily sensible. Before we discovered that wood could float and carry us to different geographic regions of the globe, humanity existed as a set of geographically confined and homogenous groups. People occupying what is now Scandinavia had light skin and similar facial features; my ancestors on the Indian subcontinent were likely brown and of medium build. These insular societies needed to stick together to survive. When the Scandinavians first met Arab traders, and the Arab traders told a story that was inconsistent with what Scandinavians believed, it made evolutionary sense to give those who formed part of your group more credibility. When there is one morsel of food remaining, you prefer to get that meat for your own rather than for a group of strangers.

Hector Garcia describes this automatic human favoring of the similar as "parochial altruism" and explains that it results from the fact that much of our evolution involved existing as members of small, discrete, and insular hunter-gatherer groups.[3] In order to survive, we had to develop unconscious moral biases towards members of our own group and against those who were not part of it.[4] These biases were evolutionarily ingrained into our processing mechanisms, and today we still have brains that are predisposed to creating in-groups and out-groups and applying the same bias structures to them.[5]

This similarity bias is unconscious,[6] automatic, connected to mood, and powerfully overrides[7] our conscious value set, causing us to have a more powerful, reflexive, and immediate response to dissimilar people or people from out-groups than we believe we would, based[8] on our genuinely held beliefs or value set.[9] It leads to what psychologists call ethical blind spots.[10] Ultimately, moral judgments and conclusions are also related to whether we like or dislike the person whose actions we are observing or who is providing the narrative.[11] This unavoidably human condition is called moral hypocrisy.[12]

The Trump campaign brilliantly and masterfully weaponized bias and the fact that threats to the system increase the tendency to justify the system.[13] As I suggested in my 2022 law review article, consider the threat to the system narratives like this, which highlight in-groups and out-groups:

> The Mexican Government is forcing *their* most unwanted people into the United States. *They* are, in many cases, criminals, drug dealers, rapists, etc.

> We'll get *them* out, secure the border, and once the border is secured, at a later date we'll make a determination as *to the rest*. But we have some *bad hombres* here and we're going to get *them* out.[14]

American society is a system of white socio-economic dominance.[15] The increased system justification created by systemic threats, such as the statement above, amplifies the statement's credibility, even if the statement is false and unsupported by data.[16] Similarly, the powerful creation of an "us" and a "them" harnesses the unconscious mechanism of moral hypocrisy, making the statement powerfully convincing and believable. These same mechanisms, giving whiteness presumed validity in American society, are the reasons it is easy, for example, to receive rap music as sexist and harmful but think of "Honky Tonk Badonkadonk" as good and clean American musical humor.

We demonstrated above how our unconscious reframing, or "meh" processing, of information allows us to falsely and powerfully demonize illegal immigrants for fentanyl deaths, even in the face of empirical evidence to the contrary. Similarly, a news story about an immigrant committing a crime facilitates our unconscious and visceral association of immigrants with crime—an association that, like the narrative of immigrants bringing in most of the fentanyl, is also false.

The truth is that studies consistently demonstrate that there is no associated increase in crime with undocumented immigration.[17] Moreover, there is no measurable difference in the crime rates of cities characterized as sanctuary cities and those considered inhospitable to undocumented immigrants.[18] One study even demonstrates that increases in the numbers of undocumented immigrants actually resulted in reduced arrest rates for crimes associated with drugs and impaired driving.[19]

At some visceral level, we don't need these studies to know this is true. Even as a legal immigrant, during the time I had only my green card but not yet my citizenship, I made sure to behave uber-cautiously and to go above and beyond reasonable behavior to avoid getting in trouble. There is even more motivation for an undocumented immigrant to avoid criminality and remain as inconspicuous and invisible as possible because, even though sometimes deportation isn't immediate, criminality or causing any sort of "trouble" completely sabotages their chances of becoming a legal American citizen. If you want to understand the reality of illegal immigrants in this country, as opposed to believing untruths, watch the movie *A Better Life* by Chis Weitz.

Despite these documented truths, the same human cognitive mechanisms that justify societal structures, resulting in us believing false narratives associating illegal immigrants with fentanyl deaths and increased crime, also prevent us from accepting the truth of other narratives—such as the narrative that mass killings are a white[20] male[21] crime.

However, when one immigrant commits a crime, that entire genre of crimes becomes labeled as an "immigrant crime," and every immigrant is stereotyped as being like that criminal—even though all demographics commit that type of crime. The reflexive solution that appeals to us viscerally when an immigrant commits a crime is that we should close the border. For example, on December 22, 2024, when the illegal Guatemalan immigrant committed the heinous crime of setting a woman on fire on a New York subway train, the new Trump border czar, Tom Horman, said, "Here's another example of an illegal alien killing an American citizen. It's almost a daily occurrence now, because a historic number of criminal aliens are walking the streets, because of this administration's policy in sanctuary jurisdictions and lax immigration enforcement."[22]

But where was that same stereotyping of white males as a dangerous group when:

1. Ted Bundy killed 30 women across several states in the 1970s.[23]
2. Jeffrey Dahmer killed 17 males between 1978 and 1991, dismembering and eating their bodies.[24]
3. John Wayne Gacy murdered 33 teenagers in the 1970s in Illinois.[25]
4. Dennis Rader, also known as the BTK Killer, killed 10 people in Kansas between 1974 and 1991.[26]
5. Adam Lanza killed 20 children and six adults in Connecticut during the Sandy Hook Massacre.[27]
6. Dylan Roof killed nine churchgoers in Charleston, South Carolina, in 2015.[28]
7. James Holmes injured 70 people and killed 12 in the cinema shooting in Aurora, Colorado, in 2012.[29]

8. Scott Peterson, in 2004, murdered his pregnant wife in California.[30]
9. Chris Watts, in 2018, murdered his wife and their two daughters in Colorado.[31]
10. Timothy McVeigh bombed the Federal Building in Oklahoma City in 1995, killing 168 people, 19 of whom were children. and injuring hundreds of others.[32]
11. Patrick Crusius shot and killed 23 people and injured countless more in an El Paso Walmart in 2019.[33]
12. Robert Bowers, in 2018, shot killed 11 people in a synagogue in Pittsburgh.[34]
13. Stephen Paddock, shooting from a hotel window during a Las Vegas music festival in 2017, shot and killed 60 people and injured hundreds.[35]

This list of horrific crimes committed by white males in America is endless, but even if I listed the countless others, including but not limited to Dylan Klebold and Eric Harris in Columbine, James Alex Fields in Charlottesville, and John Timothy Earnest in Poway, there is no way we would feel comfortable calling the next mass murder a white male crime and brand the entire demographic of white males defective and undesirable. Further consider that white males have been responsible for all the assassination attempts on American presidents except for the attempts to assassinate Gerald Ford and Harry Truman. Both of Gerald Ford's assassination attempts were carried out by white women with guns and Harry Truman's assassins were Puerto Rican.[36]

Yet all it takes is one Fox News story about an immigrant committing a crime for the truth not to matter. Our unconscious mind and limbic brain-based reframing of reality to favor the "us" powerfully and reflexively makes us viscerally feel that immigrants are criminals that need to be kept out of the country, and to make America great again, we must vote for the politicians that will ensure this. *This is* moral hypocrisy and the "meh" relegation of information that does not fit the bias-consistent narrative, favoring the societal status quo. Even now that we know the immigrant narrative is false, the truth causes us stress and feels uncomfortable in our brains, making it still almost impossible for us to behave and vote in accordance with that truth.

Nothing illustrates our cognitive frailties and the associated unconscious racism and xenophobia more than my own reaction to the horrific New Orleans New Year's Day attack that killed 15 people when I found out it was a Muslim who drove a car into a crowd of people celebrating on Bourbon Street.[37] My brain immediately and forcefully rang the alarm bell, trying to *falsely* label all Muslims as dangerous. However, my brain never tried to label white people the same way when a white male, Robert Card, shot and killed 18 people in Lewiston, Maine, in October of 2023.[38] I did not even remember this had happened until I began to research it. But I can remember almost every single act of mass violence committed by a person of color.

It's especially interesting that the BBC's headline of the Robert Card murders tries to make excuses for the white male's behavior, as the headline provides: "Maine mass shooter's brain showed signs of injury, doctors say." This, even though the article under the headline unequivocally provides, and I quote: "Dr McKee *did not find evidence of chronic traumatic encephalopathy (CTE) in Card's brain.*"[39]

So entrenched is our erroneous association of immigrants with criminality that the same unconscious processing that I describe above as impacting me also seems to have impacted President Trump and Vice President J.D. Vance. They simply assumed that the New Orleans terrorist was an immigrant and suggested that the terrorist act was evidence of the need to close the Southern border.[40] The inconvenient and cognitively uncomfortable truth, however, is that he was an American citizen who received his citizenship like most Americans—by being born in the USA. In addition to being born and raised in Texas, he had served our country as a soldier in the U.S. Army.[41]

It is also worth noting that a study by M. Steven Fish at the University of California found that the murder rate in predominantly Muslim countries is 2.4 murders for every 100,000 people, compared to 7.5 murders per 100,000 people in countries that are not predominantly Muslim.[42] This data challenges the notion that Muslims are more violent than non-Muslims. However, data is irrelevant to unconscious processing heuristics.

In Chapter 11, I explain in detail the cognitive mechanisms that powerfully motivate us to stereotype immigrants as criminals when one immigrant commits a crime, while simultaneously excusing every instance of white crime as atypical, abnormal, or exception-to-the-rule behavior for white males. These mechanisms explain why we can honestly believe we aren't racist or xenophobic, yet feel powerfully motivated to vote for a convicted felon simply because he invents the fiction that immigrants are eating our pets—thereby comfortably distracting us from the complexity of social issues by providing a demographic for you to focus on and be angry at.

But it is worth mentioning the role of white privilege, or white normativity, again and asking you to review my explanation of white privilege in Chapter 5 in the context of World War II. In societies where white people are viewed as the norm, their culpable actions are often judged as individual actions rather than as representative of the white population as a whole. Darker-skinned immigrants enjoy no such privilege.

Of course, we know by now our reaction to this truth is MEH! But an even more difficult truth to accept is the fact the United States is responsible for much of the shit in the countries Donald Trump designated as "shithole countries."

In 2018, then-President Trump broadly labeled non-European immigrants as coming from "shithole countries" and contrasted them with Norwegians. What President Trump failed to acknowledge is that many of these illegal immigrants come from countries that were deliberately destroyed by U.S. foreign policy, which supported brutal, genocidal regimes.

After Mexico, the three countries that were the source of the most illegal immigrants in 2021were Guatemala, El Salvador, and Honduras.[43] What is almost never acknowledged is that American policy in each of these countries is largely responsible for the instability there and the reason people are fleeing.

Guatemala

Guatemala was the source of 780,000 illegal immigrants in 2021.[44] In 1954, the United States government and the CIA led a coup to depose the democratically elected President Jacobo Árbenz Guzmán. Juan Gonzalez, in his book *Harvest by Empire*, explains that Guzmán was only the second democratically elected leader in Guatemalan history. He came to power because of a push by the country's middle class to change the long tradition of dictatorships, which had left almost 70% of the population unable to read and 80% barely subsisting in rural areas.[45]

The social inequity was especially stark in the statistics surrounding land ownership. In a country with very fertile soil, almost 75% of the arable land was owned by less than 3% of the landowners, and only a small fraction was cultivated.[46] The previous dictatorships forced the natives to work for these large landowners.

Inspired by Roosevelt and New Deal socioeconomics, Guzmán tried to resolve the inequity plaguing Guatemalan society by passing laws authorizing the government to buy from the large landowners all idle, privately owned land larger than 600 acres that was not being cultivated.[47] One of the large landowners was the United Fruit Company.

The United Fruit Company was an American multinational corporation formed in 1899. It owned vast tracts of land in Central America, where it developed a thriving banana trade. Today, it is known as Chiquita Brands International. The company monopolized the banana trade in Guatemala, Honduras, and Costa Rica, which is why these countries are referred to as "Banana Republics."[48]

The United Fruit Company expertly developed an American market for their bananas by combining cruise tourism to Guatemala with banana marketing.[49] Cruise ships, designated as a members of "The Great White Fleet," transported American tourists to the countries in Latin America controlled by the United Fruit Company.[50] By doing this, the United Fruit Company hoped to entrench itself as a good corporate entity and to create and capitalize on an association between their bananas and the adventurous spirit of America.[51]

When American passengers arrived in these countries, part of the itinerary included a carefully staged tour of the banana plantations and manufacturing facilities, making it seem as though the locals were happy working for the company and that everything was "just peachy" (to use another fruit pun).[52] American tourists would leave these tours completely ignorant of the harsh and oppressive practices the laborers were subject to and oblivious to the corruption that allowed these conditions to exist.[53]

These tours, combined with advertising in America, romanticized the reality of the exploitation occurring and made Americans perceive Central America as a happy, wild place where the locals joyously participated in the banana industry.[54] This simultaneously created a demand for cruise tourism and for the fruit coming from this seemingly harmonious and happy part of the world.[55]

Guzmán's land buyback resulted in United Fruit Company losing 600,000 acres of mostly unused land. The Guatemalan government paid them $1.2 million for the land, which was the approximate value of the land according to the company's internal accountants.[56] In response, the United States State Department, apparently acting on behalf of the United Fruit Company, suggested to Guzmán that the company should have been paid $16 million for the land.[57] Guzmán refused, and the United States government developed a plan for the armed overthrow of Guzmán.[58] At the time, the Secretary of State was John Foster Dulles, and his brother, Allen Dulles, was the CIA director.[59] Before entering government service, both Dulles brothers were partners in the main law firm that the United Fruit Company used in the United States.[60]

In summer of 1954, on the advice of the Dulles brothers, President Eisenhower authorized "Operation Success," giving the green light for the CIA to arrange the armed overthrow of the democratically elected Guzmán.[61] The CIA even selected the Guatemalan military officer Carlos Castillo Armas to lead the coup and trained and financed the Guatemalan soldiers needed for it in nearby Nicaragua.[62] Planes piloted by the CIA supported the invasion.[63] Armas eventually became known as the Butcher of Zacapa because of his brutality and his willingness to "turn the whole country into a cemetery" to achieve the U.S. goals in Guatemala.[64]

The anti-democratic coup was violent, and the government installed by the CIA subjected Guatemalan citizens to an unparalleled reign of terror for decades.[65] The American-funded and American-trained terrorists committed atrocities, such as dropping mutilated bodies from helicopters onto crowds at sporting events, to intimidate the population and cut out the tongues of people resisting them.[66]

The newly installed government was immediately supported by copious American aid, and in return, it suppressed trade unions and returned over 1 million acres of land to the United Fruit Company.[67] That was essentially the end of democracy in Guatemala.[68] By 1985, 75,000 people had been killed as a result of the U.S.-backed anti-democracy coup in Guatemala.[69]

The United States, therefore, made Guatemala a "shithole" country by overthrowing its democratically elected government and installing a brutal dictator to ensure the profitability of an American multinational company with deep ties to the United States government. We are the reason they need to flee their country and come illegally to ours.

But this truth—that when it suits the needs of powerful private citizens, America will act and has repeatedly acted antidemocratically—is hard or impossible to accept because it causes significant dissonance with the dominant and comfortable narrative of America as the beacon for and protector of democracy in the world. When our unconscious brain is forced to choose between this palliative narrative, which makes us cry with pride at the uniqueness of the unwavering and absolute American reverence for democracy, and the truth, it chooses the narrative that brings us more comfort. And we don't even realize our brains are doing this. From there, our conscious brain backfills the story, and we feel convinced we've made a reasoned decision supported by truth. Meh relegation at work.

Honduras

In 2021, 564,000 illegal immigrants were Honduran.[70] The story of how Honduras became a "shithole" country is as *bananas* as the story of Guatemala. It begins with a 1954 strike by banana workers against the United Fruit Company.[71] The strike involved as many as 25,000 workers or 15% of the entire Honduran workforce.[72]

The United States exerted pressure on the Honduran government to resolve the strikes because it viewed the striking workers as a potential inroad for communism in Latin America, given the rise of leftist governments in the region. This was unacceptable in the Cold War era. However, the Honduran government was essentially pro-U.S. at the time,[73] and the U.S. did not directly orchestrate an overthrow of the government in response to the perceived threat to U.S. interests. Still, it had troops at the ready on two ships in the Gulf of Honduras in case the strikes spun out of control.[74] But this is only the beginning of U.S. involvement in Honduran affairs, whether in the name of fighting communism or protecting the corporate interests of American corporations.

During the Cold War in the 1980s, Honduras became an important American ally in the effort to prevent the spread of communism in Latin America.[75] The United States used Honduras as a base for the Contra rebels fighting the government of Nicaragua and trained "anticommunist" death squads in the country, the most infamous of which was Battalion 316.[76] This battalion abducted, tortured, and killed people they believed were communist sympathizers.[77]

According to the *Baltimore Sun*:

> Newly declassified documents and other sources show that the CIA and the U.S. Embassy knew of numerous crimes, including murder and torture, committed by Battalion 316, yet continued to collaborate closely with its leaders.
>
> In order to keep U.S. dollars flowing into Honduras for the war against communism in Central America, the Reagan administration knowingly made a series of misleading statements to Congress and the public that denied or minimized the violence of Battalion 316.[78]

In the name of suppressing communism in the 1980s, we trained the army of a Central American country to kidnap, torture, and murder its citizens, thereby actively promoting authoritarianism, and stymied socioeconomic growth and democracy in the country.

Any attempt to firmly reestablish stability and security in Honduras was shattered when the democratically elected president, Manuel Zelaya, was overthrown in a coup in 2009. Members of the new regime included prominent figures from the infamous U.S.-funded and trained Battalion 316.[79]

The United States acted reluctantly to condemn the coup or even officially declare it a military coup because they suspected Zelaya leaned left.[80] Instead, by November 2009, the United States announced it would recognize the legitimacy of any government elected in the shadow of the military coup and continued to provide military aid.[81]

Honduras is yet another country whose potential stability and viability was thwarted by U.S. anticommunist interests. While the U.S. has the right to protect its interests against communism, it is alarmingly disingenuous to pretend that we had nothing to do with catalyzing the conditions that have resulted in Hondurans desperately leaving their country and coming to the U.S. as illegal aliens. We are reaping what we helped sow.

El Salvador

In 2021, 751,000 of the illegal immigrants in the United States were from El Salvador.[82] El Salvador's story of how it came to be a nation people are fleeing from is no different. In 1980, the murder of a priest in El Salvador led to the deaths of 75,000 civilians and a 12-year civil war,[83] during which 20% of the population was displaced.[84] However, the murder itself was just the trigger point for a decades-long struggle between right-wing and leftist groups in the society.[85] Using the now-familiar justification of containing communism, the United States trained and supported the military in its fight against the leftists. "The army killed men, women, and children and destroyed anything the guerillas used to survive, like animals, food, and infrastructure."[86] More than 95% of the casualties in this war were caused by the Salvadorean right-wing government, which was funded by the United States.[87]

Some commentators explain:

> The Salvadoran army did not set out to exterminate the human rights movement in El Salvador by its own volition; the U.S. political machine orchestrated the desire to suppress change and stifle the voice of the Salvadoran people by keeping Salvadoran peasants impoverished and illiterate.[88]

A battalion of government soldiers trained by the United States carried out what has become known as the El Mozote massacre.

> The U.S.-trained and funded Atlacatl Battalion of the Salvadoran Army surrounded the village of El Mozote and held every civilian at gunpoint. Men and young boys were separated and brought into rooms to be brutally tortured. Women and girls as young as six years old were brought into other rooms to be raped. In the end, every single civilian was executed. A Salvadoran Civil War survivor reported, "the soldiers killed children; they killed the elderly. If they found a pregnant woman, they cut her stomach in half. They took the fetus outside of the woman and killed them both.[89]

Of the 11 Salvadorean officers identified by the United Nations as participating in the massacre, nine were trained by the US Army in Panama, and the battalion had also competed training in Georgia at Fort Benning.[90] The United States did this. We, the greatest democracy on Earth and a country of civilized people, orchestrated this barbaric killing.

El Salvadoreans ended up fleeing a country the United States helped destroy, where, in the name of suppressing Latin American communism, the United States committed war crimes, according to legal scholars.[91]

> The U.S. will likely never be expected to apologize, nor will the state likely ever be held responsible for aiding and abetting war crimes in El Salvador during the Civil War that likens to a Latin American genocide. However, the U.S. has an opportunity to assist Salvadorans, who flee to our border due to instability and violence that we helped create. We must not turn yet another blind eye to the Salvadoran immigrants who die crossing our border or perish while in our detention centers. We not only have the opportunity but a moral obligation to prevent more deaths, to build more bridges and to destroy walls. We can't change our past, but we can improve the outcomes for those needing us in the present.[92]

Other Examples

The United States has also destroyed countries across Latin America and the Caribbean whenever those sovereign nation-states have leaned left. Here are more examples of the United States destabilizing sovereign nations simply because we disagreed with the politics of the democratically elected governments.

In 1970, in Chile, Salvador Allende was democratically elected as the Chilean leader. He was a self-proclaimed socialist who came to power with the promise of nationalizing the U.S.-owned copper companies, which were an important part of the Chilean economy.[93]

President Nixon told top U.S. officials to do whatever was necessary to prevent Allende from taking power pursuant to the free and fair elections in Chile.[94] The CIA infiltrated members of the Chilean military and explicitly assured them that the United States would support a coup to overthrow Allende.[95] The CIA even orchestrated the assassination of the then-Chilean commander-in-chief, General René Schneider.[96] Schneider was targeted because he defended the constitutional and democratic transfer of power to Allende.[97] The U.S. attempts to derail democracy in Chile initially had the opposite effect, as leaders of the military and the population rallied around Allende and defended the democratic process.[98]

Allende spent three years in power before he was overthrown in a U.S.-supported military coup. During these three years, the U.S. had spent over $8 million on covert operations to overthrow Allende, in addition to enacting economic policies that were aimed at destroying the Chilean economy.[99]

The United States of America ensured that General Augusto Pinochet came to power in a coup in 1973. During his 17-year reign in Chile, 200,000 Chileans were forced into exile, 3,400 people were "disappeared," and tens of thousands were tortured and arrested.[100] Among the 200,000 exiles were some of the most educated members of Chilean society.[101] The United States destroyed Chile's economy and society, by installing a dictator to replace the democratically elected leader. Then, when the dictator did not completely abide by U.S. wishes, they destroyed the Chilean economy by imposing economic sanctions on the country.[102]

Similarly, the United States occupied Haiti from 1915 to 1934 to protect American interests, and during that time, the United States wrought significant changes to Haiti's economy and constitution.[103] Combined with the U.S. intervention to restore Jean-Bertrand Aristide to power in 1994, this helped ensure long-term instability in the country.[104]

In 1961, the CIA orchestrated the assassination of Rafael Trujillo, the despotic leader of the Dominican Republic.[105] This led to four years of instability in the country. In 1965, the United States concluded that left-leaning forces were attempting to take power in the Dominican Republic and sent 22,000 troops to the country. This is widely believed to be one of the factors perpetuating the country's instability.[106]

In 1983, under the guise of rescuing American medical students,[107] the United States invaded Grenada after the elected prime minister, Maurice Bishop, was overthrown by a leftist coup.[108] Again, fearing Grenada would become a Communist stronghold, the United States invaded the island and restored a non-leftist government.[109]

There are many other examples of the United States destabilizing Latin American and Caribbean countries and deposing the democratically elected leaders of those countries. Perhaps the most recent and currently visible of these are U.S. efforts to destabilize Venezuela.[110] The next time you wonder why so many Venezuelans are fleeing their failed state and trying to enter the United States, understand that we caused this.[111]

The depressing reality that our unconscious mind shields us from is that, in the name of domestic security, *all countries* have done—and will continue to do—unspeakable evils to human beings, especially in other countries. The United States is no exception. But our inability to receive this information is, once again, the involuntary human limbic brain reflex of "meh relegating" information that does not justify the societal status quo. It is a lot easier and more palliative to create a simple fiction of society, which the further fictions of "bad hombres" and "immigrant criminality" reinforce. Our unconscious brain needs us to be comfortable.

But at least we now understand that comfort is caused by the fictional simplicity that our amygdala fabricates. The painful reality is that this fictional simplicity is also essential to human progress, because without it, we would be perpetually paralyzed by the intractable complexity of reality. It is unsettling and disorienting to ponder the truths written here. It is much easier to say, "Murica!" and live in that world.

Endnotes

1. David J. Bier, *Fentanyl Is Smuggled for U.S. Citizens by U.S. Citizens, Not Asylum Seekers*, CATO INSTITUTE (Sept. 14, 2022, 3:46 PM), https://www.cato.org/blog/fentanyl-smuggled-us-citizens-us-citizens-not-asylum-seekers.

2. *See* Stefan Becket, *Read the Full VP Debate Transcript from the Walz-Vance Showdown*, CBS NEWS (Oct. 2, 2024, 10:18 AM), https://www.cbsnews.com/news/full-vp-debate-transcript-walz-vance-2024/. Senator Vance said:

> Ninety-four executive orders suspending deportations, decriminalizing illegal aliens, massively increasing the asylum fraud that exists in our system, that has opened the floodgates. And what it's meant is that a lot of fentanyl is coming into our country. I had a mother who struggled with opioid addiction and has gotten clean. I don't want people who are struggling with addiction to be deprived of their second chance because Kamala Harris let in fentanyl into our communities at record levels. So you've got to stop the bleeding. You've got to re-implement Donald Trump's border policies, build the wall, re-implement deportations. And that gets me to your point, Margaret, about what do we actually do? So we've got 20, 25 million illegal aliens who are here in the country. What do we do with them? I think the first thing that we do is we start with the criminal migrants. About a million of those people have committed some form of crime in addition to crossing the border illegally. I think you start with deportations on those folks, and then I think you make it harder for illegal aliens to undercut the wages of American workers. A lot of people will go home if they can't work for less than minimum wage in our own country. And by the way, that'll be really good for our workers who just want to earn a fair wage for doing a good day's work. And the final point, Margaret, is you ask about family separation. Right now in this country, Margaret, we have 320,000 children that the Department of Homeland Security has effectively lost. Some of them have been sex trafficked, some of them hopefully are at homes with their families, some of them have been used as drug trafficking mules.

In response Tim Walz said:

> But look, we all want to solve this. Most of us want to solve this. And that is the United States Congress. That's the Border Patrol agents, that's the Chamber of Commerce. That's most Americans out here. That's why we had the fairest and the toughest bill on immigration that this nation's seen. It was crafted by a conservative senator from Oklahoma, James Lankford. I know him. He's super conservative, but he's a man of principle, wants to get it done. Democrats and Republicans worked on this piece of legislation. The Border Patrol said, this is what we need in here. These are the experts. And the Chamber of Commerce in the Wall Street Journal said, pass this thing. Kamala Harris helped get there. Fifteen hundred new border agents, detection for drugs, DOJ money to speed up these adjudications on this. Just what America wants. But as soon as it was getting ready to pass and actually tackle this Donald Trump said "No," told them to vote against it because it gives him a campaign issue.

3. Hector A. Garcia, *God, Satan, and Our Moral Bias: Can Science Explain Our Moral Bias Toward God Over Satan*, PSYCH. TODAY (Aug. 2, 2015), https://www.psychologytoday.com/us/blog/alpha-god/201508/god-satan-and-our-moral-bias.

4. *Id.*

5. *Id.*

6. *See* Bernard J. Luskin, *MRIs Reveal Unconscious Bias in the Brain*, PSYCH. TODAY (Apr. 7, 2016), https://www.psychologytoday.com/us/blog/the-media-psychology-effect/201604/mris-reveal-unconscious-bias-in-the-brain#:~:text=Unconscious%20bias%20has%20been%20identified,neuroscientists%20as%20real%20and%20measurable.

7. B. Keith Payne & C. Daryl Cameron, *Divided Minds, Divided Morals: How Implicit Social Cognition Underpins and Undermines Our Sense of Social Justice*, *in* HANDBOOK OF IMPLICIT SOCIAL COGNITION: MEASUREMENT, THEORY, & APPLICATIONS 445 (Bertram Gawronski & Brian Keith Payne eds., 2010) ("Implicit reactions are often hierarchical, dividing the world into 'us' and 'them[].'").

8. Konrad Bocian & Bogdan Wojciszke, *Self Interest Bias in Moral Judgments of Others' Actions*, 40

PERSONALITY & SOC. PSYCH. BULL. 898, 906 (2014). People tended to have a positive attitude about another when they felt, among other things, "similarity" about the actor. This similarity leads to the unconscious creation of in-groups and out-groups with more favorable moral judgments towards members of the in-group.

9. *See* Luskin, *supra* note 6.

10. Jerry Kang, *Trojan Horses of Race*, 118 HARV. L. REV. 1489, 1591 (2005).

11. Bocian & Wojciszke, *supra* note 8, at 906.

> When the observers were induced to dislike an actor, the self-interest bias disappeared, and the actor remained immoral in the eyes of those who disliked her.... This result has some disconcerting implications, which is typical for the self-interest bias. When self-interest is involved, individuals may reframe others› counter normative behaviors as virtuous. For example, a librarian waiving a fee may be reframed as an authority figure who exhibits prosociality toward a beleaguered student—a generous act of human-to-human kindness. A student who cheats on a task during a psychology experiment may be viewed as someone displaying a small, virtuous act of rebellion against a powerful, capricious-seeming authority figure (the experimenter). It is possible that the participants were not viewing the actor's act as immoral.

12. *Id.*

13. JOHN T. JOST, A THEORY OF SYSTEM JUSTIFICATION 106–107 (2020).

14. Rory D. Bahadur, *Law School Rankings and the Impossibility of Anti-Racism*, 53 ST. MARY'S L. J. 991, 1045 (2022) (quoting Michelle Ye Hee Lee, *Donald Trump's False Comments Connecting Mexican Immigrants and Crime*, WASH. POST (July 8, 2015), https://www.washingtonpost.com/news/fact-checker/wp/2015/07/08/donald-trumps-false-comments-connecting-mexican-immigrants-and-crime/?noredirect=on&utm_term=.e53366e44d9; Carolina Moreno, *Here's Why Trump's 'Bad Hombres' Comment Was So Offensive*, HUFF. POST (Oct. 26, 2016), https://www.huffingtonpost.com/entry/heres-why-trumps-bad-hombres-comment-was-so-offensive_us_5808e121e4b0180a36e9b995).

15. David R. Williams, Naomi Priest & Norman Anderson, *Understanding the Association Between Race, Socioeconomic Status and Health: Patterns and Prospects*, 35 HEALTH PSYCH. 407, 408–9 (2016).

> Data on median household income tell a similar story. Asians have the highest median household income in the U.S. but Hispanics earn 70 cents and blacks earn 59 cents for every dollar of income that whites receive. However, income differences markedly understate racial differences in economic status. Net

worth, a measure of wealth, captures the economic assets and reserves that a household has. Wealth facilitates the ability of a household to both plan for the future and cushion shortfalls in income. Racial differences in wealth are striking. For every dollar of wealth that whites have, Asian households have 83 cents but blacks have 6 cents and Hispanics have 7 cents.

16. *See infra* Chapter 10.

17. Brianna Seid, Rosemary Nidiry & Ram Subramanian, *Debunking the Myth of the 'Migrant Crime Wave'*, Brennan Center For Justice (May 29, 2024), https://www.brennancenter.org/our-work/analysis-opinion/debunking-myth-migrant-crime-wave?ms=gad_illegal%20immigrant%20crime_700983500566_8628877148_163578260112&gad_source=1&gclid=EAIaIQobChMIztKp58m3iAMVh3J_AB0Jpw12EAAYASAAEgKnMvD_BwE.

18. *Id.*

19. *Id.*

20. Statista Research Department, *Number of Mass Shootings in the United States Between 1982 and September 2024, by Shooter's Race or Ethnicity*, Statista (Dec. 9, 2024), https://www.statista.com/statistics/476456/mass-shootings-in-the-us-by-shooter-s-race/ ("Between 1982 and June 2024, 81 out of the 150 mass shootings in the United States were carried out by White shooters.").

21. Statista Research Department, *Number of Mass Shootings in the United States Between 1982 and September 2024, by Shooter's Gender*, Statista (Dec. 9, 2024), https://www.statista.com/statistics/476445/mass-shootings-in-the-us-by-shooter-s-gender/.

Since 1982, an astonishing 144 mass shootings have been carried out in the United States by male shooters. In contrast, only four mass shootings (defined by the source as a single attack in a public place in which four or more victims were killed) have been carried out by women.

22. Jennie Taer & Chris Nesi, *Trump's Board Czar Slams Gov. Hochul for Bragging About Better Subway Safety After Illegal Migrant Allegedly Set a Passenger on Fire*, New York Post (Dec. 23, 2024, 3:55 PM), https://nypost.com/2024/12/23/us-news/border-czar-homan-slams-hochul-over-nyc-subway-safety-boast/.

23. Wikipedia, *Ted Bundy*, https://en.wikipedia.org/wiki/Ted_Bundy (last visited Jan 16, 2025).

24. Wikipedia, *Jeffrey Dahmer*, https://en.wikipedia.org/wiki/Jeffrey_Dahmer (last visited Jan 16, 2025).

25. Wikipedia, *John Wayne Gacy*, https://en.wikipedia.org/wiki/John_Wayne_Gacy (last visited Jan 16, 2025).

26. Wikipedia, *Dennis Rader*, https://en.wikipedia.org/wiki/Dennis_Rader (last visited Jan 16, 2025).

27. Wikipedia, *Sandy Hook Elementary School shooting*, https://en.wikipedia.org/wiki/Sandy_Hook_Elementary_School_shooting (last visited Jan 16, 2025).

28. Wikipedia, *Dylann Roof*, https://en.wikipedia.org/wiki/Dylann_Roof (last visited Jan 16, 2025).

29. Wikipedia, *James Holmes (mass murderer)*, https://en.wikipedia.org/wiki/James_Holmes_(mass_murderer) (last visited Jan 16, 2025).

30. Wikipedia, *Murder of Laci Peterson*, https://en.wikipedia.org/wiki/Murder_of_Laci_Peterson (last visited Jan 16, 2025).

31. Wikipedia, *Watts family murders*, https://en.wikipedia.org/wiki/Watts_family_murders (last visited Jan 16, 2025).

32. Wikipedia, *Timothy McVeigh*, https://en.wikipedia.org/wiki/Timothy_McVeigh (last visited Jan 16, 2025).

33. Wikipedia, *2019 El Paso Walmart shooting*, https://en.wikipedia.org/wiki/2019_El_Paso_Walmart_shooting (last visited Jan 16, 2025).

34. Wikipedia, *Pittsburgh synagogue shooting*, https://en.wikipedia.org/wiki/Pittsburgh_synagogue_shooting (last visited Jan 16, 2025).

35. Wikipedia, *Stephen Paddock*, https://en.wikipedia.org/wiki/Stephen_Paddock (last visited Jan 16, 2025).

36. Darlene Superville & Christina A. Cassidy, *A Look at the History of Presidential Assassination Attempts in America*, AP News (July 14, 2024, 3:18 PM), https://apnews.com/article/presidential-assassinations-lincoln-mckinley-garfield-kennedy-175d046b694ec8b370ba60bf2b001d76#. Oscar Collazo and Griselio Torresola appear to be phenotypically white but what these two Puerto Rican nationalists self-identified as is beyond the scope of this book.

37. Pierre Thomas, Josh Margolin, Aaron Katersky, Luke Barr, Bill Hutchinson & Meredith Deliso, *New Orleans Truck Attack Suspect: What We Know About Shamsud-Din Jabbar*, ABC News (Jan. 2, 2025, 4:25 PM), https://abcnews.go.com/US/suspect-new-orleans-attack-bourbon-street/story?id=117247072.

38. Brandon Drenon, *Robert Card: Maine Mass Shooter's Brain Showed Signs of Injury, Doctor Says*, BBC News (Mar. 7, 2024), https://www.bbc.com/news/world-us-canada-68503159.

39. *Id.*

40. Josh Fiallo, *Trump Uses 'Terror' Attack by U.S. Army Vet to Stir Up Anti-Immigrant Hate*, Yahoo! News (Jan. 1, 2025, 7:30 PM), https://www.yahoo.com/news/trump-uses-terror-attack-u-013035416.html?guccounter=1&guce_referrer=aHR0cHM6Ly93d3cuZ29vZ2xlLmNvbS8&guce_referrer_sig=AQAAABUInU-aP2_O0M9CBRkGOXvxhyWhWXdHoY53HXwXPOuP9hd6iS-NUWV2tosQVRsbsXq6fZ6zMjv04gDNwc3fy8WgaboWsaqbSOzIHlfcPN8VeL5t2b0VEYhCcYdX3K1C88ie3xMr5YdHw8o884-fgC1rU79py0wZ0Llobc1BKJuF.

41. Thomas et al., *supra* note 37.

42. Zack Beauchamp, *This Study Obliterates the Myth That Muslims Are More Violent*, Vox (Jan. 30, 2015, 11:10 AM), https://www.vox.com/2015/1/30/7951309/islam-violence (citing a study by M. Steven Fish).

43. Marcus Lu, *Charted: Unauthorized Immigrants in the U.S., by Country of Origin*, Visual Capitalist (June 22, 2024), https://www.visualcapitalist.com/unauthorized-immigrants-in-the-u-s-by-country/.

44. *Id.*

45. Juan Gonzalez, Harvest of Empire 152–154 (2d ed. 2022).

46. *Id.*

47. *Id.*

48. Wikipedia, *United Fruit Company*, https://en.wikipedia.org/wiki/United_Fruit_Company#:~:text=The%20company%20was%20formed%20in,Colombia%2C%20and%20the%20West%20Indies (last visited Jan. 16, 2025).

49. Lindsey Morey, *Blood for Bananas: United Fruit Central American Empire*, Wash. State Univ. (Fall 2014), https://history.wsu.edu/rci/sample-research-project/ (last visited Jan. 16, 2025) (citing Catherine Cocks, Tropical Whites: The Rise of the Tourist South in the Americas 37 (University of Pennsylvania Press, 2013).

50. *Id.*

51. *Id.*
52. *Id.*
53. *Id.*
54. *Id.*
55. *Id.*
56. Gonzalez, *supra* note 45, at 150.
57. *Id.* at 152–153.
58. *Id.* at 153.
59. *Id.*
60. *Id.*
61. *Id.*
62. *Id.*
63. *Id.*
64. *Id.* at 154.
65. *Id.*
66. *Id.* at 153.
67. *Id.*
68. *Id.*
69. *Id.* at 154.
70. Lu, *supra* note 43.
71. Gavin Musynske, *United Fruit Company Laborers Campaign for Economic Justice, Honduras, 1954*, GLOBAL NONVIOLENT ACTION DATABASE (Dec. 12, 2009), https://nvdatabase.swarthmore.edu/content/united-fruit-company-laborers-campaign-economic-justice-honduras-1954#:~:text=The%20government%20created%20progressive%20labor,a%20workforce%20of%20over%20100%2C000).
72. *Id.*
73. Emilee Haines, *General Strike of 1954*, COW LATIN AMERICA (May 1, 2020), https://cowlatinamerica.voices.wooster.edu/archive-item/general-strike-of-1954/#:~:text=Former%20lawyer%20for%20the%20United,Honduran%20people%20during%20his%20presidency. The president Juan Manuel Gálvez Durón was a former lawyer for United Fruit Company.
74. ASS'N FOR DIPLOMATIC STUD. & TRAINING, *Cleaning up America's Backyard: The Overthrow of Guatemala's Arbenz*, https://adst.org/2016/06/cleaning-americas-backyard-overthrow-guatemalas-arbenz/ (last visited Jan. 16, 2025). This is referred to as Operation PBSUCCESS.
75. THE CTR. FOR JUST. & ACCOUNTABILITY, *Honduras*, https://cja.org/where-we-work/honduras/ (last visited Jan. 16, 2025).

> With the communist Sandinista government entrenched in Nicaragua and the outbreak of the Salvadoran civil war in 1981, Honduras would be transformed into a staging ground for covert operations. The U.S. poured military aid and advisors into the Honduran army and set up base camps for the Contras—a right-wing paramilitary force cultivated by the U.S. to overthrow the Sandinistas in Nicaragua.

76. *Id.*
77. *Id.*; Gary Cohn & Ginger Thompson, *Unearthed: Fatal Secrets When a Wave of Torture and Murder Staggered a Small U.S. Ally, Truth Was a Casualty. Was the CIA Involved? Did Washington Know? Was the Public Deceived? Now We Know: Yes, Yes and Yes.*, BALTIMORE SUN (Oct. 23, 2018, 4:48 PM), https://www.baltimoresun.com/1995/06/11/

unearthed-fatal-secrets-when-a-wave-of-torture-and-murder-staggered-a-small-us-ally-truth-was-a-casualty-was-the-cia-involved-did-washington-know-was-the-public-deceived-now-we-know-yes-yes-and-yes/.

78. Cohn & Thompson, *supra* note 77.

79. The Ctr. for Just. &Accountability, *supra* note 75.

80. Alexander Main, *Honduras: The Deep Roots of Resistance*, Dissent (2014), https://www.dissentmagazine.org/article/honduras-the-deep-roots-of-resistance/.

81. *Id.*

82. Lu, *supra* note 43.

83. Brenna Dilley & Kristina-Aiad Toss, *Aiding and Abetting Terror in El Salvador: Holding the United States Responsible for War Crimes Committed During the Salvadoran Civil War*, IPM (2020), https://ipmconnect.org/wp-content/uploads/2020/02/US-Aiding-Abetting-Salvadoran-Civil-War.pdf.

84. *Id.*

85. *Id.*

86. *Id.* at 3 (citing Erik Ching, *Setting the Stage: El Salvador's Long Twentieth Century*, *in* Stories of Civil War in El Salvador: A Battle Over Memory 35. (Chapel Hill: University of North Carolina Press, 2016).

87. *Id.*

88. *Id.* at 6 (citing Seth G. Jones, Olga Oliker, Peter Chalk, C. Christine Fair, Rollie Lal, & James Dobbins, *Securing Tyrants or Fostering Reform? U.S. Internal Security Assistance to Repressive and Transitioning Regimes*, 22–3. (RAND Corporation, 2006).

89. *Id.* at 10 (citing Anna-Catherine Brigada, *Salvadorans Await Justice in Civil War Killings as One of Its First Victims Sainted*, The Guardian (Oct. 14, 2018), https://www.theguardian.com/world/2018/oct/14/el-salvador-oscar-romero-civil-war-saint-justice; Report of the UN Truth Commission on El Salvador, Doc. S/25500 (1993); *See also* Leigh Binford, The El Mozote Massacre: Human Rights and Global Implications. Revised and Expanded Edition 75 (University of Arizona Press, 2016).

90. Dilley & Toss, *supra* note 83.

91. *Id.*

92. *Id.*

93. James Doubek, *The U.S. Set the Stage for a Coup in Chile. It Had Unintended Consequences at Home*, NPR (Sept. 10, 2023, 6:00 AM), https://www.npr.org/2023/09/10/1193755188/chile-coup-50-years-pinochet-kissinger-human-rights-allende.

94. *Id.*

95. *Id.*

96. National Security Archive, *The CIA and Chile: Anatomy of an Assassination*, https://nsarchive.gwu.edu/briefing-book/chile/2020-10-22/cia-chile-anatomy-assassination (last visited Jan. 16, 2025).

97. *Id.*

98. *Id.*

99. Doubek, *supra* note 93.

100. Rachel Sauer, *'The Dictatorship Left a Lot of Scars'*, Colo. Arts & Sciences Mag. (Sept. 26, 2023), https://www.colorado.edu/asmagazine/2023/09/26/dictatorship-left-lot-scars.

101. Doubek, *supra* note 93.

102. *Id.*

103. Off. of the Historian, *U.S. Invasion and Occupation of Haiti, 1914–34*, https://history.state.gov/milestones/1914-1920/haiti (last visited Jan. 16, 2025).

104. Mark Weisbrot, *America's Subversion of Haiti's Democracy Continues*, The Guardian (Mar. 13, 2012), https://www.theguardian.com/commentisfree/cifamerica/2012/mar/13/america-subversion-haiti-democracy.

105. Peter Kross, *The CIA Assassination of Rafael Trujillo*, Warfare History Network (Nov. 2013), https://warfarehistorynetwork.com/article/the-cia-assassination-of-rafael-trujillo/#:~:text=John%20F.,dissidents%20in%20the%20Dominican%20Republic.

106. Salvador E. Gomez, *The US Invasion of the Dominican Republic: 1965*, Sincronía (1997), http://sincronia.cucsh.udg.mx/dominican.html.

107. Dana Hornig, *The Truth Emerges About Grenada*, Cape Cod Times (Nov. 2, 2007, 2:15 AM), https://www.capecodtimes.com/story/opinion/2007/11/02/the-truth-emerges-about-grenada/52752749007/.

108. Britannica, *The U.S. invasion of Grenada [1983]*, https://www.britannica.com/event/U-S-invasion-of-Grenada (last visited Jan. 16, 2025).

109. U.S. Dep't. of State, *Grenada (10/04)*, https://2009-2017.state.gov/outofdate/bgn/grenada/47463.htm#:~:text=Following%20a%20breakdown%20in%20civil,evacuated%2C%20and%20order%20was%20restored (last visited Jan. 16, 2025).

110. Espinoza Martínez & Kleidy Yanira, *The US Methods and Goals to Destabilize Venezuela*, Globalistic & Globalization Stud. (2021), https://www.sociostudies.org/almanac/articles/the_us_methods_and_goals_to_destabilize_venezuela/.

111. Edward Hunt, *The U.S. Economic War on Venezuela Has Fueled Migrant Crisis*, Foreign Policy in Focus (Jan. 18, 2023), https://fpif.org/the-u-s-economic-war-on-venezuela-has-fueled-the-migrant-crisis/.

CHAPTER 8

Changing Demographics Don't Change Systemic Structure

The United States is on its way to a significant demographic shift. According to the Brookings Institution, white people will no longer comprise the largest group in the U.S. population by 2045.[1] However, this demographic change alone will not change the system, as my experiences in the Caribbean demonstrate.

In the summer of 2010, Washburn Law School launched a program we called the Summer in Barbados. At the time, I was a junior professor, and I assisted a senior professor with the formation of the program. The program involved teaching two summer semesters at Cave Hill Faculty of Law in Barbados. The classes were composed of law students from the University of the West Indies and American law students. Each class was co-taught by a Washburn Law professor and a law professor from the University of the West Indies. The classes were designed to be comparative law courses, exposing students from each institution and region to the way topics of law varied by region. Another aim of the program was to give American (predominantly white) law students the experience of living in a country where they were the minority. This was my first time back in the Caribbean as an adult, apart from visiting home after immigrating, and it was sobering. I quickly discovered that, even though it had remained invisible to me while I lived in the region, racism and system justification resulted in a hierarchy of white dominance and superiority—even in Barbados, where 92.4% of the population is of African descent and only 2.7% of the population is white.[2]

Barbados was one of the many British islands in the Caribbean where the white-owned sugar plantations were worked by African slaves. These slaves were eventually emancipated, and Barbados gained independence from England in 1966. Today, the island boasts a well-educated population, with a literacy rate of 99.7%.[3] Despite these impressive demographics, the white supremacy of colonialism still persists, as the following illustrates.

Our students lived in the dormitory at the university, and the dormitory support staff was predominantly of African descent. It quickly became apparent to me and the other (white) Washburn professor who was with me at the time that if we needed dormitory support or assistance with room issues, such as sheets, pillows, etc., the staff's response varied significantly depending on who made the request. When I (a brown man) asked the staff for assistance, their response was generally dismissive, often brushing me off and effectively communicating that my requests were a "bother."

On a hunch, after years of living in the United States, I asked my white Washburn colleague to try dealing with the dormitory support staff instead of me. Their response to her was the equivalent of a salute—an enthusiastic and bustling eagerness to please. In fact, they even addressed her as "Miss." I was appalled at their eagerness to please whiteness. Each of the three times I have returned to Barbados to teach, we experienced the same pattern. By the most recent visit, I was able to joke with my white colleague that they should handle all interactions with the dormitory support staff because, well, "you know."

Additionally, in the summer of 2010, after my class was over, my white wife and daughter flew down from Kansas, and we spent a week at an all-inclusive on the island before returning home. The resort catered mostly to Virgin Atlantic customers flying in from England. One day there was a barbeque on the beach at lunchtime—and I mean *on the beach*. The grill was in the sand, and a Black Barbadian was grilling hamburgers. People were coming straight out of the ocean, stopping by the grill, and being served hamburgers, and proceeded to eat them right there on the beach.

When I arrived at the grill, the grill attendant told me that I could not be served food until I had changed my clothes and dried off. From her tone, it felt as though she was saying, "I have to serve the white people, but there's no way I'm doing the same for you. You're just like me, fucker." Right behind me in line was my white wife, still dripping wet in her bathing suit. She was served her hamburger without any issues. She later commented to me then that she would never return to Barbados, and since then, she has steadfastly refused to accompany me whenever I've gone there for work.

Then, on that same trip, we left the all-inclusive resort to get a meal that I thought was fantastic, one I had before my wife and daughter arrived. It was at a restaurant near the base of the hill leading to the university, a place the then-dean of the law school had taken me to. The restaurant has since closed I think, but on that day in 2010, they served a buffet of Barbadian food, including the best pepper pot I have ever had. When we arrived in my rental car, the restaurant was packed, and the security guard directed me to park on an elevated part of the parking lot.

We parked, entered the restaurant, and left about an hour and a half later. When I came out of the restaurant, the parking lot was empty, and the tires on my car were slashed. I went into that restaurant and asked if anyone knew what had happened. A white Barbadian woman, who appeared to be the owner or a senior member of staff said, "That's what happens when you park where you are not supposed to."

The Black Barbadian staff standing behind her had looks of helplessness on their faces. It seemed they knew if they came out and said that she (the white woman) had slashed the tires, they would lose their jobs. Meanwhile, the white Barbadian all but admitted, "I did it." She spoke with impunity, fully aware that no one would ever say otherwise and that the police probably would not care. It was the most self-confident white supremacy I had ever experienced—and I've traveled extensively.

My suspicions were confirmed when I called the rental car company to ask for assistance. The rental contract specified that the renter would be responsible for all tire damage. However, when the representative from the rental car company arrived at the restaurant and heard what had happened—and who had spoken to me from the restaurant—he said, "We won't charge you for the tires. We all know what happened here. Sorry that happened to you."

I mentioned my experiences and my thoughts about what I described as the worship of white people in Barbados to a Barbadian professor I taught a subsequent course with. He is now deceased but eventually went on to become a judge on the Barbados Court of Appeals. In response to my observations of white worship on the island, he said, "It takes a lot of effort for people to break their habits and routines and while the very well-educated and successful Black Barbadians are strong and put people in their place when they need to be put in their place, the majority of the population isn't there yet."

Sir Hilary Beckles, one of the most respected Barbadian historians, agrees with me. He argues, "that the white inheritors of The First Black Slave Society remain both dominant and unrepentant in today's Barbados. For all the *de jure* political power that black descendants have achieved, *de facto* economic power has not shifted."[4] Additionally, a working paper by Colin Constantine demonstrates that the plantation economy in Barbados was unique in that the white plantation owners banded together to ensure that they and their descendants would continue to own most of the land on the island.[5] What I experienced in Barbados was the reality that "old colonial oligarchy in Barbados has transformed itself into a post-colonial oligarchy."[6]

Of course, I thought this racist hierarchy did not exist on my island of Trinidad, where the national anthem expressly provides, "Here Every Creed and Race Find an Equal Place." For me, Trinidad meant growing up on an island where the only difference between the races and the religions was whose house we ate at for Divali, Eid, Christmas, and so on. The island prides itself on being one of the most cosmopolitan and racially tolerant societies in the world. Alas, this too is a lie. I first began to think about the privilege of being white in Trinidad while in Barbados in 2010.

As we worked to establish the program in Barbados, we visited various hotels and small guest houses before settling on the university dorms for the students' accommodation. One of the hotels we considered was owned by a white Barbadian who had the same surname as some white students I went to primary school with as a child in Trinidad. I mentioned this to her, and she said, "That shouldn't be surprising because the dad of the kids you went to school with is my cousin. The ______ family was originally a plantation owning family in Nevis and then as the industry dried up there, we took our wealth and moved all over the Caribbean, including Trinidad, and bought land everywhere."

It was then, and *only* then, as an adult, that I realized that the ancestors of some of the people I considered exactly like me—and whom I loved as people in Trinidad—were the very people some of my ancestors would have been enslaved by and worked as indentured laborers for. Suddenly, it dawned on me that white privilege and a history of white supremacy was the reason so many of the houses on the resort islands off the coast of Trinidad were owned by white people, and why so many of the expensive recreational hobbies on the island, like powerboat racing, were dominated by white people. They were different from me, and pretending that they weren't was a convenient delusion that I had perpetuated. To this day, I don't know if most of the island continues to perpetuate this delusion just to keep the peace or to cater to this section of the population—one that clearly still benefits from the legacies of slavery and indentureship in the Caribbean—by avoiding anything that might make things "awkward."

When I was last in Trinidad in 2024, I found myself, like most Trinidadians often do, hanging with a group of people from all ethnicities and backgrounds without even really being consciously aware of it. That is "normal ting, man." But one of the white people made a comment that, before I became a critical race scholar, would not even have registered with me. He said, "Nothing good ever comes out of Africa." I bit my tongue, feeling enraged and wanting to scream, "Except centuries of labor that allows you to be incredibly wealthy today." Not to mention some of history's most brilliant sociopolitical minds, as well as the ancestors of the greatest cricket team the world has ever seen. The blindness of the privilege is simply overwhelming, and if you disturb the illusion of racial harmony by pointing it out, you will be labeled the disruptive asshole. Such is the entrenchment of privilege and the deference shown to it.

I am still struggling to come to terms with what this all means and experiencing existential dissonance over my blindness to it for so many decades. Maybe it was a clear example of how system justification blinds us to reality, as I describe in Chapter 1?

In 2024, to try to sort out the reality, I asked a variety of Trinidadians via email:

> Trinidad's colonial history includes Spanish rule from 1509, the arrival of French settlers in 1777 and British rule from 1797 until independence in 1962. Please describe how today's Trinidad is shaped by colonialism, the majority of which was British and included slavery and emancipation of African slaves in 1838, East Indian indentureship from 1845–1907, and all events including all migrations through independence in 1962 and the lingering effects of these realities postindependence.

Interestingly, most responses mentioned white supremacy. For example, one response included the following observation:

> While the conception of colonialism may seem rooted in Economics—slavery, indentureship and other forms of rigid, brutal hegemony, invasion, plunder, transfer of wealth ... the basis for all of this was crude racism and dominance of a ruling class, evolving from the belief held throughout Europe in a sacred royal class, buttressed by the belief in the Divine Right of Kings/Queens to rule over others and supported absolutely by the various Christian religions of Europe. All this could be summed up in two words—white supremacy.[7]

Another response included the following observation:

> And perhaps it is physical proximity or the presence during the War Years and the oil boom years—Trinidad is becoming increasingly influenced by American culture and lifestyle.... Maybe it is also partly determined by our colonial past where we are subliminally following the patterns of the White Master, believing what they have and do is superior.[8]

One of the most powerful responses I got was as follows: "The saddest part of the legacy of colonialism for me is the devaluing of self, having been brainwashed to believe that whatever was brought by colonialism was and is superior to anything the indigenous and ancestral cultures had to offer."[9]

It was only then that I realized that the oft-stated expression we always justified as a joke growing up, "when you're white you're right," was a reflection of a white supremacy that was rendered invisible by system justification. It was also then that I thought about the social media responses to crimes in Trinidad against white people and those against non-white people. Crimes against white individuals invariably prompted an outpouring of sympathy, with sentiments like hoping no harm would come to that "pretty" girl. Meanwhile, crimes against non-white individuals typically elicited responses suggesting that crime only affected families involved in criminal activity or that "dey have to be in ting for that to happen."

Even though it took me fifty years and a whole heap of education to understand how system justification manifested itself in Trinidad, it seems everybody in Trinidad besides me was aware of this systemic reality. Upon further probing, it also became clear that everybody in Trinidad seemed to understand something it took me half a century to grasp: "The system will never change." This is the reality even in a country where white people make up less than 1% of the population and multiracial people comprise almost a quarter, making Trinidad the most ethnically diverse country in the English-speaking Caribbean.[10]

As Monique Kelly states in her research, which investigated the impact of race in Trinidad on socioeconomic outcomes and their evolution post-independence, even today—almost 186 years after the abolition of slavery and 104 years after the formal end of Indian indentureship in Trinidad—"White advantage remains prevalent, as the economic, political, and social values of the regions are based on the assumed superiority of Whites."[11]

Even though system justification in Trinidad makes it uncomfortable for us to stop perpetuating the bullshit illusion that "all ah we is one," the truth is that recent research proves:

1. Whites had the highest mean years of education, with Blacks and East Indians reporting the lowest.[12]
2. Blacks earn significantly less monthly income overall when compared to Whites, Chinese, Syrian/Lebanese, Mixed-others, and racial others. However, Blacks earn more monthly personal income than East Indians. Although Syrian/Lebanese had the largest increase . . . whites had the most personal income, and East Indians had the least.[13]

Kelly concludes what we don't want to admit in the tranquil utopia of racial equity that our limbic brains force us to perceive Trinidad as: that even today, white advantage, rooted in historical marginalization, continues in Trinidad.[14] Similarly, white supremacy remains entrenched in predominantly Black South Africa, even thirty years after the end of apartheid.[15]

That is a long way of saying systems don't change on their own, and a shift in the racial composition of American society will not, by itself, bring about systemic change. Rather, systemic change usually requires more disruptive and acute upheaval to the status quo—such as the disruption caused by the American War of Independence or the American Civil War. There are very few, if any, examples of systemic change without significant social disruption. *Make no mistake I am against and not advocating for violent social upheaval*, but the reality is that systemic change is never comfortable or polite—it involves discomfort.[16] For example, the discomfort of thinking deeply about what I just wrote about Trinidad and Barbados, rather than just ignoring it or "meh relegating" it for the sake of comfort while socializing in a multiracial environment and deciding what the next drink should be.

My friend and legal scholar Ali Khan is fascinated by the idea of whiteness in America. He reflects deeply on the fact that so many white people who were oppressed, discriminated against, enslaved, and considered the lowest rung of society in their native Europe could sail across the ocean and, based solely on the color of their skin, suddenly be seen as—and see themselves as—entitled to supremacy over non-white people. The following examination of history hopefully describes how this transformation occurred.

There is no need to document what whiteness means and entitles people to because that is already so well-established in the scholarship and research.[17] I have already explained in Chapter 5 that Jewish scholar Eric Goldstein confirms the American decision to rescue and resettle the Jewish Holocaust victims after World War II is an example of this benefit conferred by whiteness.[18] However, it is worth exploring how this entitlement developed and to carefully examine how it became so entrenched and so foregone a conclusion that, for example, Trinidadians and African Americans—jokingly or sadly—depending on the context, say without any trepidation or curiosity as to why it is so, "When you are white you're right." In other words, why is whiteness and white superiority apparently baked into the genes of colonial societies and America? It's ironic that Caribbean history provides an explanation for the phenomenon of whiteness in America. The first prime minister of Trinidad and Tobago suggests the most helpful framing of this issue: "slavery was not born of racism: rather, racism was the consequence of slavery."[19]

Robert Baird suggests that whiteness, as we see it today, was born in the latter part of the seventeenth century and developed as a way to justify "the enslavement of Africans" in the British colonies.[20] Baird explains that, up until early in the seventeenth century, an English person might have noted that they had white skin but would not have associated the whiteness of their skin with any greater entitlement to resources or as the basis of a common identity.[21] While an English person might have identified as English and had some commonality with other European nations, that commonality would not then have been expressed as whiteness.[22] Instead, what most Europeans of the time used to separate themselves from other societies was Christianity.[23] For instance, Europeans were largely Christians, while Ottomans were Muslim.[24]

Baird points out a fact that I was previously unaware of: white Europeans of the poorer classes provided the labor for the sugar cane plantations in the British West Indies and the Americas before the African slave trade began.[25] Like the Black slaves who came after them, they were subject to brutal living conditions and cruel treatment. The only thing preventing these white Europeans from being subjected to a lifetime of bondage was their Christianity, as the law forbade the lifetime bondage of Christians except in the case of criminals and war prisoners.[26] However, despite this distinction, the conditions were so harsh and appalling that, by the middle of the sixteenth century, white laborers became increasingly unwilling to come to the Caribbean to work on the plantations.[27] As a result, plantation owners began to rely more heavily on the African slave trade to provide labor for their plantations.[28]

The Africans were not Christians, and so any protections European laborers were entitled to did not inure to the African slaves.[29] The plantation owners were astute and realized that there were far more laborers and slaves working the plantation than there were plantation owners.[30] To prevent these two laborer groups from aligning and violently resisting the relatively few plantation owners, they began to use religion as the basis for a textbook application of divide and conquer.[31]

By emphasizing to the Europeans that, as Christians, they were entitled to better or at least slightly different treatment than the non-Christian African slaves, the plantation owners sought to ensure that the Europeans laborers would see themselves as superior to or different from the Africans and would not unite with them to overthrow the plantation owners.[32] While religion was the initial distinguishing factor, skin color eventually came to be associated with the distinction in entitlement.[33]

By referring to the work of historian Katherine Gerbner, Baird suggests that the plantation owners deliberately switched the basis of the entitlement from religion to skin color to avoid problems maintaining the religious-based distinction.[34] These problems arose due to the late-1600s push by many religious leaders and abolitionists to convert the African slaves to Christianity.[35] The issue was that European laws prohibited the enslavement of Christians, which would have effectively prohibited the enslavement of Africans once they converted to Christianity.[36]

Initially, Barbadian plantation owners tried to pass laws prohibiting the conversion of African slaves to Christianity, but the religious hierarchy in England denied this request.[37] Once African slaves were allowed to become Christians, the law had to change to perpetuate the strife between workers to prevent them from unifying to overthrow the plantation owners.[38] Because the Christian versus non-Christian dichotomy could no longer serve this purpose, as Blacks were now allowed to convert to Christianity, skin color became the dividing line.[39] By the late 1600s in Jamaica, the laws governing slaves and servants shifted, and the identity of the slightly more privileged class of workers changed from Christian to white.[40] Laws in parts of the Americas adopted this change, with the same shift in terminology appearing in South Carolina codes governing labor.[41]

This concept of "white" as meaning more entitled to privilege quickly took hold because it facilitated increased supply of labor from Africa, as these "non-white" laborers could be enslaved.[42] Baird mentions that Theodore Allen, a historian, posits, "The plantation bourgeoisie deliberately extended a privileged status to the white poor of all categories as a means of turning to African slavery as the basis of its system of production."[43] Whiteness, as an economic tool, was incredibly efficient, and the concept spread like a religion across the world.[44]

From its inception, therefore, the concept of whiteness has always meant white supremacy. It has always meant that, based on skin color or the social construct of race, some people were considered superior to others and more deserving than others.[45] According to Baird, government officials of the time framed whiteness as: "race implies difference, difference implies superiority, and superiority leads to predominance."[46]

Ali Khan also notes that poor and wretched Europeans were also brought to United States as debt servants to work for the venture capitalists who essentially founded America.[47] Just as the East India Company was formed for venture capitalists to participate in and profit from the spice trade in India on behalf of the crown, the Virginia Company of London was established in 1606 so venture capitalists could profit from industries in what was then described by the British as "savage" America.[48] Other similar stock companies were formed to establish settlements in America, and these entities resorted to all measures, including human trafficking, to obtain the labor necessary to operate.[49]

Because of religious strife in Europe, there was a ready supply of labor in the form of people from various European countries, including England, Germany, and among others Scotland.[50] As is typical with indentured labor, venture capitalists offered these Europeans passage to the New World in exchange for a fee, which they could work off during an "indenture," hence they were known as indentured or debt laborers. Entire European families found their way to America in this fashion, and more than half of all the labor in the American colonies consisted of these European laborers.[51]

At this point, Africans, Europeans, and people from wherever labor could be obtained worked alongside each other under similar conditions.[52] In fact, when Massachusetts legalized the institution of slavery in 1641, non-white people were enslaved[53] because it was illegal under English law to enslave Christians, which most European laborers were. However, this wasn't about color or race at the time—it was about labor. Presumably, the white laborers would have also been enslaved were it not for the religious laws protecting them as Christians, *not* as white people.

And once it was decided that Christianity was the chosen distinction to perpetuate disunity among the laborers, the powerful merchants grafted the story of Noah and his son Ham, which I mention in Chapter 2 onto their chosen and contrived distinction. The result is that the meritless, skin-color-based distinction created in the 1600s appeared to carry divine provenance. Perhaps it is that divine provenance that is responsible for the myth's durability, such that today the distinction still exists with a fancy new name: systemic racism.

But up until 1785, British ships continued to bring white European debt laborers to the colonies. When Britain banned the transport of debt laborers on their own ships, vessels from other countries began bringing them to the Americas. These Europeans continued to work alongside Africans and anyone else the venture capitalists could find to provide labor, often under similar conditions. At this point, it was religion—not skin color—that prevented Europeans from being enslaved.

When these Europeans completed the repayment of their indenture-based debt, they began to marry and reproduce. However, class, wealth, and status distinction prevented them from mixing with the descendants of the aristocratic venture capitalists.[54] They remained a separate group of lower-status white people and referred to by derogatory terms such as white trash, rednecks, okies, hillbillies, and similar to distinguish them from the aristocratic and identify them as debt workers or the descendants of debt workers.[55]

The reality is that the invention of whiteness as meaning "more entitled than darker skinned people" is something the plantation owners and American aristocrats invented to create division and make management of labor easier. By fostering this division, they ensured that their laborers would not unite and depose them. It was divide and conquer at its finest. The concept of whiteness as superior was, and remains, a brilliantly manipulative strategy that money merchants and corporations continue to exploit today. The reality, however, is that:

> Millions of Americans, the progenies of slaves and [white] debt servants, should [recognize] all forms of racism as a cruel ploy that money merchants, venture capitalists, entrepreneurs, and morality-free politicians exploit to divide and rule vulnerable people [who have been manipulated into forgetting the] historical mistreatment of their forefathers and foremothers. Most Americans, regardless of race, religion, national origin, and gender, have much [more] in common than idiotic racial distinctions invented to separate them.[56]

Rather than racial difference, the unique beauty and meaning of America lies in the absence of an immovable class-based barrier preventing upward mobility, regardless of where one starts on the socioeconomic ladder. Absent systemic racism—the current iteration of the deliberate and manipulative perpetuation of the original divide-and-conquer strategy—this ideal should hold true for all Americans, regardless of skin color. However, as long as our institutions remain designed to strip the majority of American white people of the ability to remember that, apart from divide-and-conquer strategies of wealthy individuals seeking to become even richer, they are no different than people of color, this ideal will not be equally true for people of color—especially the descendants of African slaves.

Some suggest changing American demographics and the inevitable minority/majority cliché will necessarily end systemic racism,[57] but this is grossly erroneous. It hasn't changed it in the Caribbean, and it was also not true in the colorism observed in phenomena based on skin color, such as the brown paper bag test in New Orleans.[58] This occurred even in a society where there is an abundance of mixed-race people referred to then by the now-derogatory term "mulatto."[59]

The brown paper bag test was a practice used by African Americans to discriminate against each other based on skin tone.[60] Mixed-race individuals with lighter skin tones, who were said to be at least as light skinned as a brown paper bag, were admitted to clubs and entitled to privileges that darker-skinned people were not.[61]

This illustrates the extent to which the greed of businesspeople and their manipulative decision to baselessly and arbitrarily distinguish Black from white in the seventeenth century—solely to ensure their wealth was not threatened—has infected America and much of the West. It is the reason "white is right" and the reason, as Monique Kelly provides in her study, even in Trinidad where whites comprise less than 1% of the population, assumptions of white superiority define and shape social values, politics, and economics.[62]

This nonsense has indeed been baked into our DNA, as religion and the story of Ham combined with wealth, power, and race have rendered the differential treatment of people based on skin color seemingly unassailable. I will not apologize for challenging the reader, as I did in Chapter 2, to consider the massive role religion has played throughout history to make cruelty and murder appear divine. Time and demographic change will not dilute these hierarchies. Something more conscious and deliberate is required.[63]

Endnotes

1. William H. Frey, *The US Will Become 'Minority White' in 2045, Census Projects*, Brookings (Mar. 14, 2018), https://www.brookings.edu/articles/the-us-will-become-minority-white-in-2045-census-projects/.

2. Barbados Integrated Government, *Demographics*, https://www.gov.bb/Visit-Barbados/demographics (last visited Jan. 18, 2025).

3. American Association of Collegiate Registrars and Admission Officers, *Barbados*, https://www.aacrao.org/edge/country/barbados#:~:text=Barbados%20is%20an%20island%20of,literacy%20rates%20in%20the%20world (last visited Jan. 18, 2025).

4. Asa Cusack, *Trouble in Paradise: The Hidden Impacts of Increasing Inequalities in Barbados*, LSE (Aug. 18, 2017), https://blogs.lse.ac.uk/latamcaribbean/2017/08/18/trouble-in-paradise-the-hidden-impacts-of-increasing-inequalities-in-barbados/.

5. Collin Constantine, *A Community Divided: Top Incomes in CARICOM Member States* (Griton Coll. Univ. of Cambridge, Working Paper Apr. 2017).

6. Cusack, *supra* note 4.

7. Survey Response from Rodney Yamin Ali (2024).

8. Survey Response from Shareeda Narsiah (2024).

9. Survey Response from Ingrid Kemchand (2024), B.A. French and Spanish, Hons. 1st Class, M.Ed. University of the West Indies (2024).

10. Monique D. A. Kelly, *The Changing Terrain of Racial Inequality in Trinidad and Tobago*, 86 Rsch.in Soc. Stratification & Mobility 1, (2023). Explaining that Trinidad "boasts the largest ethnoracially diverse population" in the English-speaking Caribbean.

11. *Id.*

12. *Id.* at 4–7.

13. *Id.* at 8.

14. *Id.* at 9–10.

15. Shola Lawal, *South Africa: 30 Years After Apartheid, What Has Changed?*, Aljazeera (Apr. 27, 2024), https://www.aljazeera.com/news/2024/4/27/south-africa-30-years-after-apartheid-what-has-changed.

16. *See* Sophia Wushanley, *Real Change Is Uncomfortable*, The Daily Pennsylvanian (Mar. 1, 2015), https://www.thedp.com/article/2015/03/sophia-wushanley-real-change-uncomfortable.

17. *See* Cheryl I. Harris, *Whiteness as Property*, 106 Harv. L. Rev. 1707, 1707 (1993).

18. *See* Eric L. Goldstein The Price of Whiteness: Jews, Race, and American Identity (Princeton University Press, 2019).

19. Robert P. Baird, *The Invention of Whiteness: The Long History of a Dangerous Idea*, The Guardian (Apr. 20, 2021), https://www.theguardian.com/news/2021/apr/20/the-invention-of-whiteness-long-history-dangerous-idea.

20. *Id.*

21. *Id.*

22. *Id.*

23. *Id.*

24. *Id.*

25. *Id.*

26. *Id.*

27. *Id.*

28. *Id.*
29. *Id.*
30. *Id.*
31. *Id.*
32. *Id.*
33. *Id.*
34. *Id.*
35. *Id.*
36. *Id.*
37. *Id.*
38. *Id.*
39. *Id.*
40. *Id.*
41. *Id.*
42. *Id.*
43. *Id.*
44. *Id.*
45. *Id.*
46. *Id.* (quoting the Victorian Prime Minister Benjamin Disraeli).
47. L. Ali Khan, *White Servitude in America*, CounterPunch (Dec. 3, 2015), https://www.counterpunch.org/2015/12/03/white-servitude-in-america/.
48. *Id.*
49. *Id.*
50. *Id.*
51. *Id.*
52. *Id.*
53. National Park Service, *Slavery and Law in 17th Century Massachusetts*, https://www.nps.gov/articles/000/slavery-and-law-in-early-ma.htm (last visited Jan. 18, 2025).
54. Khan, *supra* note 47.
55. *Id.*
56. *Id.*
57. *See* Richard Alba & Christopher Maggio, *Demographic Change and Assimilation in the Early 21st-Century United States*, 119 Proc. of the Nat'l Acad. of Sci. of the U.S.A. 1 (2022).
58. Wikipedia, *Brown paper bag test*, https://en.wikipedia.org/wiki/Brown_paper_bag_test (last visited Jan. 17, 2025).
59. Wikipedia, *Mulatto*, https://en.m.wikipedia.org/wiki/Mulatto (last visited Jan. 17, 2025).
60. Wikipedia, supra note 47.
61. *Id.*
62. *See* Kelly, *supra* note 10.
63. *See* John Chenault, *Western Christianity and the Origins of Antiblackness, Eurocentrism, and White Supremacy*, Univ. of Louisville 375 (2022). John Chenault explains the fundamental role of Western Christianity in creating and perpetuating systemic racism.

> Western Christian intellectuals never intended for Enlightenment principles to be applied to non-Christian, "non-white" men, or to women of any hue. Those deemed sub-human and irrational (the latter of which applied even to

"White" women) lacked the basic cognitive and physical characteristics and qualities for inclusion in [the] category of humankind. The confluence of historical events, theo-politics, and whiteness/antiblackness ideology in the Christian Intellectual Tradition lead directly to this finding.

CHAPTER 9

Three Other Things That Don't Change Systemic Structure

White People Who Passionately Mean Well

Recently, a student of color came to my office and asked if I had time to discuss something that was driving her insane. She explained that a white student said the following to her: "Don't worry, I'm an ally so I got your back." She told me that she did not even know how to respond to what was, to the white person, an obviously powerful pride-inducing revelation about themselves. She then asked me, "Just what the fuck does 'I'm an ally mean'?" We both laughed heartily—the kind of laugh that typifies the saying "If you don't laugh you will cry." Our interaction represented our recognition of the reality of how hopeless systemic reform can often seem.

It's not enough that you march in support of George Floyd. Feeling good about the fact that you marched to protest the George Floyd murder is, in reality, a distraction—one that makes you feel good about a performative and ineffectual gesture. As I've spent the first part of this book explaining, systemic racism and systemic hierarchies depend on us being distracted from reality by the powerful emotional bait our limbic brains deploy to refocus us on palliative illusions. As I stated in a previous publication:

> Systemic racism is not at all impacted or diminished because Derek Chauvin got convicted. And while it is easier to focus on the happy by focusing on the result in that trial rather than the deeply entrenched nature of systemic racism, that trial needs to be considered in light of the fact that there were 10 million arrests in 2019 in the United States.
>
> While we can use the George Floyd result as a motivating symbol in the fight against racism, do not mistake this emotionally powerful, beneficial symbolism for actual societal change and progress.[1]

Similarly, your beliefs, your heartfelt support for, and your comforting of colleagues of color who experience microaggressions or racism does nothing to ameliorate systemic racism. These gestures simply serve to help white people justify their perceptions of themselves as just and moral. They are performative gestures that do nothing to ameliorate racism. It's akin to offering to keep someone in your thoughts when they've suffered a loss—it does nothing for that person but makes you feel good because you are pretending to do something. And you need to stop shedding tears when people call you out on the uselessness of these performative gestures. Being called out is not personal.

White people are so accustomed to "mattering" because the world consistently validates their feelings and individuality so powerfully that it becomes nearly impossible for most of them to comprehend how their personal motives and feelings are incapable of creating systemic change. This level of *individual* irrelevance is difficult, if not impossible, for many white people to accept. Yet accepting it is a necessary condition for achieving systemic reform.

Systemic change requires a shift in societal power structures and norms, and it must be uncomfortable. If you feel morally certain about the "goodness" of your actions, you need to step back and really question whether that action has any impact on inequity or whether those actions are merely palliative and perpetuating the comfortable fiction all human brains create. Actions that push back against systemic structure are uncomfortable precisely because system justification powerfully normalizes and renders moral the policies, structures, and assumptions that perpetuate systemic discrepancies. Reformative actions feel uncomfortable, abnormal, and wrong because they challenge the system our limbic brains are wired to reinforce and they confront those in power who seek to maintain the status quo.

Frederick Douglass reminds us that there can be no systemic power shift without discomfort and agitation:

> If there is no struggle, there is no progress. Those who profess to favor freedom and yet deprecate agitation are men who want crops without plowing the ground. They want rain without thunder and lightning. They want the ocean without the roar of its mighty waters.
>
> The struggle may be a moral one or it may be a physical one, or it may be both moral and physical, but it must be a struggle. Power concedes nothing without a demand. It never has and it never will. Find out just what a people will submit to, and you have found out the exact amount of injustice and wrong which will be imposed upon them; and these will continue till they are resisted with either words or blows, or with both. The limits of tyrants are prescribed by the endurance of those whom they oppress.[2]

If what you consider your well-meaning gestures of antiracism don't involve you experiencing agitation and discomfort then, despite your firm belief in the altruism and prosocial nature of your gesture, it benefits you only. And if you continue to be satisfied with good, moral gestures as the limit of your ability to effectuate systemic change, then you are now aware you are effectuating no change except to your own well-being and comfort, and your perpetuation of the systemic hierarchy is no longer unconscious.

So, get over yourselves. I know you are not used to the world not revolving around the way you feel, but the way you feel—and whether you're trying to be kind to people of color or not—is irrelevant to resolving systemic racism. But even when white people understand this reality and are willing to make the sacrifices that would impact systemic inequity, the system punishes them.

Individual Attempts to Reform the System

a. Kendra Schwartz

In 2023, I witnessed behavior by a young white woman that gave me hope that we can reach a place in society where we all internalize and understand what systemic change requires. On that day, I was a passenger in Dean Michael Hunter Schwartz's car when his daughter Kendra called from Philadelphia to tell him that she was involved in an automobile accident. The parties to the accident had already agreed that she was not at fault, and she called asking if she should make a police report. Dean Schwartz jokingly mentioned that in his car there were two torts professors (me and another dear friend), so she should ask us.

The entire conversation was on speakerphone, and I was adamant that she should make sure the police came to the scene and that a report memorializing the attribution of fault was generated, just in case the other party later recanted their admission of liability. She seemed inexplicably hesitant to do this, and I wondered—though not because of anything specific about Kendra, but because I have a 20-year-old driver away at college (who, let's just say, isn't as skilled as Danica Patrick)—whether the hesitancy to call the police represented a disconnect between what really happened and what was being reported.

What Kendra said next had a profound impact on me. She said, "I am not willing to call the police because the other driver is black, and I don't trust the Philly police with Black people. Things could go south." This young woman was willing to risk the other party in the accident changing their story and finding herself having to file a claim with her insurance—likely resulting in an increase in premiums—or paying for the repairs herself, rather than risk exposing a Black man to police interaction. She was willing to impose a cost on herself and justified that cost because she believed it was necessary given the systemic racism frequently associated with interactions between police and people of color. Unless your antiracism also involves this self-imposition of cost and sacrifice, you can keep it. Instead, find other ways to feel good about yourself other than pretending you are contributing to antiracism.

But even these individual actions aren't enough, because the system ensures that gestures like these will likely be punished. The system gave

Kendra a choice: call the police and attempt to maintain the status quo of systemic inequity, or do something meaningful and risk putting herself in a vulnerable position. The risk materialized. The other party in Kendra's accident changed his story after the fact, but even though there was no police report, the evidence was so overwhelming that the insurance company correctly concluded the other driver was at fault.

An even more graphic and far-reaching example of how individual sacrificial deeds to ameliorate systemic inequities are severely punished by the system is found by examining legal education.

b. Legal Education

Nine years ago, *The Washington Post* reported that law is "the least diverse profession in the nation."[3] At that time, 88% of lawyers were white, and less than 2% of partners and 3% of associates in major law firms were Black.[4] The situation has not improved significantly today.[5] The reasons are explicit and implicit racism.[6] We have known for years, and it is beyond debate, that the metrics that we use to rank applicants to law school, rank law schools, and to test competency to practice law are racist. Yet, we continue to abide by these metrics.[7]

The most common metric for deciding whether applicants to law schools will be admitted is the Law School Admission Test (LSAT). Copious studies demonstrate this exam is a racially exclusionary test that disenfranchises Black applicants from access to legal education.[8] The validity of the test is also questionable on its own, but especially so considering the racist exclusion it causes while its ability to predict law school success remains highly suspect.[9]

The continued use of the test is so incredulous that Sandra Simpson explains, "It defies logic: why do law schools continue to use standardized admission tests when that process harms diversity?"[10] The answer, as Simpson explains, is because we prefer to have a standard that allows us to compare people, even if that standard is racist and perpetuated by racist ranking systems. As I have explained countless times in this book so far, our brains prefer to create simple and straightforward fictions rather than confront the paralyzing complexity of reality.

The continuing use of the LSAT is driven by ABA requirements, which mandate that accredited law schools use a "valid and reliable admissions test."[11] If schools choose to use a test other than the LSAT, they must demonstrate the validity and reliability of the alternative test.[12] Additionally, the ABA signals its favoritism for the LSAT by requiring law schools to publicly publish, in accordance with ABA Standard 509, the LSAT scores of its entering classes annually. The ABA also refuses to accredit any law school whose LSAT scores are lower than 140.[13] This practice misleads law school applicants into believing that the LSAT scores of the entering cohort are an expression of the school's efficacy.

This, even though the test is of questionable predictive value and reduces Black enrollment significantly. For over 50 years, we have been aware that Black applicants perform poorly on the LSAT—not because of ability or capacity, but due to "prior educational disparities, socioeconomic status, biased questions, family structure, and stereotype threat."[14] Rather than respond to this reality, it is much easier and requires less work for the ABA to pretend law school admission is a meritocratic process. Because of system justification, society—including those disenfranchised by the test—buys into this meritocracy-based lie.[15]

Remember, meritocracy is,

> one mechanism by which inequality and status differences are maintained in America. Subtle cues to meritocracy in the cultural environment may encourage members of low status groups to construe personal and group disadvantage as deserved and to minimize the perception that such disadvantage is due to discrimination. These system justifying responses to meritocracy cues may be most likely precisely when [they should be] least like[ly] ... to occur: in the presence of clear, meritocracy-violating inequality.[16]

The reality of racism is that "55% of black applicants in the 135–149 LSAT band did not receive offers to law schools while only 39% of white applicants in the same band did not receive offers. This contradicts what most people assume; that black applicants in the lower LSAT range have advantages over white applicants."[17]

The cognitive comfort of order created by the illusion of meritocracy causes us to "meh relegate" reality and instead buy into the comforting delusion that the system is valid and makes sense. However, the racist and exclusionary reality of the LSAT is exacerbated by its inclusion in perhaps the most insidious example of systemic racism in any educational arena: the *U.S. News and World Report Ranking*.[18]

The U.S. News Law School Rankings is an annual ranking of law schools that wields significant influence in legal education, despite being profoundly flawed.[19] As I mentioned above and explained in great detail in my 2022 law review article *Law School Rankings and the Impossibility of Anti-Racism*,[20] schools put an enormous amount of effort to recruit students with entering credentials that result in an increased ranking in *U.S. News*. While *U.S. News* has recently reduced the impact of entering credentials in its methodology, schools still generally rank higher if they are more selective and admit students with a higher median LSAT. Make no mistake, these rankings have a firm grip on the structure of legal education. The often-unspoken truth, according to the dean of Yale Law School, Heather Gerken, is that: "The U.S. News rankings are profoundly flawed—they disincentivize programs that support public interest careers, champion need-based aid, and welcome working-class students into the profession."[21] Together, the LSAT and *U.S. News* rankings combine to suppress Black enrollment in law schools.

But an even more harmful expression of systemic racism—and the one most responsible for racial exclusion in the legal world—is the bar examination. Let's begin by stating a truth that is often hard to acknowledge: "*The Bar examination was never designed to test competency but, from the beginning, was an exam designed to limit entry into the law profession and reduce competition among lawyers.*"[22] In some cases, the bar exam was adopted by states to expressly impede the practice of law by African Americans. For instance, in 1950, the title of the bill to adopt the bar exam in South Carolina was described by members of the legislature as a bill to "'bar Negroes and undesirable whites' from becoming lawyers."[23] The current bar examination, despite never being shown to correlate with a person's competence or readiness to practice law, remains a powerful racist tool for excluding people of color from the practice of law.

But this should not come as a surprise, as robust research demonstrates both that the ABA itself was, until fairly recently, a racist institution, and the bar exam simply reflects this racist reality. Devito, Hample, and Lain, in their 2022 article, illustrate this point, stating:

> At the end of the nineteenth century and into the beginning of the twentieth, critical race theorist Roithmayr argues, leaders in the legal profession were troubled by the possibility of im-

> migrants and non-Whites entering the field. At the same time, the American Bar Association (ABA) became instrumental in the push for limiting which applicants to the bar would actually be accepted, with anti-immigrant and racist sentiments shaping the measures proposed and supported by the ABA. Law and society scholar Friedman, in describing the origin of the ABA and its motivations for developing formal bar admission requirements, emphasizes the pervasiveness of exclusionary beliefs among ABA members and leaders, pointing to the role that such beliefs played in discussions surrounding the prospect of a formal bar.
>
> Throughout this period, the ABA was an all-White organization that actively excluded persons who were not "White" from membership. For example, in 1912, the ABA mistakenly admitted three Black lawyers to the association and justified revoking their admission by explaining that they wanted to keep "pure the Anglo-Saxon race."
>
> * * *
>
> Thus, throughout the first half of the twentieth century, there was widespread sentiment that the profession should be limited to Whites. Raising admission standards, including through use of the bar exam, was a mechanism for achieving this goal.[24]

Other scholars demonstrate that "The American bar exam is an initiation rite that bars diversity in the legal profession."[25] The racist and exclusionary nature of the bar exam is documented by so many studies that I don't need to replicate or rehash here—a simple Google search will reveal the uncontroversial nature of this reality.[26]

Even though we know this about the bar exam and even though there isn't a single study suggesting that the bar exam measures the competency to practice law, almost every state in the union mandates that lawyers pass a bar examination to practice law. The ABA continues to support the bar exam, perpetuating the fantasy that the exam measures anything relevant to the practice of law or lawyer competence.[27]

It is heartbreaking to know we live in a world where money and system justification of an unproven examination render invisible the systemic injustice and disparate impact of the bar exam on people of color.

In light of everything this book has demonstrated about how we reframe reality and "meh relegate" disconcerting truths, it should come as no surprise that "many law professors who sincerely believe they are anti-racist [will continue to] assist the same private Wisconsin corporation—with a history of racist exams and secrecy to"[28] perpetuate the monopoly on admission to practice law and the racist exclusion the bar examination represents.

Again Derrick Bell, the father of critical race theory, reminds us that "racism is not a passing phase but a permanent feature of American life, and that the path is marked not by real progress but by occasional short-lived judicial or legislative victories that serve to obscure the underlying truth even more."[29]

And *U.S. News*' baseless but influential ranking of law schools relies on bar passage as a major indicator of a law school's rank. As a result, schools tend to hinge admission decisions on an applicant's likelihood of passing the bar. Given the racist reality that the bar exam has historically excluded—and continues to exclude—people of color, law schools tend to be very careful about admitting students of color.

But even more alarming is the fact that the ABA conditions law school accreditation on a school's bar passage rate. This means that schools are punished when they attempt to compensate for systemic inequities by moving beyond racist admission criteria, as those same racist admission criteria correlate with which students will pass the racist bar examination. In doing so, the ABA and *U.S. News* perpetuate race-based exclusion from the practice of law. They continue to do this with impunity because system justification makes it so much easier and more comfortable for us to cloak the reality of this racism in the fiction of meritocracy.

Law schools are, therefore, punished in the rankings for taking individual action to account for the reality of systemic inequity in our society. Nothing illustrates the futility of individual action, even when well-intentioned and meaningful, to address systemic inequity more clearly.

At this point, it is important to consider the discord and disruption that rejecting the system would cause. Consider what would happen if we decided to do away with the bar examination and the current admission metrics. Where would that leave us? It would leave us in a state of discord, confusion, and widely divergent standards for admission to law school and to the practice of law. It is much more convenient to have a streamlined system that we all abide by, even if we know the system is baseless. And it is especially easy to have faith in the system when the baseless system buttresses stereotypes of white intellectual superiority and Black inferiority, which remain the conclusions of the unconscious processing heuristics responsible for our societal implicit biases.

And in case it appears that I am overstating how entrenched these race-based intellectual biases are, it is worth remembering that, until recently, the absence of Black NFL quarterbacks was thought to reflect the reality that Black people didn't have the intellectual ability to be a quarterback.[30] This bias also led to Black NFL players being paid significantly less than white players in the settlement of brain injury claims because the methodology used to determine the level of cognitive impairment a player suffered "assumed Black players started out with lower cognitive function."[31]

We don't see the racism and systemic hierarchy in legal education because acknowledging it would lead to greater discord and less social stability than unconsciously reframing the system as meritocratic. Like all other information that doesn't conform to the systemic hierarchy, we "meh relegate" it to the realm of the insignificant. As humans, we have evolved to avoid letting facts and reality disrupt our palliatively harmonious reconstructions of reality. Knowing all these facts about the bar examination will result in little change because system justification creates a "juggernaut"[32] that is dishearteningly unstoppable. The Faculty, Alumni, & Students Opposed to Racial Preferences ("FASORP") lawsuit against Northwestern is another example of how deeply entrenched systemic racism is and how presumptively normative it appears.

c. FASORP v. Northwestern

Northwestern University School of Law, a well-known law school in Chicago, Illinois, implemented a robust affirmative action plan to mitigate the effects of centuries of systemic inequity based on race in the United States. The plan was specifically designed to identify where barriers and disparities might exist in recruitment and employment activities and to take steps to remove those barriers and disparities.[33]

Essentially, Northwestern was acutely aware of the "meh relegation" associated with systemic inequity and sought to move beyond the palliative fictions of colorblindness and racial equity our brains create to distract us from the harsh reality of socially acceptable, insidious discrimination. This plan was an attempt to realistically address the disparity that had arisen due to various forms of discrimination—whether based on sex, race, ethnicity, disability, or religion.

These disparities manifest themselves as equitable, fair, and just, because, as addressed in Chapters 2 and 3, they appear to be based on meritocratic norms. The truth, however, is that the very metrics used to assess the qualifications of faculty candidates are racist metrics posing as meritocratic indicators.

For example, an accepted and entrenched indicator of faculty qualification is law review placement. Legal faculty are expected to research and publish academic articles in law reviews. Law reviews are student-run journals, found at all law schools, with their staff composed of the most academically gifted students.

Twice a year, faculty members at all the U.S. law schools deposit their research papers into national pools that the law journals have access to. Law reviews then select faculty publications and make offers to the faculty members they would like to publish. The higher the ranking of the school associated with the journal that publishes a faculty member's work, the more prestigious and important that faculty member's publication is deemed to be.

When hiring faculty candidates, law schools examine the ranking of the journals where the faculty member has published, using that metric as perhaps the most important factor in selecting candidates. Some of my own colleagues, who powerfully professes their own anti-racism, suggest, for example, that an unavoidable reality of legal academia is that these publication metrics are the currency of the legal academia realm.

However, it is beyond question that these publication metrics are both a product of systemic racism and also a mechanism that perpetuates systemic racism. Before delving into the racist nature of these rankings, it is important to note one absurdity that the legal academy consistently "meh relegates" because it would disrupt systemic structure: the individuals who are judging the quality and merit of the scholarship of established legal academics are second-year law students, because these students make up the editorial staff of the various law journals!

In terms of the racist nature of publication metrics in the legal academy, it is important to note that the three most significant factors for deciding whether a paper will be published are: the law school the author attended, the law school the author teaches at, and the popularity or fame of the judge the author clerked for.[34]

A 2022 survey demonstrated that over 75% of all law school professors attended and graduated from the highest-ranked law schools in the country.[35] I created the following table in a previous article to demonstrate the economic and racist realities of this dynamic.

DEMOGRAPHICS OF THE FOURTEEN LAW SCHOOLS GRADUATING 76% OF LAW PROFESSORS[36]

	U.S. News 2021 Rank	% Black	Current Annual Tuition
Yale	1	7.49	$68,117
Stanford	2	8.50	$66,396
Harvard	3	8.10	$67,081
Columbia	4	8.79	$74,995
Chicago	4	6.43	$69,975
NYU	6	7.30	$71,304
Penn	7	7.43	$68,130
Virginia	8	5.63	$67,000
Northwestern	9	5.39	$68,800
Michigan	9	4.54	$65,698*
Berkeley	9	5.17	$61,487
Duke	12	6.63	$66,120
Cornell	13	6.40	$70,724
Georgetown	14	9.15	$63,528

* This figure represents the average cost of in-state, full-time student tuition and out-of-state, full-time student tuition displayed as $64,198 and $67,198, respectively. *Id.*

In 2022, the average African American enrollment at the law schools considered the most highly ranked was 6.92%, even though at the time African Americans made up 13.4% of the U.S. population.[37] To reiterate, the ranking of the school the author attended is one of the most important metrics affecting the ranking of the law journal that elects to publish that author. Since the ranking of the journal publishing the author is perhaps the most important metric in determining whether that author will be hired as a law faculty member, most law faculty are selected from the schools that have the lowest enrollment of African Americans in the country. By contrast, the only schools enrolling Black students at 13%, or the percentage of the U.S. population that identifies as Black, are the schools that are so poorly regarded that they are considered "unranked."[38] I shouldn't need to explain that economic realities prevent many Black students from attending these fourteen law schools as well, but I will anyway.

The average income and wealth of Black families is much lower than that of white families. As of 2022, the median wealth disparity between Black and white households was over $240,000.[39] Specifically, Black median wealth was $44,890, while median white wealth was $285,000.[40] As a result, most Black families cannot afford college, much less an expensive Ivy League education.[41] Furthermore, LSAT scores correlate closely with socioeconomic status, as the most important preparation steps for scoring well on the LSAT—such as the ability to afford tutors, preparation books, and time off from work to prepare—require financial resources.[42] A high LSAT score[43] and the elite nature of the undergraduate college attended[44] are two of the factors that are most likely to get a student into an elite law school. It should, therefore, be no surprise that the average annual tuition at the most highly regarded schools in the table above was $67,811, while at the schools where the African American enrollment was 10% or higher, the average annual tuition was $36,264.[45]

As Debra Cassens explains:

> More than three-quarters of the students at the nation's top 20 law schools come from the top one-fourth of the socioeconomic population, and well over half of the students at these schools come from the top 10 percent, according to the study by UCLA law professor Richard Sander. Just 2 percent come from the bottom quarter.[46]

The second factor in the ranking of a law professor's scholarship—the ranking of school the author teaches at—also perpetuates the racist reality explained above of selecting publications based on the school the author attended. This is because the most highly ranked schools tend to hire professors who attended the most highly ranked schools. According to Eric Segall and Adam Feldman, "almost ninety-five percent of the professors at the top ten highest-rated schools who received law degrees in the United States obtained their degree at one of those same schools."[47]

Finally, the third most important factor for deciding the ranking of the school where a legal scholar is published is the popularity or fame of the judge the legal scholar clerked for. To understand the racist nature of this metric, it is important to remember that, after passing the bar, a lawyer can choose not to go into private practice and instead become a research assistant or clerk for a judge. Clerking is considered prestigious, but it is also usually a financial sacrifice, as clerkships are usually low-paying positions or non-paying positions. As a result, the only people who usually can afford to clerk after graduating are those who have the financial wherewithal to forego a higher salary even after three years of expensive legal education—during which time they would not have been able to earn a substantial income.

Not surprisingly, given the racial lines along which wealth is distributed in America, clerking is an option that results in most judicial clerks being white. In fact, only 4.1% of clerks were Black, and a recent article published by the ABA noted that almost 80% of law clerks were white.[48]

So, the most important metric for ranking legal faculty candidates, the ranking of the school at which your legal scholarship is published, is itself comprised of three racist metrics which largely ensure that whiteness and wealth are the most important factors in assessing a faculty candidate's qualifications. As Aaron Taylor poetically describes, legal rankings and the metrics underlying them represent "continued propagation of a system that rewards privilege under the guise of meritocracy."[49]

The research is unequivocal that, in the education and school environments, system justification is especially potent, allowing a powerful belief in school meritocracy to persist despite clear and overwhelming evidence to the contrary. For example, according to Virginie Wiederkehr:

> [A]dmitting that school success would be determined not only by merit, but also by social group belonging (e.g., social class, gender) would question the legitimacy of those who are in a high status position and, thus, would threaten the social order. By promoting BSM, the school system is particularly efficient in justifying the social order. Indeed, by making people believe that school success is a result of individual merit, the school transforms, in some way, social class or gender dif-

> ferences into individual merit differences and, thus, into differences that appear to be legitimate, equitable, and fair. Such an idea is congruent with the theory of social reproduction (Bourdieu et al., 1990), according to which school promotes BSM precisely to make people accept—whatever their own status—that high status groups are more "valuable" than low status groups and, thus, deserve a higher status position within the social hierarchy. As such, BSM is a key element for maintaining the social order and rationalizing the unequal position between individuals from high vs. low status groups.[50]

Northwestern recognized the gross and entrenched systemic inequity in traditional law school faculty hiring practices and how easily these inequities can be framed as meritocracy. Determined to address this disparity, Northwestern decided to include additional metrics in the faculty hiring process. "As a result, Northwestern implemented a policy that allows them to see what racial, ethnic, sexes, or other groups are underrepresented in their student body and faculty, and to actively seek to hire or admit individuals that would correct those under-representations. This is all "to maintain a University community that is based on equal opportunity, reflects the diversity of American society, and improve[] opportunities for women, minorities, veterans and individuals with disabilities."[51]

The result was the system pushing back against attempts to disrupt systemic inequity. On July 2, 2024, the 60th anniversary of the 1964 Civil Rights Act, a group called FASORP filed a discrimination lawsuit against the Northwestern School of Law, claiming that their affirmative action plan was discriminatory.

The FASORP claim against Northwestern Law alleged that Northwestern discriminated against white males when making faculty hiring decisions and publication decisions for their student-led law reviews.[52] The complaint accused Northwestern of violating the law by "hiring women and racial minorities with mediocre and undistinguished records over white men who have better credentials, better scholarship, and better teaching ability."[53] As my explanation above demonstrates, the word "better" in the complaint is simply a proxy for whiteness, given the entrenched systemic inequity powerfully posing as meritocracy in legal education hiring. This is another powerful illustration of "meh relegation." The word "better" feels powerfully moral and empirically valid, even though—or perhaps because—it masks the fact that Northwestern's policies were put in place to overcome the underrepresentation of certain groups that have been undeniably oppressed and discriminated against for the entire history of our nation.

FASORP claimed that Northwestern discriminated against multiple white male professors in making its hiring choices for the law school. One of the professors that was allegedly discriminated against was described as "a highly desirable and sought-after faculty candidate at any law school" whose "accomplishments exceed those of nearly every professor currently on the Northwestern Law School faculty."[54] Another white male professor allegedly discriminated against was described as "another famous and distinguished legal scholar" whose "accomplishments exceed those of nearly every professor currently on the Northwestern Law School faculty."[55]

Additionally, FASORP claimed white male professors, described with the language from above, were not hired solely because they were white males. FASORP asserted that instead of hiring the more *qualified* white men, they hired individuals who were not nearly as qualified as the white men. They described one hire as a Black female who "would never even have been considered ... if she had been white or a member of a different race, and ... was hired over white male candidates who were vastly more *capable* and qualified than she was."[56] Hopefully, by now, the palliative, system justifying illusions created by the words "qualified" and "capable" should appear conspicuous and obvious.

Remarkably FASORP did not limit its criticism to Northwestern's efforts to diversify faculty hiring, but also criticized Northwestern's decision to fund a Center for Racial and Disability Justice. The professor who started the center was described as "a black affirmative action hire ... [who] would have never been considered for an appointment at Northwestern if she had been white."[57] Further, FASORP described Northwestern's actions as wasting "money on this useless center to pander to an affirmative-action hire who never deserved her appointment in the first place."[58]

But most remarkably, given all the racist and socioeconomic inequity wrapped up in the selection of authors for placement in law reviews, FASORP also claims that "[t]he student editors of the *Northwestern University Law Review* also discriminate on account of race and sex."[59] They allege that the law review members "give discriminatory preferences to articles written by women, racial minorities, homosexuals, or transgender people, while rejecting far *better* articles written by white men."[60] Consider the system justification and self-reinforcing systemic inequity evident in the confidence with which FASORP deploys the word "better."

This lawsuit exemplifies the reality that we are living in a post-truth society. It was filed by a group of people who are likely aware of the race-based systemic inequities Northwestern is attempting to address and move beyond. Yet, our own need to "meh relegate" these realities away means that lawsuits like these, which blatantly ignore reality, need only employ racist and conclusory language like better, qualified, and capable. Once these terms are used, our palliative need to create an imaginary meritocracy makes it almost impossible to acknowledge that the core concepts of merit and quality, as used by FASORP, are meaningless and meritless outside of their powerful ability to invoke a cyclic perpetuation of systemic racism.

These are just a few examples of the harsh and weaponized language that was used by FASORP to describe what they claim is discrimination by Northwestern. All of this, of course, is aimed at attacking Northwestern's efforts to remove disparities and barriers that have arisen over years of systemic inequality. It is worth noting that the language cited above came from the complaint filed by FASORP. System justification ensures that a few selectively presented facts, intertwined with the charged language in the complaint, powerfully lead readers and arbiters to draw incorrect conclusions about Northwestern and its hiring, promotion, and law review selection processes.

Not only does FASORP seek the court's help in putting an end to Northwestern's attempts to remedy systemic inequity by taking "race, sex, sexual orientation, or gender identity" into consideration when making staff decisions, but they also want the court to appoint an individual to monitor and oversee Northwestern's staffing and review operations. They also, incredulously, want Northwestern to pay the attorneys' fees for the cost of FASORP bringing the case.[61] At its core, FASORP's lawsuit seeks not only to stop Northwestern from actively trying to right a tangible and documentable historical wrong but they also want Northwestern to be punished for doing so.

Ultimately, individual attempts to remedy the systemic racial subordination of people of color to whites are pointless and ineffective, no matter how well-intentioned or altruistic those efforts may be. What is needed to address systemic inequity is system-wide disruption. The system must be uprooted and completely restructured.

One way to make the difficult and uncomfortable discourse related to systemic racism more meaningful is to engage in discourse without charged adjectives or emotion-generating phraseology. In other words, meaningful discourse means language must be weaponized less. We often use language that evokes emotion and system justification to derail meaningful debate on systemic inequity. This language emotionally and powerfully mandates the conclusions we seek, allowing us to avoid ever having to debate the actual merits of our positions.

Weaponized Language

If you learned just one thing from reading this book so far, it should be that humans unconsciously, and for evolutionarily valid reasons, create comfortable fictions that prevent us from constantly confronting the dishearteningly complex and harsh nature of reality. Part of this fiction creation involves the establishment of powerful notions of right, wrong, moral, and immoral. As a result, individuals in society feel passionately certain about many societal issues. For example, most people have strong and even absolute views on abortion, gun control, trans athletes, and the Black Lives Matter movement. The strong feelings people have for these issues are reflected in the frequent heated and angry debates about these issues.

Debaters have grown accustomed to using adjectives that assume a conclusion rather than relying on thought, facts, and the truth, or understanding the complexity of these issues they try to paint as one-sided and absolute. The adjectives I am referring to are, for example, sexist, racist, privileged, transphobic, antisemitic, and gun nut. People deploy these adjectives in debates about complex issues as a short cut for thoughtful and meaningful debate. By employing these adjectives to describe their opponents, they seek to brand the person with the opposing viewpoint as too morally defective to meaningfully participate in the debate and imply that, for "normal or moral" people, there can only be one answer. I experienced this recently as follows:

A while ago I circulated the following question to people I trusted:

> I was wondering if anyone could explain the transgender athletic laws that are currently popping up across the country, one of which is now at our Governor's desk here in KS. From what I can tell, the bills generally seek to prevent people who were born biologically male from participating in female youth athletic events. I am asking for this presentation because I generally run screaming away from bills proposed by the typical lot who proposed this one, and of course, I know there probably is some ulterior motive other than protection of athletes and parity involved.
>
> BUT as a former girls' youth competitive soccer coach and the father of a female teen soccer player who tore her ACL, and given the copious scientific evidence about how uniquely dangerous the game of soccer is for females post puberty (https://research.uncg.edu/news/how-puberty-can-impact-teens-knees/ and https://pubmed.ncbi.nlm.nih.gov/22784194/), I would absolutely object to males and females on the same competitive team playing against each other at the teen competitive level. The boys'/men's game and the girls'/women's game is completely different, and after the age of 14, the coaching techniques for them are also different.
>
> So, I am asking an honest question here from a position of ignorance, seeking to learn what I am missing, knowing that I must be missing something when I say that, at least for competitive teen youth soccer, I have no objection to prohibiting biological males from playing against biological females. The dangers are just too high.
>
> All I ask is that there be no reflexive anger and shaming sent my way because of my genuine ignorance and curiosity.
>
> Thanks,
>
> Rory

One of the responses I got to the above question was, "What can I say man, your question shows that you are sexist and that's all there is to it."

And in case you decide to follow my accuser and label me sexist, and therefore unworthy of engagement, be aware that, despite my question, I firmly believe that for some, gender and sexuality are definitely fluid and non-binary. No one should be forced to live their life having to bear, for society's comfort, the unbearable burden of the internal dissonance associated with pretending to be someone they are not.

My question had to do solely with the athletic safety of teenagers. If, instead of short-circuiting the discourse with the use of the adjective sexist, that person had said to me, "Let me hear your thoughts. I think you are wrong, but I'll share mine with you and we might learn something from each other," we could have been able to discover any erroneous assumptions we each had. Instead, like many of us in society, we don't want to do the intellectual lifting necessary for these debates. All we really want to do is use adjectives to bully people with opposing viewpoints into submission. This approach is more comfortable and simpler than genuinely taking the opportunity to understand whether some of the assumptions you rely on to frame your view of the world are unsustainable. So powerful is the human need for comfort that we perpetuate deliberate ignorance through adjective deployment rather than learning through informed exchanges.

This athletic debate is not simple if we are honest. In a world where adjectives were restricted, such that I received a response that fostered more debate rather than one labelling me as sexist, I might start by saying that, from the perspective of soccer and other sports that involve sharp or cutting movements, female participants are four to six times more likely to injure their ACLs, and girls suffer these injuries eight times as often as boys.[62] This is alarming on its own, but when a female athlete returns to playing the sport, they have a 30% chance of suffering another ACL injury.[63]

Scientific studies suggest that physiological changes associated with puberty are responsible for teenaged girls suffering increased rates of ACL injuries as compared to boys.[64] Prepuberty, both boys and girls tend to have femurs that, together with the bones of the lower leg, form a straight line from hip to foot. Post-puberty, this angle changes for girls as female hips become wider during puberty.[65] Consequently, the femur, which originates in the hip socket is now angled inward from the hip to the knee, rather than remaining in a straight line.[66]

This angle, known as the valgus angle, changes during puberty for girls but not for boys, who do not experience the same changes in hip shape.[67] This inward angled femur that is thought to make the knee less stable and more prone to collapse on itself.[68] If you think of a completely collapsed knee as one where the femur forms a 90-degree angle with the lower leg bones, the increased valgus angle in post-pubertal female athletes can be visualized as a head start on knee collapse.

Female athletes suffer ACL injuries at alarming rates when they are playing against other females. Males, however, do not develop increased valgus angles after puberty,[69] so their ability to cut and turn like they did pre-puberty remains the same. This lack of change is not associated with the same increased post-puberty risk of ACL injury that girls experience.

In my opinion, not only is it unfair to ask teenaged girls to compete against teenaged boys given the reality of the difference in movement mechanics, but it is unsafe. Subjecting these girls to an environment where they would have to change direction and pivot even more extremely than in all-female sports to be able to competitive with the male athletes—who did not experience post-puberty hip shape changes—poses significant risks.

To which the other person/people in the conversation would probably respond that not all females experience the hip shape changes noted above, and we don't ban these females who have less than typical hip shape changes during puberty from playing female soccer. Furthermore, they might point out that there are some biological females with the musculature and testosterone ratios more typical of men. Conversely, the reverse is also true: there are men with very low testosterone ratios and wider hips than society tends to associate with men.

To which an appropriate response might be that, yes, the policy of separating the athletes by biological sex is not a perfect way to achieve parity, safety, and fairness, and yes, it results in a lot of gender stereotyping. However, the perfect should not be the enemy of the good. From a utilitarian perspective, the net benefits to girls who want to play sports is higher if we continue to apply the imperfect divider of biological sex.

A response to this could be that, by acknowledging that there are many exceptions to the physical post-puberty characteristics that society uses to define the binary sexes, I am implicitly admitting that perhaps these categories aren't as well-defined and separate as I am suggesting. And therefore, by continuing to rely on binary notions of sexuality, I am discriminating against all atypical and intersex athletes.

I would concede that this is a possibility, but I would also point out that, rather than calling someone sexist for doing the research and trying to genuinely articulate and support a viewpoint, they should also understand that by suggesting that all people must accept the lack of gender divisions in sport, they are asking for a complete and utter disruption of what admittedly may be a contrived normal. And the difficulty of abandoning such a contrived normal might be more fully appreciated if they came from a family that now owns land previously taken from Native Americans and if their family benefited from decades of farm subsidies to accumulate intergenerational wealth—or, in other words, if they read Chapter 5.

But ultimately, I would also need to do some research comparing the number of male-to-female trans athletes seeking to participate in female sports like wrestling, soccer, football, and basketball—where strength, speed, and musculature are an advantage—with female-to-male trans athletes seeking to do the same. If the former is significantly larger, then the *perception* of trans athletes as seeking to have their cake and eat it would also need to be addressed.

The truth is that, at the end of the day, I lean heavily towards not allowing trans athletes to participate in teen competitive sports, but that may be my own palliative simplification of the issue. Without a policy on this, we would face athletic anarchy. If we didn't arbitrarily draw a line, then none of the established athletic leagues and sport competitions would exist.

The honest question I am asking myself, as a human forming an opinion on this, is how much of my conception of *normal*—and the comfort I and like-minded people derive from it—am I willing to abandon? Without the perhaps contrived simplicity of binary gender in sports, we would have to reconceptualize almost all the organizations and structures that currently govern sport worldwide, leading to significant disruption of the current normal.

While I remain convinced that no system is perfect, this isn't a disruption of the normal that I personally think should happen. However, that doesn't mean I am not open to learning why I am wrong. My desire for the normalcy here is no less selfish and self-serving than the normalcy of those who believe farm subsidies are different from welfare, that athletes kneeling for the flag are unpatriotic, or that white addicts should be labelled as victims while Black addicts are crackheads.

Language choice is important in other areas as well. The use of adjectives and language that hijack our unconscious processing systems—making informed and real analysis of the issues impossible—is exemplified by phrases like "Black Lives Matter," describing something as antisemitic, or the debates about gun control and abortion.

The "Black Lives Matter" movement was designed to raise awareness of the indisputable fact, as established throughout this book, that America historically and to this day dehumanizes non-white people. This dehumanization is so deeply entrenched in societal norms that most of us fail to even recognize it is happening. Once again, our unconscious reframing of reality renders this reality invisible while simultaneously perpetuating it, because this reframing is cognitively effortless. But what if we chose the slogan "Black Lives *Also* Matter" instead of "Black Lives Matter"? This way, the movement would acknowledge that America already recognizes the value of non-Black lives. Would brilliant racists not have been able to co-opt the message to deliberately and falsely suggest that the intended message of the movement is that "Only Black Lives Matter," as easily as they did?

By hijacking the message through the language used to title the movement, racists were able to prevent a significant sector of the population—who might otherwise be receptive to the message—from even being able to hear the message the movement's title was meant to convey. By portraying the message as a threat to the system, they were able to generate widespread resentment for the movement and increased anger towards Black people with zero conscious effort. Instead, system justification and bias did the work for them, much in the same way the Trump campaign brilliantly employed the phrase "bad hombres" to create passionate but baseless fear and resentment of immigrants as discussed in Chapter 7. Admittedly the truth is probably that systemic racism would result in powerful negative responses to the movement no matter what language was used to describe the Black Lives Matter movement.

The word antisemitic is also another word that capitalizes on system justification. For example, in this book, I have done a significant amount of historical research pointing out that the concepts of terrorist, barbarian, freedom fighter, entitlement to property, and others have been traditionally employed to create a distinction in rights and entitlement between white people and people of color. Because some of the historical truths I uncovered question the accepted moral absolutism of the established narrative surrounding the Israel/Palestine dispute, someone will likely untruthfully label my work as antisemitic. The erroneous and misleading use of the word to describe this book will lead to sudden silence and spinelessness of many people who agree with my work. Furthermore, many others who have never even seen this book will feel powerful and substantial hatred for me.

This is the power of using language that buttresses systemic hierarchies. To avoid the discomfort, inconvenience, and unsettling complexity of reality, we resent even truthful information that threatens the comfort and stability of the simple and absolutist fictions we unconsciously create and hold dear. This "meh relegation," however, is an essential aspect of humanity. "Meh relegation" is also important in gun control debates.

The Second Amendment to the Constitution of the United States expressly provides: "A well-regulated Militia, being necessary to the security of a free State, the right of the people to keep and bear Arms, *shall not be infringed*."[70]

There has been much debate about whether the right to bear arms exists outside of the militia context, but the current Supreme Court interpretation of the amendment establishes two things clearly. First, the right to bear arms is a fundamental right, and second, it includes the right to bear arms to defend oneself in the home.[71] This right also extends beyond the home,[72] and the exact parameters of the right are currently being litigated in upcoming cases. The right to bear arms in America is so fundamental that "when the plain text of the Second Amendment covers the regulated conduct, the Constitution presumptively protects it; to justify a regulation of that conduct, the government must demonstrate that a challenged law is consistent with the nation's historical tradition of firearm regulation."[73] Liberal arguments for banning or regulating gun ownership to the point of essential oblivion also rely on fictions and delusions, much like many of the issues discussed throughout this book.

Consider this: the news media has created the impression that, because Americans own guns, the chances of being shot in America are higher than anywhere else. This fiction is so pervasive that my family from Trinidad and Jamaica often express fear of being shot as a rationale for not visiting the United States. The reality, however, is that chance of being murdered by a gun in Trinidad and Jamaica is 4.5 and 4.3 times higher respectively compared to the United States.[74] Both Trinidad and

Jamaica, as former British colonies, are countries where gun ownership is largely illegal. Another statistic of the anti-gun movement is that 54% of gun deaths in the United States are suicides, not homicides.[75]

I ask any of the American anti-gun advocates to spend a week in Trinidad or Jamaica outside of an all-inclusive or other artificially safe environment. None of them can ever understand the constant and oppressive fear residents of these countries experience, because the only people with guns in these countries are criminals. Criminals who freely ignore the illegality of gun ownership. When arriving at your home at night and opening the gate, you are acutely aware—and the armed criminals know you are aware—that you are helpless to defend yourself. As a law-abiding citizen, you cannot own a gun. It is with impunity and little fear of resistance that the armed criminal approaches the homeowner or vehicle owner. Only after experiencing that absolute feeling of helplessness and complete inability to deter or defend against criminals should a person be deemed qualified to advocate against gun ownership.

Consider that on February 22, 2017, in Olathe, Kansas, a white man entered a bar and shot two South Indian patrons after yelling, "Get out of my country." One of the men was injured, and the other died. That was the day I decided to sign up for firearm use and safety classes and to earn my concealed carry license. The Second Amendment affords me the right to defend myself against crazy racists who might try to kill me and, as described below, attacking dogs.

I am an avid walker, covering four to six miles every day for exercise. In April 2024, I was visiting my in-laws in rural central Florida and was walking in the small town they live in with my permitted 9mm pistol, essentially in a fanny pack. As I approached the end of my walk, a large canine ran out of a yard and attempted to attack me. It was one of those canines that is so powerful and formidable that it would likely have been impossible to defend against the animal unarmed without getting bitten. I yelled and screamed at the dog, but it would not stop. Just as it got to within six feet of me, I drew my firearm and shot the dog. Thankfully, the magnificent animal—who was perhaps just trying to be protective—did not die but was only injured.

If I had not had my firearm with me, I would have been severely injured, possibly permanently maimed, or completely at the mercy of whether the homeowner decided to vaccinate his dog against rabies, for example. However, I also need to describe this dog attack story in detail to reemphasize the difference between individual racism and systemic racism.

The neighborhood my in-laws live in consists of small, modest houses aligned along a small road. I needed to walk approximately a fourth of a mile along this small road to reach the main boulevard of the town where there was a sidewalk that I could walk on for approximately one and a half miles in either direction. Between my in-laws' house and the main road were approximately 15 houses, some with fenced yards and others without. From the moment we first drove into the neighborhood, one house stood out to me. Its yard was cluttered with old furniture, appliances, and various mechanical equipment. Two signs in the yard immediately caught my attention and sparked a mild sense of panic. One sign read, "Ammunition is expensive, so there will be no warning shots fired." The other said "Trump 2024." Because of my own stereotype and biases, I thought to myself, "Here in rural Florida, this is probably the last house a brown guy like me should be found near."

Yet, this is the house from which the dog charged at me. When that dog came at me, the world seemed to slow down around me. Except for the tiny sphere of space that the dog and I occupied, the entire rest of the world seemed to be made of a thick, gelatinous, and blurred bubble, with time operating differently. Everything in my immediate bubble seemed absurdly slow and clear—similar to how the Flash perceives the world when the movie shifts to his perspective. When I grabbed the pistol and took the safety off, it felt as if I was watching someone else do it. A dissociated part of my brain noted without emotion, "Amazing how he (really me) is operating on automatic and removing the safety and holding the gun properly and lining up the shot." That same part of my brain was simultaneously terrified and disgusted, noting, "He is performing so automatically, without hesitation, a series of actions designed solely to lethally incapacitate a beautiful sentient being like this dog." Another part of my brain chimed in with, "Okay so now I understand the concept of muscle memory due to repetitive practice, and this series of events is as a result of the amount of time 'he' spends at the range practicing." In this surreal environment, I discharged the weapon, but my adrenaline and heightened state were such that I never heard the loud bang. My only knowledge that the animal was shot was that it lurched to its right and had a look of horrified shock on its face.

Once the animal was no longer trying to attack and was headed back to the yard, the world seemed to become normal again. The gelatinous periphery of my world once again became temporally consistent, real, and discernable. A neighbor was the first to tell me that he saw what happened, and I shouldn't worry because it was clear I was defending myself. I don't remember what I said to him, but my immediate reaction was to call 911. I then had a surreal conversation with the dispatcher, who mentioned that I should make sure the firearm was unloaded and away from my body when the officers arrived, so they would not feel as though they were in danger when they approached the scene. While I was still on the phone with the dispatcher, the owner of the dog emerged rapidly from the house. My immediate thought was, "Shit this Trumper is gonna go nuts because Brown dude shot his dog out here in the boonies." What happened next, however, perfectly illustrates the difference between individual and systemic racism.

The dog owner came up to me while I was still on the phone with the dispatcher and said, "Mister, are you alright? I am so sorry for what happened here. These dogs usually have a boundary collar on them that prevents them from leaving the yard. I just got home, and I forgot to put it on." His wife was equally apologetic, as was another neighbor who was also a close friend of theirs. The dissonance between what my own bias and stereotype predicted would occur and what actually happened was almost paralyzing for me. In my stupefied state of amazement, I said, "Sir, you know I shot your dog right?" He responded, "Yes, but you had no choice given what happened and the dog will survive because it was a clean through-and-through to the right of anything vital. I would have done the same thing in your shoes. It's why we have guns and why we practice with them."

He further, disarmingly, said, "It's obvious you practice as well to be able to hit the dog under such pressure and I know, because I have a lot of guns and am licensed to have even atypical weapons and have a grandkid who is a competitive shooter who I taught how to shoot."

In the meantime, the police dispatcher informed me that they were dealing with a domestic dispute and that it would be a while before officers could arrive. In the half an hour it took them to show up, this man and I struck up a conversation. It turns out we had much in common—we had both worked in the Alaskan fishing industry, among other shared experiences.

When the two police officers showed up, one of them got out of his truck and, said in a strong Southern accent, "Hey [used homeowner's name familiarly], how's it going? Long time no see." They had a short exchange about how they knew each other. The police officer then, half-jokingly, said, "I was expecting to arrive here and have to separate the two of you from trying to kill each other, instead here you are just chatting and the only thing missing from this shooting the breeze session is a cold beer for each of you." The homeowner then again said, "He did nothing wrong. I would have done the same thing in his situation. This was our fault, and the dog was where it shouldn't have been."

My ultimate point being that this homeowner had every opportunity to retaliate and even to lie about what happened, given the remoteness of the area and his friendship with the police. But instead, he behaved like my third-world stereotype of the American—honest, honorable, and faithful to justice. I left there genuinely struggling to reconcile my bias with the reality of the honesty and compassion of this Trump supporter.

Here was a man who was voting for the guy who ran a campaign on hatred of immigrants, xenophobia, bullying, lying, and behaving in the most un-American fashion. Yet, on an individual level, this man behaved towards me with more compassion, honesty, justice, and grace than I could ever have imagined anyone doing in a similar situation. Yet, I am sure this man experienced no dissonance between how differently he behaved towards me, the difference in values he demonstrated at a time when he would have been excused for not demonstrating them, and the man he was strongly supporting for president.

When I'm walking in the less rural and more suburban neighborhoods here in Kansas, generally occupied by educated and self-proclaimed progressive and tolerant people, I constantly worry about what the situation will be if I am forced to shoot a 120-pound Perro de Presa Canario attacking me that broke free from the leash held by a 100-pound severely liberal, Democrat, Lululemon wearing, yoga practitioner with a ball cap and a ponytail pulled through the back of the cap. I often think that once that person cries when the police show up and falsely claims, "The dog was so sweet, he never previously attacked anyone," I would be fucked. Unconscious hierarchies would render my credibility nonexistent compared to the dog owner's. It's why I now walk with a live streaming GoPro.

The point being that our individual, conscious value set is often irrelevant and dissonant with our unconscious, evolutionarily driven limbic brain mechanisms that operate to reinforce societal hierarchies. Consider the 2020 Central Park interaction, where Amy Cooper called the police and lied, claiming she was being attacked by a Black man who had told her to leash her dog.[76] When she found out that her lies were captured on camera, she publicly apologized to everyone.[77] I believe she was sincere and truthful when she said, "I'm not a racist. I did not mean to harm that man in any way,"[78] further explaining that she also meant no harm to African Americans. Consciously, she may not be a racist. I can imagine so many people just like her, crying and feeling so genuinely passionate about equality as they marched to protest George Floyd's murder. Yet, she likely still remains confused about how when the rubber met the road and her limbic brain engaged, she probably acted completely opposite to her genuinely held belief set. It's the same feeling I get when I observe passionately anti-racist, progressive people decide not to vote for a qualified, diverse candidate, because (insert here a legitimate reason based on real and tangible metrics, the racist nature of which metrics are "meh relegated" into oblivion at the time). Unless we begin to understand the cognitive complexity of human beings, we will be stuck in a fruitless cycle of trying to remedy inequality by addressing only the conscious brain.

Similarly, when I visit Trinidad, I do not walk for exercise because there is no way I can defend myself against the powerful dogs that are irresponsibly owned in almost every wealthy residential area in the country. Nor can I defend myself against a criminal who, in the cool predawn hours—ideal for walking—might decide to make me a target.

Should reasonable restrictions on the right to own a gun include a requirement that everyone owning a gun must go through a background check? Should the right to own a gun include the right to have a bazooka as home defense? Should the right to own a gun include assault rifle ownership? And should there be a training requirement in firearm safety for people who own a handgun? The answers to these questions are more complex than we would like to acknowledge. Artificially simplifying the issues by using weaponized language involves far less cognitive effort and is more comfortable than dealing with the paralyzing and complicated minutia and hair-splitting intricacies involved in realistically trying to resolve these disputes on the merits.

By minimizing the issues in this fashion, humans reframe their environments as more orderly and hence more manageable than they are. This sense of order and manageability is what facilitates human social progress. We can move forward socially because we artificially allow ourselves to ignore the discord and complexity of reality and interpret our positions as stable, established, or fixed. Directional changes, such as moving forward, can only occur in relation to such established positions. This false certainty of our current positions—or the present—is what allows us to move on from the present or to engage in what we humans call progress.

But the issue is incredibly complex if we get beyond weaponized language and emotion. The existence of a right does not imply that there is an absolute right to own a gun. All rights are subject to reasonable regulations. For example, even though the First Amendment guarantees freedom of speech, hate speech is still prohibited, and you can't yell "fire" in a crowded theater when there is no fire. Additionally, as demonstrated in the chapter on the bans on critical race theory, lawmakers often interpret rights flexibly when it suits them.

Of course, unconscious racism and white supremacy leads to the other argument most gun control advocates make: "Well, you should not compare the United States to these undeveloped countries" (read uncivilized non-white countries) "but only to the other high-income or developed countries." In this context, the level of gun violence in the United States "stands out" as high.[79] But this should not be surprising, because the United States' firearm ownership rate is five times higher than that of Germany and France, for example.[80]

We can argue numbers back and forth, but ultimately, the United States is a country whose founding document promotes gun ownership. This reality is where we should proceed from in the gun debates. There is an express constitutional provision which provides for gun ownership. However, it is also illustrative of how our unconscious cognitive mechanisms prevent us from experiencing dissonance with our conscious belief sets when we should experience dissonance to consider that most anti-gun advocates are also prochoice advocates. Yet, none of the prochoice, anti-gun individuals likely experience any cognitive dissonance as they argue forcefully for a tenuous interpretation of the Constitution to recognize a non-express right to abortion, while simultaneously remaining furiously certain about the absoluteness of their argument that we should ignore an express right to own guns. These same prochoice individuals posit:

> It's no coincidence that that the same politicians passing abortion bans are refusing to take action on gun safety—they only care about controlling our bodies, our lives, or our futures.... The *hypocrisy* of this public health issue is deadly.[81]

Hypocrisy indeed. I point out this inconsistency even though I believe *nothing* should stand in the way of women having the freedom to make the private and sometimes impossibly difficult decision about whether they should terminate a pregnancy.

Our unconscious reframing renders us blind to our own hypocrisy time and time again. This lack of cognitive dissonance in the incongruity of our positions is the power of unconscious processing and system justification. The adjectives we use catalyze this blindness, making the debates less cognitively taxing. Adjectives like "gun nut" and "sexist pig" artificially narrow the breadth of legitimate considerations in these complex debates, making the "correct" outcome seem more absolute than it truly is.

Endnotes

1. Rory D. Bahadur, *An Immigrant Contextualizes the George Floyd Verdict*, Washburn Law Journal Blog (Apr. 25, 2021).

2. Social History for Every Classroom, *Frederick Douglas Declares "There Is No Progress Without Struggle"*, https://shec.ashp.cuny.edu/items/show/1245 (last visited Ja, 19, 2025) (quoting Frederick Douglass).

3. Deborah L. Rhode, *Law Is the Least Diverse Profession in the Nation. And Lawyers Aren't Doing Enough to Change That*, The Washington Post (May 27, 2015), https://www.washingtonpost.com/posteverything/wp/2015/05/27/law-is-the-least-diverse-profession-in-the-nation-and-lawyers-arent-doing-enough-to-change-that/.

4. *Id.*

5. Scripps News Staff, *There Is a Lack of Diversity in the Law Profession*, Scripps News (Feb. 22, 2022, 7:47 PM), https://www.scrippsnews.com/us-news/in-the-loop/there-is-a-lack-of-diversity-in-the-law-profession.

6. Sybil Dunlop & Jenny Gassman-Pines, *Why the Legal Profession Is the Nation's Least Diverse (And How to Fix It)*, 47 Mitchell Hamline L. Rev. 129, 141 (2021).

7. *See* Rory D. Bahadur, *Law School Rankings and the Impossibility of Anti-Racism*, 53 St. Mary's L. J. 991 (2022).

8. *See* LaTasha Hill, *Less Talk, More Action: How Law Schools Can Counteract Racial Bias of LSAT Scores in the Admissions Process*, 19 Univ. Md. L.J. Race Relig. Gender & Class 313 (2020); Scott Jaschik, *Do Law Schools Limit Black Enrollment with LSAT?*, Inside Higher Ed (Apr. 14, 2019), https://www.insidehighered.com/admissions/article/2019/04/15/study-argues-law-schools-limit-black-enrollment-through-lsat; Jay Rosner, *Op-Ed: The Legal Profession Lacks Diversity, and the LSAT Makes Matters Worse*, Los Angeles Times (Dec. 13, 2022, 3:04 AM), https://www.latimes.com/opinion/story/2022-12-13/lsat-law-school-diversity-aba.

9. Jaschik, *supra* note 8.

10. Sandra L. Simpson, *The Ultimate Logic Question: Why Continue to Use the LSAT When the Test Harms Diversity?*, 90 Tenn. L. Rev. 1 (2023).

11. *Id.* at 17.

12. *Id.* at 17–18.

13. *Id.* at 19.

14. Hill, *supra* note 8, at 313.

15. Shannon K. McCoy & Brenda Major, *Priming Meritocracy and the Psychological Justification of Inequality*, 43 J. Experimental Soc. Psych. 341, 341 (2007).

16. *Id.*

17. Aaron N. Taylor, *The Marginalization of Black Aspiring Lawyers*, 13 FIU L. Rev. 489, 497 (2019).

18. Bahadur, *supra* note 7.

19. Miles J. Herszenhorn & Nia L. Orakwue, *Rejecting the Rankings: Why Harvard and Yale Led a Widespread Boycott of U.S. News After Decades-Long Criticism*, The Harvard Crimson (May 25, 2023), https://www.thecrimson.com/article/2023/5/25/us-news-rankings-harvard-feature/#:~:text=%E2%80%9CThe%20U.S.%20News%20rankings%20are,Law%20School%20Dean%20John%20.

20. Bahadur, *supra* note 7.

21. Herszenhorn & Orakwue, *supra* note 19.

22. Rory D. Bahadur & Kevin Ruth, *Bad Math, Bar Sauce and the ABA as a Shill for the NCBE*, 66 How.L.J. 323, 385 (2022) (emphasis added).

23. Roger M. Baron Vermillion, *Do Bar Exams Preserve White Privilege?*, YANKTON DAILY PRESS & DAKOTAN (Feb. 22, 2022), https://www.yankton.net/opinion/editorials/article_39f57fec-9450-11ec-af1e-1f345440e452.html.

24. Scott Devito, Kelsey Hample & Erin Lain, *Examining the Bar Exam: An Empirical Analysis of Racial Bias in the Uniform Bar Examination*, 55 UNIV. MICH. J. L. REFORM 597, 601–2 (2022).

25. Mary Szto, *Barring Diversity? The American Bar Exam as Initiation Rite and Its Eugenics Origin*, 21 CONN. PUB. INT. L.J. 38 (2022).

26. For example, follow this link:

https://www.google.com/search?q=articles+that+suggest+the+bar+exam+is+racist&client=safari&sca_esv=6449538529ffda2f&hl=en-us&ei=-DwBZ-7HIOe4kPIPjNKrOA&oq=articles+that+suggest+the *Bad Math, Bar Sauce and the ABA as a Shill for the NCBE*, 66 How. L.J. 323, 385 +bar+exam+is+racist&gs_lp=EhNtb2JpbGUtZ3dzLXdpei1zZXJwIixhcnRpY2xlcyB0aGF0IHN1Z2dlc3QgdGhlIGJhciBleGFtIGlzIHJhY2lzdEieTVCvClifRXACeAGQAQCYAc0BoAHKHaoBBjkuMjYuMbgBA8gBAPgBAZgCGKACthLCAgoQABiwAxjWBBhHwgIFECEYoAHCAgUQIRirAsICBhAAGBYYHsICCxAAGIAEGIYDGIoFwgIFECEYnwXCAggQABgWGB4YD5gDAIgGAZAGCJIHBDcuMTegB-6DAQ&sclient=mobile-gws-wiz-serp (Results of a Google search using the following prompt: "articles that suggest the bar exam is racist".).

27. *See* Bahadur & Ruth, *supra* note 22.

28. *Id.*

29. Linda Greenhouse, *The End of Racism, and Other Fables*, NEW YORK TIMES ARCHIVE (2000), https://archive.nytimes.com/www.nytimes.com/books/00/06/04/specials/bell-well.html?scp=26&sq=End%2520of%2520tenure&st=Cse.

30. WIKIPEDIA, *Racial issues faced by Black quarterbacks*, https://en.wikipedia.org/wiki/Racial_issues_faced_by_black_quarterbacks.

31. Gene J. Puskar, *NFL to Halt 'Race-Norming,' Which Assumed Black Players Had Lower Cognitive Function*, NBC NEWS (Jun. 2, 2021, 4:10 PM), https://www.nbcnews.com/news/sports/nfl-halt-race-norming-which-assumed-black-players-had-lower-n1269435.

32. Marsha Griggs, *Building a Better Bar Exam*, 7 TEX. A&M L. REV. 20 (2019).

33. NORTHWESTERN UNIVERSITY, *Initiatives*, https://www.northwestern.edu/civil-rights-office/about/initiatives/affirmative-action/ (last visited Jan. 19, 2025).

34. Deborah Jones Merritt, *Research and Teaching on Law Faculties: An Empirical Exploration*, 73 CHI-KENT L. REV. 765, 766 (1998).

35. Sarah Lawsky, *Entry Level Hiring—JD School Total and Over Time*, PRAWFSBLAWG (May 27, 2020, 6:31 AM), https://prawfsblawg.blogs.com/prawfsblawg/2020/05/entry-level-hiring-jd-school-total-and-over-time.html.

36. Bahadur, *supra* note 7, at 1016.

37. *Id.*

38. *Id.* at 1015.

39. Andre M. Perry, Hannah Stephens & Manann Donoghe, *Black Wealth Is Increasing, But So Is the Racial Wealth Gap*, BROOKINGS (Jan. 9, 2024), https://www.brookings.edu/articles/black-wealth-is-increasing-but-so-is-the-racial-wealth-gap/#:~:text=Figure%202%20shows%20that%20from,when%20the%20gap%20reached%20%24214%2C970.

40. *Id.*

41. Kelly Rosinger, *Promoting Racial Equity Through Federal State College Affordability Partnerships*, EdTrust (Feb. 27, 2024), https://edtrust.org/blog/promoting-racial-equity-through-federal-state-college-affordability-partnerships/ (explaining that "Black students are less able to afford college and more likely to be burdened by student debt than their White peers, thanks to racial housing discrimination and the racial wealth gap in the U.S.").

42. *See* Mona E. Robbins, *Race and Higher Education: Is the LSAT Systemic of Racial Differences in Education Attainment?*, Penn. Libraries Univ. of Pa. (Aug. 20, 2017).

43. ScoreItUp LSAT Prep, https://www.scoreitup.com/2020/01/top-5-law-school-admission-factors-other-than-lsat-score-and-gpa/ (last visited Jan. 19, 2025) (Explaining that LSAT and GPA are the two most important law school admission criteria.).

44. Law School Expert, *Who Gets into Top Law Schools? Understanding the Admission Criteria*, https://www.lawschoolexpert.com/who-gets-to-attend-a-top-law-school/#:~:text=Top%20law%20schools%20require%20stellar,of%20the%20law%20school%20class (last visited Jan. 19, 2025) (Explaining "Attending a prestigious undergraduate institution puts you at an advantage in the eyes of the Top Law Schools. You've been tested against the nation's best and brightest, and—presumably—engaged in rigorous coursework with renowned professors.").

45. Bahadur, *supra* note 7, at 1018.

46. Debra Cassens Weiss, *Study Finds 'Lopsided' Concentration of Socioeconomic Elites at Law Schools*, A.B.A. J. (Oct. 5, 2011), https://www.abajournal.com/news/article/study_finds_lopsided_concentration_of_socioeconomic_elites_at_law_schools#:~:text="Across%20the%20spectrum%20of%20law,University%20Law%20Review%20(PDF).

47. Eric J. Segall & Adam Feldman, *The Elite Teaching the Elite: Who Gets Hired by the Top Law Schools*, 68 J. of Legal Educ. 614, 615–16 (2019).

48. Stephanie Francis Ward, *Many Federal Judges Want Clerkship Diversity but Say the Topic Is Rarely Addressed in Court, New Study Says*, A.B.A. J. (Dec. 2, 2022), https://www.abajournal.com/news/article/many-federal-judges-want-clerkship-diversity-but-say-the-topic-is-rarely-addressed-in-court.

49. Taylor, *supra* note 17, at 497.

50. Virginie Wiederkehr, Virginie Bonnot, Silvia Krauth-Gruber & Céline Darnon, *Belief in School Meritocracy as a System-Justifying Tool for Low Status Students*, 6 Frontiers Psych. 1–3 (2015).

51. Northwestern University, *supra* note 33.

52. Compl. For Petitioner FASORP v. Northwestern Univ., (No. 1:24-cv-05558 (N.D. Ill. July 2, 2024).

53. *Id.* at 1.

54. *Id.* at 4–5.

55. *Id.*

56. *Id.* at 7.

57. *Id.* at 12.

58. *Id.* at 12–13.

59. *Id.* at 18.

60. *Id.*, italics mine.

61. *Id.* at 30.

62. Mark Cullen, *Why Female Soccer Players Are at Risk of ACL Injuries*, Mass General Brigham, https://www.wdhospital.org/wdh/services-and-specialties/orthopedic

-care/blog/why-female-soccer-players-are-at-risk-of-acl-injuries (last visited Jan. 19, 2025).

63. *Id.*

64. *See* Akhilesh Kumar Ramachandran, Jason S. Pedley, Sylvia Moeskops, Jon L. Oliver, Gregory D. Myer & Rhodi S. Lloyd, *Changes in Lower Limb Biomechanics Across Various Stages of Maturation and Implications for ACL Injury Risk in Female Athletes: A Systematic Review*, 54 Systematic Rev. 1851 (2024).

65. Center for Young Women's Health, *Why Does the Pelvic Area in Girls Widen During Puberty?* (Nov. 6, 2013), https://youngwomenshealth.org/askus/why-does-the-pelvic-area-in-girls-widen-during-puberty/ (last visited Jan. 19, 2025).

66. Ramachandran et al., *supra* note 64.

67. *Id.*

68. *See* CE Quatman & TE Hewett, The Anterior Cruciate Ligament Injury Controversy: Is "Valgus Collapse" A Sex-Specific Mechanism?, 3 Br. J. Sports Med. 328–335 (2009).

69. Ramachandran et al., *supra* note 64.

70. (Italics added)

71. *See* District of Colombia v. Heller, 554 U.S. 570 (2008); *see also* McDonald v. City of Chicago, 561 U.S. 742 (2010).

72. *See* New York State Rifle & Pistol Association v. Bruen, 597 U.S. 1.

73. David S. Sidhu, *The Second Amendment at the Supreme Court: Challenges to Federal Gun Laws*, Congressional Research Services (July 8, 2024), https://crsreports.congress.gov/product/pdf/LSB/LSB11108#:~:text=Heller%2C%20the%20Supreme%20Court%20held,is%20a%20%E2%80%9Cfundamental%E2%80%9D%20right.

74. Nurith Aizenman, *How the U.S. Gun Violence Death Rate Compares with the Rest of the World*, NPR (Oct. 31, 2023, 2:08 PM), https://www.npr.org/sections/goatsandsoda/2023/10/31/1209683893/how-the-u-s-gun-violence-death-rate-compares-with-the-rest-of-the-world.

75. John Gramlich, *What the Data Says About Gun Deaths in the U.S.*, Pew Research Center (Apr. 26, 2023), https://www.pewresearch.org/short-reads/2023/04/26/what-the-data-says-about-gun-deaths-in-the-u-s/#:~:text=Though%20they%20tend%20to%20get,)%2C%20according%20to%20the%20CDC.

76. Amir Vera & Laura Ly, *White Woman Who Called Police on a Black Man Bird-Watching in Central Park Has Been Fired*, CNN (May 26, 2020, 4:21 PM), https://www.cnn.com/2020/05/26/us/central-park-video-dog-video-african-american-trnd/index.html.

77. *Id.*

78. *Id.*

79. Katherine Leach-Kemon, Rebecca Sirull & Scott Glenn, *On Gun Violence, the United States Is an Outlier*, IHME (Oct. 31, 2023), https://www.healthdata.org/news-events/insights-blog/acting-data/gun-violence-united-states-outlier#:~:text=US%20ranks%20first.-,Rates%20of%20firearm%20homicides%20among%20high-income%20countries,populations%20over%2010%20million%2C%202021&text=Age-adjusted%20firearm%20homicide%20rates%20in%20the%20US%20are%2019,firearm%20homicide%20seen%20in%20Australia.

80. World Population Review, *Gun Ownership by Country 2025*, https://worldpopulationreview.com/country-rankings/gun-ownership-by-country (last visited Jan. 19, 2025).

81. Amy @ Planned Parenthood, *Reproductive Freedom and Gun Safety Are Connected*, Planned Parenthood (July 15, 2022), https://www.plannedparenthood.org/blog/reproductive-freedom-and-gun-safety-are-connected.

CHAPTER 10

Systemic Racism Is Quintessentially Human

It should now be clear that getting beyond the systemic status quo is difficult, if not impossible. It entails overcoming the evolutionary mechanisms essential to our success as a species. Human societies all over the planet consistently find ways to generate and justify hierarchies within societies. In this book I have focused on race as the mechanism around which the hierarchies are maintained, but in many other parts of the world, even more precipitous hierarchies are created that aren't based on race. Consider the caste system in India, Kikuyu tribalism and resource domination in Kenya, and the fate of the Uygur, Zhuang, Manchu, Hui, and Miao populations in China.[1]

This chapter is a deeper dive into the cognitive science that supports "meh relegation." The 2024 American presidential election provides an excellent opportunity for the in-depth exploration of the unconscious cognitive mechanisms that support the "meh relegation" of information I have described thus far.

Before going forward, let me be clear. Even though the results of the 2024 election terrify me as an immigrant of color, I deeply respect and honor the result as the choices of the population of an amazing country that has provided me opportunities for success that I am certain would not have materialized anywhere else. I must admit, as I write this, that I do so from a position of relative privilege made possible by my own achievement of what many people call the American Dream.

My goal in writing this book is not to appear ungrateful to America but to make people aware that systemic barriers hinder wide swaths of the population from also achieving this dream. Systemic inequity blinds us to the fact that race and skin color still impact the attainability of that dream. This racial inequity is an inconvenient truth that nothing less than our very humanity and the cognitive reality of that humanity prevents us from acknowledging or even seeing.

If mitigating that inequity is something you think is worthwhile, then this chapter is for you. Understand, however, that sometimes the truth hurts. But because this is America, two things are still true. The first is that no one can force you to believe anything or think anything—you are *free* to draw your own conclusions. The second is that information and viewpoints are freely available to the population, and censorship is un-American.[2] This second truth is the reason we have so much faith in the first truth. This chapter is just providing information, using the 2024 election as a way to contextualize that information.

Initially, if we are honest with ourselves, egalitarianism and equality have never been natural characteristics of human societies. Philosophers like Foucault and Nietzsche have long explored this unassailable reality in their writings. Even in Scandinavia, where they are proud of their egalitarianism, Danes are still curious about how many generations of a person's family have been Danish. Overcoming systemic hierarchy in human populations may very well prove impossible because that hierarchy appears to be essential to our ability to maintain stable societies. Understand that egalitarianism and equity involve reversing many cognitive traits and patterns that, for better or worse, render us essentially human. Being a liberal or feeling like you are "woke," as I have demonstrated, isn't enough. These things might satisfy your ego's need to view yourself favorably, but they have no real impact on systemic inequity.

Additionally, the complexity and magnitude of the task is often underestimated by experts in the field as well. For example, Shankar Vedantum suggested that most Republicans wished Trump would shut up about things that were untrue, such as immigrant criminality, and that he would be a better politician if he was more adept at changing his views and expression to know his audience.[3] I disagree. The reality is that the 2024 election demonstrated Donald Trump needs no real substantive views on anything. He simply needs to repeat a narrative that involves deporting immigrants falsely accused of criminality and eating domestic animals to win the presidency. This chapter explores why that is true.

The Cognitive Foundations of Systemic Inequity

Muzafer Sherif, generally regarded as the pioneer of intergroup dynamics research,[4] suggested as early as 1956 that the creation of societal groups or the formation of an "us" and a "them" is an essential part of human societal structure.[5] In 1946, he conducted an experiment where he invited 11- and 12-year-old boys who did not know each other and were considered "normal" by the standards of the day to be part of a camp. The boys were not informed that they were part of an experiment on human group dynamics.[6] Initially, the boys were allowed to mingle freely, and friendships developed, with some of the boys identifying certain other individuals as their best friends.[7]

The boys were then divided into two discrete groups, and, as far as possible, the boys identifying as best friends were placed in different groups.[8] Once the groups were established, the researchers observed that group belonging and membership became more important than the individual friendships formed before the groups were created. Hierarchies quickly developed within the groups, resulting in the emergence of leaders and followers.[9]

In fact, allegiance to the group was so powerful, and group membership was so significant, that members of each group turned against the individuals of the opposing group, even if those individuals had been identified as their best friends prior to the group division.[10] Even more interestingly, in terms of our natural tendencies to reframe reality, the researchers observed that the members of each group consistently overestimated the excellence of their group's leaders while underestimating the achievements of the lower-ranked members in a series of games designed by the camp organizers.[11]

Sherif's work also demonstrates that the boys who were initially identified as having bullying tendencies early in the camp interaction were eventually elected as the leaders of the group as intergroup competition intensified.[12] He suggested that when resources were limited, humans naturally formed groups to compete for those resources. His findings concluded by suggesting that intergroup conflict was reduced when people were motivated to work together. Sherif observed that intergroup competition decreased and cooperation increased when groups were placed in situations requiring joint effort to solve a shared problem. For example, when the researchers staged a scenario in which the truck delivering food to the camp could not move, both groups collaborated to pull the truck into camp using the same rope they had previously used to compete against each other in a tug-of-war match.[13]

Sherif's labeled these observations as Real Conflict Theory. He suggested that when resources are finite, humans naturally gravitate towards groups, leading to competition. However, when people are required to work together to achieve a common goal, intergroup cooperation increases, and the barriers between groups are reduced.

In 1979, Henri Tajfel and John Turner[14] expanded upon this research even further, demonstrating that there did not even need to be logical reasons for humans to assemble and identify as members of groups within societies—they just did so, and once they do, intergroup discrimination occurs organically.[15]

Subsequent research confirms that discriminatory behavior toward members of a different group can exist even in the absence of dislike for the out-group. All that it takes for discrimination to materialize is in-group preference.[16] The creation of groups is, in fact, essential for human identity formation. Brewer describes group creation as "the fundamental survival strategy that characterizes the human species."[17] Similarly, Worchel suggests that "it almost seems as though conflict and discrimination are natural states of human interaction and harmony and intergroup attraction are anomalies."[18] Any attempt at systemic reform must begin with an acknowledgment of this frightful reality of human nature and intergroup relations. Relying on fictions such as the innate goodness of humanity means we are relying on baseless, palliative recreations powerfully reinforced by morality, civility, and even religion.

These intergroup conflicts are understandable in the context of our evolutionary history. According to Brewer, humans are neither the strongest nor fastest animals on the planet and could not compete with the other organisms for dominance on a purely individual level. Instead, in evolutionary terms, we sacrificed individual capacity for survival in favor of forming cooperative societies, where we cooperate as groups to ensure our survival as a species. As a result, the formation of groups is a fundamental aspect of human existence. For those groups to remain stable and survive, we have evolved to trust members of our groups more than we distrust them. Without this trust, group stability would be impossible.[19]

This theory is known as the theory of parochial altruism, as described in Chapter 7. Brewer perhaps more accurately describes it as "contingent altruism."[20] A key condition of contingent altruism is that the sacrifices an individual makes for the benefit of the group will be rewarded because other like-minded individuals will similarly act for the group's benefit. Hence, groups must be discrete, confined to people who are willing to engage in this contingent or reciprocal altruism, and exclude those who will not reciprocate.[21] Additionally, group members must be able to readily identify one another.[22]

This form of altruism goes beyond simple reciprocal benefit. Tajfel's research confirms that group members will be satisfied accepting less than their fair share if the resources they are deprived of are thought to be benefitting an in-group member.[23] The same does not aways hold true, as people are not comfortable accepting less benefit than they are entitled to if the lost benefits appear to be benefitting a member of an out-group.[24] This holds true even when the in-group consists of minimally affiliated individuals.[25] Consider how much stronger this altruism would be when it based on something very visible and apparent, like phenotype or race.

At this point, it is important to brush aside the nonsensical suggestion that race is unimportant in social group theory because it is only a social construct. Many brilliant people who should know better, like economist Glenn Loury, suggest that race is merely a social construct.[26] Others argue that because it is a social construct, it should be irrelevant and unimportant.[27] However, consider that law, religion, and economics are all social constructs, and they are undeniably important. As Ande Davis explains, Kansas, for example, is a social construct—there was nothing uniquely Kansan about the land falling within the state's borders until those borders were constructed. However, for people who are within those constructed borders, a very real series of rights and laws unique to that state become impactful.[28]

Davis explains that the fact that race is only a social construct actually cuts the other way: "In sum, the proposition that race is socially constructed posits that, as race is neither a biological nor ontological fact, it was racism that necessarily preconditioned the construction of race."[29] Furthermore, the construction of race in our society "crystallized over time in European thought to represent entities who are humanoid but not fully human ('savages,' 'barbarians') and who are identified as such by being members of the general set of nonwhite races."[30]

This may be the reason ethnocentricity is an essential aspect of human groups—ethnic distinctions are easily visible and efficient.[31] Group membership reinforces itself based on the distinctive features of the group, and phenotype or race is a distinctive feature tied to our evolutionary history. For most of our evolutionary history, we existed as distinct hunter-gatherer bands separated by geographic boundaries, where phenotypic expression evolved according to geography and environmental conditions—light skin in the polar regions and darker skin in the sunnier equatorial regions, for example.

In fact, two other researchers confirm that ethnocentrism is essential to human societal structure. Sibley and Barlow demonstrate that when we consciously or unconsciously create an "us" and a "them," face recognition is much stronger, automatic, and even unconscious for members within a certain group. Phenotypic commonality is one of those natural boundaries along which groups can be constructed. Scientifically, it is well-documented that people can distinguish and recognize faces of individuals from their own race more effectively than those of other races. This phenomenon is referred to in the literature as the "other race effect."[32] It is so deeply integrated into human nature that neither positive racial attitudes to other races nor cross-racial experience has been shown to mitigate it.[33]

We should not underestimate the evolutionary entrenchment of phenotypic characterization. Humans naturally exhibit more trust and empathy toward those that are part of their group, a reality that increases in-group socialization and cooperation. Physiological reactions also differ significantly when interacting with individuals considered familiar versus those deemed different. For example, oxytocin administration, while increasing prosocial behavior toward members of the in-group, has no effect on attitudes or behaviors toward members of the out-group.[34] Sibley and Barlow further demonstrate, consistent with Sherif's findings, that individuals tend to overestimate the performance of in-group members while underestimating the performance of out-group members.[35]

Group dynamics are often considered an equilibrium between the need to belong and the need to assert individuality.[36] These tensions define the boundaries of human groups and are inescapable aspects of our humanity. For in-group membership to be meaningful in this regard, the groups themselves must remain relatively small and clearly defined.[37] For example, there is no equilibrium achieved by saying, "I am a member of the group of the people on Earth." However, there are clear advantages to being part of a more narrowly defined altruistic reciprocity unit, such as family, religion, or other smaller, cohesive groups.[38]

In-group favoritism may result in strong positive feelings to members of an in-group, but this does not necessarily equate to active hatred for the out-group.[39] Rather, it often reflects a lack of positive feelings for the out-groups. What Brewer terms "subtle racism" is not necessarily driven by overt hatred but by the absence of the benefits of the doubt or favorable presumptions being afforded to members of the out-group.[40] Brewer emphasizes that discrimination can occur not only through active dislike but also through the mere withholding of those favorable presumptions.[41] This concept aligns with my description of white privilege in Chapter 5, and clearly explains that racism need not be a conscious or active dislike for people of color to be harmful.

This reality also makes the differences in treatment of people based on in-group or out-group membership harder to observe and accept.[42] Observable actions, such as rejection or hatred, are easier to recognize and believe, but they are not necessary for disparate treatment based on group membership to exist.[43] It is far more difficult to observe things that do not happen or occur. Because the mere absence of the benefit of the doubt, lack of favoritism, leniency, or preferential attention is all that is required for different treatment to occur, they are difficult to observe and acknowledge.[44]

Crucially, the physiological differences in response to in-group and out-group members may help explain what I define as "meh relegation" of information in earlier chapters, as merit and fault attributions are affected by group membership.[45] Good behavior by an in-group member is typically judged as consistent with their character, while bad actions are often viewed as anomalies caused by external factors, such as the weather.[46]

According to Tajfel, social group formation and identification helps individuals understand or perceive their rung of the social hierarchy ladder that they belong on.[47] Humans unconsciously compare themselves to other groups, and self-esteem in society is generated in part by unconsciously distinguishing your group and locating it higher than another "inferior" group in society.[48] Tajfel also notes that sometimes the more intense competition in intergroup dynamics is between lower-status groups rather than between the lower-status and higher-status groups. By identifying as better or distinct from a group perceived as lower, individuals derive a sense of improved self-esteem and validation.[49]

Not only is intergroup discrimination organic, but disenfranchised groups in society also justify the hierarchy of the groups within the society.[50] As Tajfel explains, there is a great deal of scientific evidence that "minority or subordinate group members—such as the American Blacks, the French Canadians, the New Zealand Maoris, or the South African Bantus—frequently tend to derogate the in-group and display positive attitudes toward the dominant out-group."[51] This reality dovetails perfectly with Jost's theory of system justification, which suggests that even disaffected groups in society justify and internalize the hierarchy of the society and perceive it as just.[52]

Jost points out that this is especially true when societies are primed with what he called system-threatening messages or are told that major social change will occur. Jost conducted research in Israel where he identified two distinct social groups:[53] the Ashkenazi, who were the high-SES group, and the Sephardim, who were considered the low-SES group.[54] When Jost suggested to both groups that Israel was a secure and strong nation, he observed that the Ashkenazi showed Ashkenazi in-group favoritism, and the Sephardim showed in-group favoritism to the Sepahrdim.[55] However, when he suggested that Israel was a nation that was under imminent threat by unfriendly neighbors, both the Sephardim and the Ashkenazi demonstrated favoritism toward the Ashkenazi.[56] In other words, both the disenfranchised and high-SES groups in a society tended to favor the status quo and hierarchy when a systemic threat was perceived.[57]

System justification is also enhanced in societies like the United States that perceive themselves as meritocratic. One researcher explains that belief in meritocracy acts as the glue that holds societies together, even in the face of massive inequality.[58] This belief allows low-status groups in society to accept inequality as normative and natural.[59] Without this acceptance, it is likely there would be continuous uprising and a lack of societal stability. Other researchers suggest that this fundamental belief in meritocracy is what permits the status differences observed in American society to be maintained.[60] Furthermore, the belief in meritocracy becomes even more powerful when coupled with the belief that we live in a just world.[61] In the West, religion is often recognized as a primary source of this belief in a just world.[62]

Meritocracy is so palliative, for example, that when women are given the choice between blaming their individual shortcomings or discrimination for rejection in the context of a job interview, they are more likely to blame themselves, thereby perpetuating stereotypes of female inability more broadly.[63] McCoy and Major also observe that meritocracy is so palliative that, even in situations where it is obvious that the rules are unmeritocratic, system justification results in people perceiving the situation as meritocratic.[64]

At this point, it should be clear that egalitarianism and equality are unnatural for humans and human societal structure. The stability necessary for our very civilizations is possible only because we naturally create groups of *us* and *them*, discriminate against each other, and justify the system of discrimination powerfully and unconsciously. If we are unwilling to accept this reality about ourselves as a species, then there is little hope of ameliorating these harsh realities of human society. This reality may be impossible to admit for many people because it renders the notion that we, as a species, were created in the image of a benevolent, gentle, and loving supreme being nonsensical. Unless we admit that human history overwhelmingly confirms that, by our very nature, we are a cruel, genocidal, and hierarchical species, solutions will be impossible.

We need to recognize the universal human nature of these hierarchies as well. Again, while my focus is on America, where the hierarchies and reframing of reality occur along phenotypic and racial lines and are based on meritocracy, in other parts of the world, the hierarchies are arranged differently. In India, for example, the hierarchies are arranged along the caste system, which is largely determined by the ranking given to different occupational groups. And in the caste system, there is no meritocratic illusion that you can work your way out of your caste.

The very nature of human societies depends on recognizing and unconsciously buttressing the societal structure, or else we would not have stable long-term societies. This means that deprived groups are not always "ethnocentric," but humans are wired to sometimes be positively oriented toward and supportive of the groups that are of higher-SES, even though those groups often will be the ones depriving the very people who view them positively.[65]

Brewer's research also supports my suggestion in Chapter 4 that morality is contrived to a certain degree because she suggests that when groups become larger and approach categories, the customs and traditions that reflect the group take on a larger-than-life character and become what we call morality.[66] This is exactly what the concept of God is described as in the book *Sapiens* by Yuval Noah Harari.[67]

Perhaps when groups reach the size of nation-states, to facilitate identification as a member of a group, the group develops norms of behavior (anthems, pledges of allegiance, dress) and appearance, which make it easier to identify members of the group as the people conforming to these norms. Whiteness has traditionally been an important norm in the United States.

My own summary of the principles developed in the cognitive research I described above are:

1. Humans unconsciously and unavoidably form groups.
2. These groups are based on perceived similarity, which may range from phenotype to a belief set.
3. Once humans situate themselves in a group, they develop favorable presumptions regarding other members of the group, exaggerate the successes of group members, and minimize the culpability of group members who perform bad acts.
4. Discrimination does not require hatred or dislike for out-groups; all it requires is the favorable perception of members of your own in-group.
5. Human societal groups form and justify hierarchies between the groups, with the lower-ranked groups discriminating against each other and jostling for hierarchical position more vigorously than low-ranked groups jostle with the highest-ranked group.
6. Once groups form, they tend to favor leaders who, in an individual setting, would be considered a bully or tyrant.
7. Group members are willing to suffer loss or give up their own well-being for the benefit of other members of their own group, but not for the benefit of out-group members.

8. Once the systemic hierarchy is perceived as threatened or based on meritocracy, all groups act in a way to strongly justify the existing hierarchy.
9. Whiteness is the characteristic of the highest-ranking group in America, as I have previously explained.

These realities of humanity explain why Donald Trump was correct in 2016 when he said, "I could stand in the middle of Fifth Avenue and shoot somebody, and I wouldn't lose any voters, OK? It's, like, incredible."[68] They also explain his resounding victory in the 2024 presidential election.

The Humanity of Trumpism

The Trump team realized early on that if they framed his campaigns and presidency in terms of a threat to the system and made it about "us" versus "them," the nine principles listed above ensured people from all demographics would be unconsciously and powerfully drawn to support him, in the same way that a moth is helplessly drawn toward a light. This is not disparaging of anyone; it is simply a recognition that people are human.

Not only did Team Trump know that making the election about an illusory "us" and "them" and a completely contrived "threat to our way of life" would render the majority of Americans incapable of acting consistently with their anti-racist belief set while remaining unaware they were behaving inconsistently, but they also immediately reinforced the illusion to the voters that their choices were conscious and merit-based.

Consider that Kellyanne Conway, the day after the election, tried to assure voters that their choices were made consciously and on merit-based reasons: "She's just a flawed candidate, she doesn't speak well, she doesn't work hard. I'm not being mean or partisan. I don't know why the country would have rewarded this candidate with the big job."[69] Kellyanne Conway is simply brilliant. No one else weaponizes implicit bias and system justification so powerfully and effectively to render invisible the reality that unconscious, hierarchy-reinforcing decision-making is occurring, while at the same time convincing the decision-makers that their decisions were conscious, merit-based, and reasoned. When you are convinced part of the reason you voted for Trump was that Harris "didn't speak well," try to remember if "bigly" had the same impact on you.

This weaponization mirrors the trap that some scholars in the field fall into. For example, Vedantam acknowledges that unconscious biases are not subject to introspection but then suggests that the solution to escaping the influence of our unconscious brain is to be introspective about our biases. In proposing that "we can *choose* to allow our actions to be guided by reason rather than instinct"[70] as the solution to being governed by the conclusions of our unconscious brain, Vedantam fails to acknowledge that we can't choose reason over unconscious processing because the results of unconscious cognitive heuristics powerfully feel as if they were reasoned conclusions, and they "escape conscious awareness or control."[71] That is the meaning of not being subject to introspection.

The principle that we minimize the culpability and deficiencies of the in-group members is reflected by the fact that, were Trump not a white male, he would have been disqualified from running for office by the very party of "law and order" Republicans who supported his candidacy. Consider that, in 2023, Justin Jones, a Black member of the Tennessee legislature, was expelled from the legislature and banned from the floor because he elected to speak about gun control and the Covenant School shooting.[72] In support of their decision to expel Jones, the Republican legislators categorized his actions as "a serious breach of decorum, tantamount to an insurrection, that requires expulsion."[73] Yet Republicans did not suggest Donald Trump's incitement of the January 6, 2021, riots on the Capitol building was disqualifying. Not only did the in-group of largely white male Republicans support the president, but a whopping 56% of the electorate, of all demographics, also voted for Mr. Trump.

And this is consistent with the reality that the Trump team framed this election as a massive threat to the American way of life and the American system. On November 4 in Pennsylvania, Trump declared, "America is an occupied country."[74] He was referring to both documented and undocumented aliens and promised he would "rescue every city and town that has been invaded and conquered." He brilliantly further framed this as "military invasions without the uniforms."[75]

Once the election was presented so effectively as a threat to the American system, even lower socioeconomic and disenfranchised members of society reframed reality unconsciously to have favorable feelings toward members of the in-group or the powerful group, which in America is the white male. The reality is that people support, as group leaders, people who individually they might consider bullies or boorish.[76]

If we examine just some of the things Donald Trump has said or done, there is no argument that if he was a man of color, he would not even have been allowed to run in the 2024 race. Both liberals and conservatives would have deemed him unfit or below the dignity required for the office of president.

For example:

1. In a 2005 recording that surfaced in 2016, Trump stated that his fame allowed him to behave inappropriately with women, saying, "grab 'em by the pussy."[77]
2. During a 2015 rally, Trump appeared to mock *New York Times* reporter Serge Kovaleski, who has a congenital joint condition, by imitating his physical movements.[78]
3. After the violent white supremacist rally in Charlottesville, Virginia, Trump stated that there were "very fine people on both sides," drawing criticism for equating protesters with white nationalists.[79]
4. In a 2018 meeting discussing immigration, Trump reportedly referred to Haiti, El Salvador, and African nations as "shithole countries."[80]
5. In 2023, Trump stated that undocumented immigrants are "poisoning the blood of our country," a phrase criticized for echoing white supremacist rhetoric.[81]
6. On Veterans Day 2023, Trump referred to some of his political opponents as "vermin," a term historically used in fascist rhetoric when the Nazis described the Jewish people.[82]
7. In 2015, Trump called for a "total and complete shutdown of Muslims entering the United States," a statement widely criticized as discriminatory.[83]
8. During his 2016 campaign, Trump encouraged supporters to "knock the crap out of" protesters, offering to pay legal fees for those who did.[84]
9. In response to George Floyd protests in 2020, Trump tweeted, "when the looting starts, the shooting starts," a phrase with historical ties to racist policing originally used in 1967 by Miami police chief, Walter Headley.[85]

10. Trump was impeached for pressuring Ukraine to investigate a political rival, leveraging military aid as a bargaining chip.[86]
11. During a 2020 debate, Trump told the far-right group Proud Boys to "stand back and stand by," rather than condemning them outright.[87]
12. In 2016, Trump claimed his supporters were so loyal that he could "stand in the middle of Fifth Avenue and shoot somebody" without losing votes.[88]
13. In 2020, Trump refused to commit to a peaceful transfer of power if he lost the election, undermining democratic norms.[89]
14. In 2016 Trump reportedly asked advisors why the U.S. couldn't use nuclear weapons, raising concerns about his understanding of nuclear policy.[90]
15. In 2019 Trump tweeted that four Democratic congresswomen should "go back" to the countries they came from, despite three of them being born in the U.S.[91]
16. Trump referred to COVID-19 as the "China Virus" or "Kung Flu," a characterization widely criticized as promoting xenophobia and reflective of the historical racism against Chinese based on false assertions that they were disease-carrying dirty immigrants.[92]
17. Trump referred to Americans who died in war as "suckers" and "losers," for example when trying to downgrade John McCain's military service, though he denies making these statements.[93]
18. Trump threatened to deploy federal law enforcement to cities with Democratic leadership experiencing protests, a move seen as political intimidation by some, even though many Republican politicians had no problem with this proposed deployment.[94]
19. Trump has used terms like "thugs" for protesters and "animals" for immigrants, phrases criticized for dehumanizing rhetoric.[95]
20. Trump warned minority groups of poverty if they did not support him, which critics saw as a coercive statement.[96]

21. Trump described Baltimore, a majority-Black city, as a "disgusting, rat and rodent infested mess,"[97] which many viewed as racially insensitive.[98]
22. In a video addressing the Capitol rioters, Trump said, "We love you, you're very special," which many saw as an endorsement of violent actions.[99]
23. Beyond Charlottesville, Trump has repeatedly hesitated to explicitly denounce white supremacist and far-right groups, including his reluctance to denounce the Proud Boys directly during the 2020 debate.[100]
24. Following his 2020 election loss, Trump repeatedly claimed the election was "stolen," fueling conspiracy theories, resulting in his impeachment for inciting the Capitol riot, and continuing to cast doubt on the electoral process.[101]
25. Trump posted on social media suggesting the "termination" of constitutional rules to overturn the 2020 election results, a comment that received bipartisan criticism as unprecedented and anti-democratic.[102]
26. In 2018, under Trump's administration, a policy of family separation for migrants was enforced, leading to public outcry over humanitarian concerns and thousands of children separated from their families.[103]
27. In 2018, Trump expressed admiration for dictatorial leaders such as Kim Jong Un and Vladimir Putin, often praising them for their "strength," a departure from typical diplomatic rhetoric of democratic leaders.[104]
28. In 2021, breaking a long-standing tradition, Trump refused to attend the inauguration of his successor, Joe Biden, an action widely viewed as undermining the peaceful transition of power.[105]
29. Over the span of many years, Trump has been criticized for using terms with racial connotations for his opponents and public figures, including calling Senator Elizabeth Warren "Pocahontas."[106]
30. Trump has repeatedly called for individual journalists to be fired, often deriding news outlets as "fake news and the "enemy of the people." These comments have raised concerns about freedom of the press.[107]

31. Trump has frequently referred to the Democratic Party and Democratic lawmakers as an "enemy from within," which many view as divisive rhetoric unusual for a president. This language is seen as an attempt to delegitimize political opposition.[108]
32. Trump has made statements suggesting that undocumented immigrants receive taxpayer-funded transgender surgeries, a claim widely criticized as inflammatory and unsubstantiated. This language plays into fears regarding immigration and LGBTQ+ rights.[109]
33. During the 2024 presidential debate with Vice President Kamala Harris, Trump falsely stated that illegal immigrants from Haiti have been eating domestic pets in Springfield, Ohio. This led to bomb threats being made toward this area densely populated with immigrants.[110]

But none of this mattered because the rhetoric he employed engaged system justification by suggesting the nature of American society was under threat. Once a threat to the American system, with whiteness at the top of the hierarchy, was conveyed, it became virtually impossible for members of American society to do anything but vote for the white male instead of the woman of color who was also a daughter of the threatening immigrants of color from "shithole" countries.

As I explained in relation to World War II in Chapter 5, this is the privilege of being a white male in America or of belonging to the dominant group in any human society. This is white privilege. Van Lathan describes this brilliantly:

> It's a masterclass in white privilege. He can't say enough racist things to be a racist. He can't commit enough crimes to be a criminal. He can't fail enough times to be a failure. He can't say enough stupid things to be stupid. The idea of him overshadows any reality. The "Christian savior" who doesn't know the Bible, the adulterer who fucks porn stars and steals from charities. It's the promise of the protection of whiteness.[111]

Ta-Nehisi Coates likewise suggests, "whiteness is neither notional nor symbolic, but is the very core of [Trump's] power."[112]

At this point, many people will suggest that I am wrong because Barack Obama was a Black, two-term president. However, Obama was brilliant, and so were his advisers. They ensured Obama carefully conformed to the established norms of civility and decency and that he did not represent a threat to the system. Additionally, he rarely dwelled on or addressed systemic inequity based on race and was careful to remind people of his white Kansas mother and his white maternal grandparents, who finished raising him, at every opportunity. Similarly, he never visited or significantly engaged with his father's family in Africa until after his term in office was over.

In short, he conformed to American norms of civility. But American norms and civility are only a set of rules that white America imposes on the rest of society so that we can all comfortably remain blind to the only real rule of all human society: that might is right.[113] He sold hope and portrayed himself as an example of how it was equally possible to get ahead, no matter your race or beginning—a myth which you know is untrue after reading Chapter 2 and hearing Alosha's response to the audience member. But this myth is comfortable, and it forms the palliative glue that holds American society together, even though it is untrue. The truth is that "civility is nothing more than a sadistic expression of systemic oppression in which the oppressed and conquered agree to obey the oppressor's demand for appeasement and accept a power imbalance."[114]

Obama's civil behavior is reminiscent of how Carla Pratt describes the behavior of the Five Civilized Tribes.[115] She discusses how the tribes that migrated west on the Trail of Tears were labeled as civilized by white settlers because "they had assimilated to European ways of living by speaking English, dressing in European attire, becoming Christians, and adopting agrarian lifestyles, including the use of black slave labor to work their farms."[116] By acting in accordance with and perpetuating the norms of civility imposed by white people, these tribes benefitted because white settlers elevated them to a status that was higher than the other tribes, whom the settlers referred to as "savages."[117]

As Pratt points out, to be recognized by the federal government as a sovereign nation, the tribes had to be recognized racially as American Indian.[118] Tribal leaders recognized that intermarriage with enslaved people of African descent would create ambiguity in the racial status of the tribes, and risk the tribes being considered "Negro" rather than

American Indian.[119] Pratt describes the uncomfortable truth that, "[r]esponsible tribal leadership thus required that tribes adopt anti-black laws and customs to protect Indian identity from degradation."[120] The Five Civilized Tribes thus worked to behave like white people and adopt their norms, thereby demonstrating, "to whites in the federal government that their tribes were 'civilized' and deserving of the same status and legal entitlements as whites."[121]

But make no mistake, despite President Obama threading the systemic inequity needle so delicately, the Tea Party materialized to resist everything he proposed or did. Mitch McConnell instructed the Senate not to confirm his choice for the Supreme Court but confirmed Justice Amy Coney Barrett under almost identical situations, and the outrage and immorality was "meh relegated" into oblivion. The reality is that no matter what members of the lower-ranked groups do in human societies, that conduct will be judged by a different standard than if the actions were performed by a member of the dominant group.

President Obama, despite his honesty, morality, kindness, and compassion, commented that he faced racism as a president.[122] He said that racism was still "part of our DNA," emphasizing that societies change slowly and it was unrealistic to expect the reality of centuries of racism to be undone quickly.[123] We are still grappling with the hierarchies that were deliberately created, as I described in Chapter 8 as almost ingrained in our very genetics, and which Obama correctly identified as DNA coded.

Pratt's work also reminds us that these nine cognitive principles are not uniquely adapted to whiteness. Humans, in general, find ways all over the world—whether based on race or other factors, such as the caste system in India—to establish groups and assign hierarchies to the groups. However, in America, race happens to be the basis of group hierarchies.

Obama's presidency reinforces the reality that ethics, civility, and morality are only valued qualities for people of color if they are employed in a way that reinforces white dominant power hierarchies in American society or silences threats to them.[124] However, these concepts, like religion and ethics, become meaningless and insignificant to even religious and ethical people when systemic hierarchies are threatened. The shifting judgments and moral hypocrisy that we all experience when a system is threatened are not conscious. We remain unaware that our decision-making and judgment are inconsistent with the people we genuinely believe ourselves to be and with our own moral compasses. The brilliance of the Trump team and their knowledge of cognitive science must, once again, be acknowledged in this regard.

These cognitive principles also explain the "But I have a Black friend, so I can't be racist" phenomenon. When some of my dear friends, who happen to be white, are powerfully motivated to vote for Donald Trump but remind me that they have many friends of color, like myself, and therefore believe this means they aren't racist and aren't voting for him because of racism, it turns out that they are both correct and incorrect.

They are correct that, personally and consciously, they are not racist. They genuinely care for me, and some may have even stood up for me when they observed me being treated differently because of my race. However, they don't have to dislike me or dislike people of color to "meh relegate" all of Trump's racist actions and give him their support and their vote. According to the cognitive principles listed above, simply subconsciously identifying as belonging to the "in" group of white is all that is required for discrimination to occur.[125]

This subconscious belonging alone is enough for white people to be given the benefit of the doubt, for white successes to be exaggerated, white failures to be diminished, and the egregious and culpable actions of white people to be "meh relegated" to the realm of locker room talk.[126] So, they are correct they don't dislike people because of the color of their skin. But they are incorrect if racism is defined as giving preferential treatment to members of a white in-group, irrespective of your feelings to members of the Black or brown out-group, resulting in differential treatment and assessment of behavior, morality, decency, and qualification depending on whether the person being judged is white or not. These principles demonstrate that you can consciously like and love the darker-skinned out-groups, but that has nothing to do with whether you unconsciously give favorable presumptions to the actions of in-group members.

Ultimately, if we define racism as different treatment based on race, then to people of color, it really doesn't matter if that racism results from conscious hatred of us or whether you love us but, as a human, you are unconsciously creating in-groups versus out-groups, which leads to differential evaluations of our actions.

In fact, as I describe in the introduction, to some extent, the conscious hatred-based racism is easier for people of color to deal with than the unconscious racism based on the cognitive realities of human group dynamics, which Brewer calls "subtle racism."[127] It is simply exhausting for people to even acknowledge the existence of these unconscious heuristics. To address the racism resulting from them, you need to expend immense diplomatic effort, tact, and apology to convince, for example, the self-righteous liberal, proud of their self-proclaimed wokeness, that their actions can be just as harmful as those of consciously racist individuals.

These cognitive science principles also explain why so many people of color voted for Trump as well, and why Trump's support is perhaps the most rabid among the poor white demographic, even though he has nothing in common with them and likely is unfamiliar with their reality. As discussed in Chapter 8, whiteness became deeply entrenched as the mechanism that distinguished those entitled to more from those entitled to nothing.

For poor white people, the palliative effect of unconsciously reframing themselves as belonging to the same group as the descendants of the class of people who treated their ancestors exactly like slaves is powerful, unconscious, and provides the most important of human needs: comfort with self. Unconsciously reframing themselves as closer to the dominant group than the lower groups in society is an irresistible palliative fiction that is created unconsciously. This fiction, formed unconsciously, gives them an identity in the social hierarchy that is far more comforting than the reality—a reality in which their allegiance to the dominant class is reinforced by mechanisms deliberately designed to make them easier to manage and control. Even today, these mechanisms continue to generate allegiance to the billionaire class, which is happy to exploit and profit from them. Poor whites still feel a sense of kinship, kindness, and favoritism toward the very class of billionaires profiting from their position at the bottom of the socioeconomic ladder.

As long as Team trump paints the societal system as threatened, there will be buy-in by all demographics, as all members of society become motivated to defend systemic structure at times of perceived systemic threat. Whatever he says that aligns with the societal biases and systemic racism perpetuated by system justification does not need to be true or even real, as he is given the presumption of believability as a white male. Let the "meh relegation" of what I am saying here begin.

In the context of the Trump campaign, this perhaps helps explain why so many Americans viewed the white male as excellent on the economy, even though he inherited millions from his father and declared bankruptcy six times as a businessman.[128] Meanwhile, Kamala Harris was blamed for inflation, an unavoidable side effect of COVID-related supply disruptions, despite the fact that she and President Biden reduced inflation and provided an economic soft landing instead of the expected recession.

This group theory of overestimating the performance of in group members could also be why so many people mentioned in this election that Donald Trump was a strong leader, despite the reality being that he cozied up to dictators like Vladimir Putin and Kim Jong Un, fawning over them like an admiring child when in their presence.

So, when Trump and his advisors paint American society as threatened, even when the threats are fictional but well-articulated—such as claiming America is an occupied society with immigrants taking over and eating our pets, or a Black woman is about to run our country and labeling her as "dumb,"[129] a socialist, and the child of foreigners—system justification becomes even stronger than it normally is. As a result, even some of the lower-SES members gravitate to his message and view him more favorably than when the system isn't perceived as threatened. As I explain later, this likely accounts for why in the 2024 election cycle, almost 25% of the Black male vote[130] went to a person whose rhetoric is likely viewed as racist by most people.

Many people also seem surprised that Donald Trump received 45% of the Hispanic vote.[131] However, this should not be surprising when viewed through the lens of intergroup dynamics. This is particularly relevant for immigration. Unconsciously, the alternative for many Hispanics was either to situate themselves with those people framed as being on a low societal rung—illegal and desperate people trying to cross the border—or to align themselves with white mainstream America by labeling those individuals as evil, criminal, and socially disruptive, *unlike us*.

And given the social group theory, American citizens who are descendants of illegal immigrants granted citizenship by Ronald Reagan may be even more cognitively inclined to distance themselves from illegal immigrants. This aligns with one of Tajfel's observations, that when individuals perceive themselves as moving upwards in the social hierarchy, they view that upward movement as a personal rejection of the shortcomings of the group they are seeking to escape.[132] They view the upward movement as a result of their individual characteristics being superior to the perceived shortcomings of their group—a perception they subconsciously reinforce as they ascend.[133] This may also explain the revulsion for Black culture exhibited by figures like Clarence Thomas and Glenn Loury. If they see their success as reflective of genuine individual character, it becomes more palliative and self-assuring than viewing themselves as randomly fortunate exceptions to the norm, as Alosha described in his encounter with the audience member in Chapter 2.

But group belonging is also important for our sense of self and individuality. Self-situating unconsciously within a group is how we self-identify and understand who we are as individuals within a society.[134] Therefore, by aligning more with the more dominant in-group or white male demographic, Hispanics can enhance their sense of self and psychological well-being. This may help explain the relatively high anti-immigrant sentiment among the Hispanic population.

My father always cautioned me to examine carefully the people who I just viscerally disliked for no real discernable reason. He explained that, very often, this dislike stems from a subconscious recognition that those people remind you of yourself and the things you wish were not true about yourself. While I couldn't find the numbers, it would be interesting to see what percentage of Trump-supporting Hispanic voters were initially undocumented immigrants or are the descendants of immigrants who were initially undocumented. We should also note that, less unconsciously, according to a November 2021 Pew Research Center finding, 58% of Hispanics identified as white.[135]

Given the unconscious group-situating choice of aligning with the white politician or the "dog-eating immigrants" exemplified by Kamala Harris, intergroup dynamics renders the result predictable. Beyond group dynamics, humans also tend to leave their group individually and attempt to fit in a higher or more socially elevated group for self-esteem reasons well.[136] All of this occurs unconsciously and is an essential element of human nature. Once again, the unconscious result of aligning with "dog eaters/ex-slaves" or white America seems like a foregone conclusion, especially given the Trump team's framing of this election. Their knowledge of cognitive science should not be underestimated.

They must have celebrated when Harris entered the race and Biden decided not to run. Without a white male from the dominant group justifying the liberal viewpoint, non-white voters could no longer associate with Biden's policies while still experiencing the palliative comfort of aligning with the dominant group. Harris' intersectionality worked against the Democratic Party because she embodied everything that the unconscious mind associates with low-group status in American society. She was a woman, Black, South Asian, and the child of immigrants.

Another reality of the cognitive principles outlined here is that people are willing to sacrifice themselves to some extent for the well-being of the group they self-identify as belonging to. This was the first election after the *Roe v. Wade* decision was overturned, and the right to an abortion was central to the Democratic Party's platform. They framed what was at stake as a choice between a nationwide abortion ban and women's right to choose. Given this context, if conscious choice were the leading force behind voters' decisions, women were expected to vote overwhelmingly and at unprecedented levels for Harris.

However, that did not happen. Exit polling suggests that Kamala Harris had 13 points less support from women than Hilary Clinton and 15 points less support than Biden.[137] Additionally, in 2024, Donald Trump outperformed his 2020 numbers among young women. Perhaps nothing illustrates the combined effect of cognitive group processing than the female Hispanic vote in 2024. Hilary Clinton, a white woman running for president against Donald Trump in 2016, when the right to an abortion was a federally enshrined right, won Hispanic women by 40 points.[138] By contrast, Kamala Harris, the daughter of non-white Jamaican and Indian immigrants running just two years after *Roe v. Wade* was overturned, won the Hispanic female vote by only 24 points.[139]

There are many more examples to be had demonstrating the essential and unavoidable reality of how our unconscious cognitive mechanisms relating to intergroup social dynamics and system justification impact our choices and behavior. However, listing more of them may only strengthen your "meh relegation" of this inconvenient truth.

What also makes this difficult to overcome is that, outside of the reality of group dynamics, ego plays a role in making my theory seem implausible. It is unsettling to accept how easily the human mind can be influenced at the unconscious level. It is much more palliative to "meh relegate" this reality and soothe our egos by convincing ourselves that we are independent, reasoned decision-makers who have conscious control over our choices.

The brilliance of the Trump campaign was its ability to harness implicit bias, intergroup cognitive realities, and system justification theory to effectively lead many people to support and reinforce white supremacy without even realizing it. It is far more comforting to reframe our society as meritocratic, colorblind, kind, moral, and almost egalitarian, making it nearly impossible for our brains not to gravitate toward this interpretation over the harsh reality of systemic inequity typical of all human societies. It is much easier to selectively credit social constructs like law, economics, and justice while overlooking the fact that another social construct—race—and the cognitive reframing developed to justify the hierarchy surrounding it, provides the true explanation. In the final chapter, I will explain why it is Pollyannaish to believe that the reasoning part of our minds can eventually put an end to systemic inequity.

Endnotes

1. *See* Emily C. Hannum & Meiyan Wang, *Ethnicity, Socioeconomic Status, and Social Welfare in China* 2 (Asia-Pacific Educ., Language Minorities & Migration (ELMM) Network, Working Paper 2010) (highlighting the plight of some ethnic minority groups in China); *see also* African Studies Center, https://www.africa.upenn.edu/NEH/kethnic.htm#:~:text=While%20no%20ethnic%20group%20constitutes,its%2032%20major%20indigenous%20groups. (last visited Jan. 22, 2025) (exploring the disproportionate influence of Kenya's largest ethnic group on politics and commerce).

2. The reality may be that we are taught that censorship is un-American, but in fact, it has always been a part of America's history and remains so in its present. Those in power have always censored. The anti-DEI and CRT bans I discussed earlier are censorship. Yet, I remain hopeful that these are just anomalous exceptions to the norm of free speech. Perhaps minimizing these as exceptions is delusional on my part, but it is a delusion born of palliative necessity.

3. Shankar Vedantam & Bill Mesler, Useful Decisions: The Power & Paradox of the Self-Deceiving Brain 10 (2021).

4. Stephen Worchel & William G. Austin, Psychology of Intergroup Relations 5 (1986) (explaining that Sherif's intergroup research can be considered a "starting point" for research in the field.).

5. Muzafer Sherif, *Experiments in Group Conflict*, 195 Sci. Am. 54–59 (1956).

6. *Id.*

7. *Id.*

8. *Id.*

9. *Id.*

10. *Id.*

11. *Id.*

12. *Id.*

13. *Id.*

14. *See* Henri Tajfel & John Turner, *An Integrative Theory of Intergroup Conflict*, in Stephen Worchel & William G. Austin, The Social Psychology of Intergroup Relations (1979).

15. *Id.* at 34 (finding that "intergroup discrimination existed in conditions of minimal in-group affiliation, anonymity of group membership, absence of conflicts of interest, and absence of previous hostility between the groups.").

16. Marilynn B. Brewer, *The Psychology of Prejudice: Ingroup Love or Outgroup Hate?*, 55 J. of Soc. Issues, 429–444 (1999).

17. *Id.*

18. Worchel & Austin, *supra* note 4, at 304.

19. *Id.*

20. *Id.*

21. *Id.*

22. *Id.*

23. Tajfel & Turner, *supra* note 14, at 42.

24. *Id.*

25. *Id.*

26. Glenn Loury, *Whose Fourth of July? Black Patriotism and Racial Inequality in America: A Speech Delivered at the National Conservatism Conference* (October 31, 2021).

27. Megan Gannon & LiveScience, *Race Is a Social Construct, Scientists Argue*, SciAm (Feb. 5, 2016), https://www.scientificamerican.com/article/race-is-a-social-construct-scientists-argue/.

28. *See* Ande Davis, *Inventing New Devils: Seeing through the Futility of Anti-Critical Race Theory Laws*, Northeastern Univ. L. Rev. (forthcoming 2025) (citing Charles W. Mills, The Racial Contract 23 (1997)), available at https://papers.ssrn.com/sol3/papers.cfm?abstract_id=5254270.

29. *Id.*

30. *Id.*

31. Brewer, *supra* note 16.

32. Hoo Keat Wong, Alejandro J. Estudillo, Ian D. Stephen & David R. T. Keeble, *The Other-Race Effect and Holistic Processing Across Racial Groups*, Scientific Reports (2021).

33. Worchel & Austin, *supra* note 4, 272–273.

34. *Id.*

35. *Id.*

36. Brewer, *supra* note 16.

37. *Id.*

38. *Id.*

39. *Id.*

40. *Id.*

41. *Id.*

42. Marilynn B. Brewer, *Intergroup Discrimination: Ingroup Love or Outgroup Hate?*, in The Cambridge Handbook of the Psychology of Prejudice 90–104 (Chris G. Sibley & Fiona Kate Barlow eds., 2017) .

43. *Id.*

44. *Id.*

45. *Id.*

46. Tajfel & Turner, *supra* note 14, at 40.

> Social categorizations are conceived here as cognitive tools that segment, classify, and order the social environment, and thus enable the individual to undertake many forms of social action. But they do not merely systematize the social world; they also provide a system of orientation for self-reference: they create and define the individual's place in society.

47. *Id.*

48. *Id.* at 40.

> The evaluation of one's own group is determined with reference to specific other groups through social comparisons in terms of value-laden attributes and characteristics. Positively discrepant comparisons between in-group and out-group produce high prestige; negatively discrepant comparisons between ingroup and out-group result in low prestige.

49. *Id.* at 44.

> It follows that self-esteem can be enhanced by comparing with other lower-status groups rather than with those of higher status. This is consistent with the fact that competition between subordinate groups is sometimes more intense than between subordinate and dominant groups—hence, for example, lower-class or "poor white" racism.

50. *Id.* Explaining "In other words, deprived groups are not always ethnocentric in the simple meaning of the term; they may in fact, be positively oriented toward the depriving out-group."

51. Tajfel & Turner, *supra* note 14, at 36–37.

52. *See generally* John T. Jost, A Theory of System Justification 6 (2020).

53. *Id.* at 106–107

54. *Id.*

55. *Id.*

56. *Id.*

57. *Id.*

58. Ana Filipa Madeira1, Rui Costa-Lopes, John F. Dovidio, Gonçalo Freitas & Mafalda F. Mascarenhas, *Primes and Consequences: A Systematic Review of Meritocracy in Intergroup Relations*, 10 Frontiers Psych. 1, 16 (2007).

59. *Id.*

60. Shannon K. McCoy & Brenda Major, *Priming Meritocracy and the Psychological Justification of Inequality*, 43 J. of Experimental Soc. Psych. 341–351 (2007).

61. *See* Katherine Stroebe, Tom Postmes, Susanne Täuber, Alwin Stegeman & Melissa-Sue John, *Belief in a Just What? Demystifying Just World Beliefs by Distinguishing Sources of Justice*, Plos One (Mar. 24, 2015), https://journals.plos.org/plosone/article?id=10.1371/journal.pone.0120145.

62. Matthew O. Hunt, *Status, Religion, and the "Belief in a Just World": Comparing African Americans, Latinos, and Whites*, 81 Soc. Sci. Q. 325–343 (2000). Although he questions the assumption of religion as the major source of belief in a just world, Hunt acknowledges:

> Religious involvement represents one of the most often cited explanations for just-world beliefs. Past research reports positive correlations with church attendance (Rubin and Peplau, 1975; Zweigenhaft et al., 1985), as well as with the "belief in an active God" (Rubin and Peplau, 1975). Such results have led some researchers to argue that the belief in a just world represents an expression of religious faith—particularly Judeo-Christian themes connecting "sin and suffering," "virtue and grace," and the notion that moral behavior is rewarded while transgressions are punished. Beyond the general religion link, several studies suggest that the belief in a just world may be especially strongly tied to Protestant themes emphasizing connections between a "work ethic," worldly success, and salvation (Lerner, 1980; Ma and Smith, 1985; Smith and Green, 1984; Wagstaff, 1984).

63. McCoy & Major, *supra* note 60.

64. *Id.*

65. Tajfel & Turner, *supra* note 14, at 36–37.

66. Brewer, *supra* note 16.

67. *Id.*; *see also* Yuval Noah Hararai, Sapiens: A Brief History of Humankind 111 (2015).

68. Colin Dwyer, *Donald Trump: 'I Could ... Shoot Somebody, and I Wouldn't Lose Any Voters*, NPR (Jan. 23, 2016, 5:00 PM), https://www.npr.org/sections/thetwo-way/2016/01/23/464129029/donald-trump-i-could-shoot-somebody-and-i-wouldnt-lose-any-voters.

69. *Kellyanne Conway 'Personally' Thanks 'The View,' Oprah for Donald Trump Victory*, Fox News (Nov. 6, 2024), https://www.foxnews.com/video/6364278046112.

70. Shankar Vedantam, The Hidden Brain: How Our Unconscious Minds Elect Presidents, Control Markets, Wage Wars, and Save our Lives 254 (Spiegel & Grau 2010).

71. *See* Calvin K. Lai, Kelly M. Hoffman & Bryan A Nosek, *Reducing Implicit Prejudice*, 7 Soc. & Personality Psych. Compass 315–330 (2013). Keith Payne & C. Daryl Cameron, *Divided Minds, Divided Morals: How Implicit Social Cognition Underpins and Undermines Our Sense of Social Justice*, *in* Handbook of Implicit Social Cognition: Measurement, Theory, & Applications 445 (Bertram Gawronski & B. Keith Payne Eds. 2010) ("Implicit reactions are often hierarchical, dividing the world into 'us' and 'them[]'" Modern research in the field for example renders Vedantam's suggestion that we reason our way out from under the results of unconscious processing even less plausible by suggesting humans have no free will. Robert M. Sapolsky, Determined: A Science of Life Without Free Will (Penguin Press New York 2023).).

72. Chas Sisk, *Tennessee Lawmakers Debated Expelling Three Democratic House Members*, All Things Considered (Apr. 6, 2023), https://www.npr.org/2023/04/06/1168490358/tennessee-lawmakers-debated-expelling-three-democratic-house-members.

73. *Id.*

74. Eric Bradner & Kate Sullivan, *Trump Describes US as an Occupied Country in Dark Closing Message Focused on Immigration*, CNN (Nov. 5, 2024, 2:10 AM), https://www.cnn.com/2024/11/04/politics/donald-trump-closing-message/index.html.

75. *Id.*

76. Muzafer Sherif, *Experiments in Group Conflict*, 195 Sci. Am. 54–59 (1956).

77. Jessica Taylor, *'You Can Do Anything': In 2005 Tape, Trump Brags About Groping, Kissing Women*, NPR (Oct. 7, 2016, 6:05 PM), https://www.npr.org/2016/10/07/497087141/donald-trump-caught-on-tape-making-vulgar-remarks-about-women.

78. Maggie Haberman, *Donald Trump Says His Mocking of New York Times Reporter Was Misread*, NYTimes (Nov. 16, 2015), https://www.nytimes.com/2015/11/27/us/politics/donald-trump-says-his-mocking-of-new-york-times-reporter-was-misread.html.

79. Ayesha Rascoe, *A Year After Charlottesville, Not Much Has Changed for Trump*, NPR (Aug. 11, 2018, 6:59 AM), https://www.npr.org/2018/08/11/637665414/a-year-after-charlottesville-not-much-has-changed-for-trump.

80. Ali Vitali, Kasie Hunt & Frank Thorp V, *Trump Referred to Haiti and African Nations as 'Shithole' Countries*, NBC News (Jan 12, 2018, 6:47 AM), https://www.nbcnews.com/politics/white-house/trump-referred-haiti-african-countries-shithole-nations-n836946.

81. Chris Michael, *Trump Tells Rally Immigrants Are 'Poisoning the Blood of Our Country'*, The Guardian (Dec. 16, 2013), https://www.theguardian.com/us-news/2023/dec/16/trump-immigrants-new-hampshire-rally.

82. Sara Dorn, *Trump Compares Political Foes to 'Vermin' on Veterans Day—Echoing Nazi Propaganda*, Forbes (Nov. 12, 2023, 10:53 AM), https://www.forbes.com/sites/saradorn/2023/11/12/trump-compares-political-foes-to-vermin-on-veterans-day-echoing-nazi-propaganda/; *see also* Holocaust Encyclopedia, *Victims of the Nazi Era: Nazi Racial Ideology*, https://encyclopedia.ushmm.org/content/en/article/victims-of-the-nazi-era-nazi-racial-ideology (last visited Jan. 22, 2025).

83. Rebecca Shabad, *Donald Trump Calls for "Total and Complete Shutdown" of Muslims Entering U.S.*, CBS News (Dec. 7, 2015), https://www.cbsnews.com/news/donald-trump-calls-for-total-and-complete-shutdown-of-muslims-entering-u-s/.

84. Daniel White, *Donald Trump Tells Crowd to 'Knock the Crap Out of' Hecklers*, TIME (Feb. 1, 2016), https://time.com/4203094/donald-trump-hecklers/.

85. Olivia Eubanks, *The History of the Phrase 'When the Looting Starts, the Shooting Starts' Used by Trump*, ABC NEWS (May 29, 2020, 4:34 PM), https://abcnews.go.com/Politics/history-phrase-looting-starts-shooting-starts-trump/story?id=70950935; *see also* Barbara Sprunt, *The History Behind 'When the Looting Starts, the Shooting Starts'*, NPR (May 29, 2020, 1:13 PM), https://www.npr.org/2020/05/29/864818368/the-history-behind-when-the-looting-starts-the-shooting-starts.

86. Zachary B. Wolf & Sean O'Key, *The Trump-Ukraine Impeachment Inquiry Report, Annotated*, CNN (Dec. 3, 2019), https://www.cnn.com/interactive/2019/12/politics/trump-ukraine-impeachment-inquiry-report-annotated/.

87. Sarah McCammon, *From Debate Stage, Trump Declines to Denounce White Supremacy*, NPR (Sept. 30, 2020), https://www.npr.org/2020/09/30/918483794/from-debate-stage-trump-declines-to-denounce-white-supremacy.

88. Ali Vitali, *Trump Says He Could 'Shoot Somebody' and Still Maintain Support*, NBC NEWS (Jan. 23, 2016), https://www.nbcnews.com/politics/2016-election/trump-says-he-could-shoot-somebody-still-maintain-support-n502911.

89. Michael Crowley, *Trump Won't Commit to 'Peaceful' Post-Election Transfer of Power*, NYTIMES (Sept. 23, 2020), https://www.nytimes.com/2020/09/23/us/politics/trump-power-transfer-2020-election.html; Aamer Madhani & Kevin Freking, *Trump Won't Commit to Peaceful Transfer of Power If He Loses*, AP News (Sept. 23, 2020), https://apnews.com/article/election-2020-virus-outbreak-voting-elections-voting-fraud-and-irregularities-8bb28627b03474a3a5ce2454ae3d1639.

90. Matthew J. Belvedere, *Trump Asks Why US Can't Use Nukes: MSNBC*, CNBC (Aug. 3, 2016), https://www.cnbc.com/2016/08/03/trump-asks-why-us-cant-use-nukes-msnbcs-joe-scarborough-reports.html.

91. Katie Rogers & Nicholas Fandos, *Trump Tells Congresswomen to 'Go Back' to the Countries They Came From*, NYTIMES (July 14, 2019), https://www.nytimes.com/2019/07/14/us/politics/trump-twitter-squad-congress.html.

92. Katie Rogers, Lara Jakes & Ana Swanson, *Trump Defends Using 'Chinese Virus' Label, Ignoring Growing Criticism*, NYTIMES (March 18, 2020), https://www.nytimes.com/2020/03/18/us/politics/china-virus.html.

93. Glenn Kessler, *The Murky Facts About Trumps Failure to Visit American War Dead Near Paris*, WASHINGTON POST (Apr. 22, 2024). https://www.washingtonpost.com/politics/2024/04/22/murky-facts-about-trumps-failure-visit-american-war-dead-near-paris/.

94. Martin Pengelly, *Trump Threatens to Deploy More Federal Agents to Protest Despite Reports of Violence*, THE GUARDIAN (July 20, 2020), https://www.theguardian.com/us-news/2020/jul/20/trump-federal-agents-violence-portland-protests.

95. Gram Slattery, *Trump's 'Bloodbath' and Other Rhetoric Inflame His 2024 Campaign Trail*, REUTERS (March 22, 2024), https://www.reuters.com/world/us/bloodbath-vermin-animals-trumps-rhetoric-trail-2024-03-22/.

96. Brian Naylor, *Read Trump's Jan. 6 Speech, a Key Part of Impeachment Trial*, NPR (Feb. 10, 2021), https://www.npr.org/2021/02/10/966396848/read-trumps-jan-6-speech-a-key-part-of-impeachment-trial.

97. Meridith McGraw, *President Trump Heads to Baltimore, a City He Called a 'Rodent Infested Mess'*, ABC NEWS (Sept. 12, 2019, 4:03 PM), https://abcnews.go.com/Politics/president-trump-heads-baltimore-city-called-rodent-infested/story?id=65570278.

98. Veronica Stracqualursi, *Trump Attacks Another African American Lawmaker, and Calls Baltimore a 'Disgusting, Rat and Rodent Infested Mess'*, CNN (July 28, 2019, 11:03 AM), https://www.cnn.com/2019/07/27/politics/elijah-cummings-trump-baltimore/index.html; Naomi Larsson Piñeda, Baltimore Residents: Trump's Attacks 'Denigrate, Dehumanize Black People', The Guardian (July 31, 2019), https://www.theguardian.com/us-news/2019/jul/31/trump-baltimore-racist-attacks-residents-respond.

99. Brett Samuels, *Trump Tells Rioters to 'Go Home' While Stoking Election Fury*, The Hill (Jan. 6, 2021), https://thehill.com/homenews/administration/532976-trump-tells-rioters-go-home-we-love-you/.

100. *Trump Now Tells Far Right to 'Stand Down' Amid White Supremacy Row*, BBC (Sept. 30, 2020), https://www.bbc.com/news/election-us-2020-54359993.

101. *Jan. 6 Riot Was 'Fueled by Lies' from Trump, Special Counsel Says*, NYTimes (Aug. 1, 2023), https://www.nytimes.com/live/2023/08/01/us/trump-indictment-jan-6.

102. Kristen Holmes, *Trump Calls for the Termination of the Constitution in Truth Social Post*, CNN (Dec. 4, 2022), https://www.cnn.com/2022/12/03/politics/trump-constitution-truth-social/index.html.

103. Human Rights Watch, *Q&A: Trump Administration's "Zero-Tolerance" Immigration Policy*, (Aug. 16, 2018), https://www.hrw.org/news/2018/08/16/qa-trump-administrations-zero-tolerance-immigration-policy (last visited Jan. 22, 2025); Terry Gross, How The Trump White Hosue Mislead *t*he World About Its Family Separation Policy, NPR (Aug. 11, 2022), https://www.npr.org/2022/08/11/1116917364/how-the-trump-white-house-misled-the-world-about-its-family-separation-policy.

104. Julian Borger, *Donald Trump Hails 'Great Leader' Kim Jong-Un at Hanoi Summit*, The Guardian (Feb. 27, 2019), https://www.theguardian.com/us-news/2019/feb/27/donald-trump-hails-great-leader-kim-jong-un-at-hanoi-summit.

105. Kaitlan Collins & Kavin Liptak, *Trump Tweets He Is Skipping Biden's Inauguration*, CNN (Jan. 8, 2019), https://www.cnn.com/2021/01/08/politics/donald-trump-next-steps/index.html.

106. Jordyn Phelps, *What's Behind Trump's 'Pocahontas' Taunt of Warren*, ABC News (Oct. 16, 2018, 5:16 PM), https://abcnews.go.com/Politics/trumps-pocahontas-taunt-warren/story?id=58530657; Allie Malloy, Trump Resumes 'Pocahontas' Moniker After Warren DNA Test, CNN (Oct. 16, 2018), https://www.cnn.com/2018/10/16/politics/trump-warren-tweet-dna-test/index.html.

107. Hadas Gold & Kristen Holmes, *Trump Campaign Denies and Revokes Journalists' Election Night Credentials After Critical Coverage*, CNN (Nov. 7, 2024), https://www.cnn.com/2024/11/05/media/trump-revokes-journalists-election-night-credentials/index.html; Nataly Pak & Matt Seyler, *Trump Calls 'Fake News' Media 'The Real Enemy of the people' Over Putin Summit*, ABC News (July 19, 2018), https://abcnews.go.com/Politics/trump-calls-fake-news-media-real-enemy-people/story?id=56687436.

108. Veronica Stracqualursi, *Trump Suggests Using Military Against 'Enemy from Within' on Election Day*, CNN (Oct. 14, 2024), https://www.cnn.com/2024/10/13/politics/trump-military-enemy-from-within-election-day/index.html.

109. Kiara Alfonseca, *A Look at Trump's 'Transgender Operations on Illegal Aliens' Debate Claim*, ABC News (Sept. 11, 2024, 1:57 PM), https://abcnews.go.com/Politics/trumps-transgender-operations-illegal-aliens-debate-claim/story?id=113584635.

110. Patrick Aftoora Orsaogos & Michael Rubinkam, *Springfield Facing Threats from Overseas After Trump's Lies About Haitians, Ohio Governor's Office Says*, PBS (Sept. 17,

2024), https://www.pbs.org/newshour/politics/springfield-facing-threats-from-overseas-after-trumps-lies-about-haitians-ohio-governors-office-says; Merlyn Thomas & Mike Wendling, *Trump Repeats Baseless Claim About Haitian Immigrants Eating Pets*, BBC (Sept. 15, 2025), https://www.bbc.com/news/articles/c77l28myezko.

111. The Quintessential Gentleman (@theqgentleman), Instagram (Oct. 21, 2024), https://www.instagram.com/theqgentleman/reel/DBzBuaYP6N0/.

112. Robert P. Baird, *The Invention of Whiteness: The Long History of a Dangerous Idea*, The Guardian (Apr. 20, 2021), https://www.theguardian.com/news/2021/apr/20/the-invention-of-whiteness-long-history-dangerous-idea.

113. *See* Rory D. Bahadur, *Civility as Morally Justified Oppression*, 30 Tex. J. Civ. On C.L. & C.R. 89 (2025).

114. *Id.*

115. Carla D. Pratt, *Indianness as Property*, 105 Boston U. L. R. 311 (2025).

116. *Id.*

117. *Id.*

118. *Id.*

119. *Id.*

120. *Id.*

121. *Id.*

122. Michael Martin, *Obama on Racial Issues During His Presidency Through Lens of His New Memoir* (Nov. 16, 2020), https://www.npr.org/2020/11/16/935475339/obama-on-racial-issues-during-his-presidency-through-lens-of-his-new-memoir, explaining

> But I think that what did happen during my presidency was, yes, a backlash among some people who felt that somehow, I symbolized the possibility that they or their group were losing status not because of anything I did but just by virtue of the fact that I didn't look like all the other presidents previously.

See also Peniel Joseph, *Obama's Effort to Heal Racial Divisions and Uplift Black America*, Washington Post (Apr. 22. 2016), https://www.washingtonpost.com/graphics/national/obama-legacy/racism-during-presidency.html, explaining

> If racial conflict, in the form of birthers, tea partyers and gnawing resentments, implicitly shadowed Obama's first term, it erupted into open warfare during much of his second. The Supreme Court's 2013 decision in the *Shelby v. Holder* case gutted Voting Rights Act enforcement, throwing into question the signal achievement of the civil rights movement's heroic period.

123. Michael D. Shear, *Making a Point, Obama Invokes a Painful Slur*, NYTimes (June 22, 2015), https://www.nytimes.com/2015/06/23/us/obama-racism-marc-maron-podcast.html.

124. *See* Bahadur, *supra* note 113.

125. Marilynn B. Brewer, *Intergroup Discrimination: Ingroup Love or Outgroup Hate?*, in The Cambridge Handbook of the Psychology of Prejudice 90–104 (Chris G. Sibley & Fiona Kate Barlow eds., 2017).

126. *Id.*

127. Brewer, *supra* note 16.

128. Rick Newman, *We're Watching Trump's 7th Bankruptcy Unfold*, Yahoo!finance (Oct. 13, 2020), https://finance.yahoo.com/news/were-watching-trumps-7th-bankruptcy-unfold-171903858.html?guccounter=1&guce_referrer=aHR0cHM6Ly93d3cuZ29vZ2xlLmNvbS8&guce_referrer_sig=AQAAABUInU-aP2_O0M9CBRkGOXvxhyWh

WXdHoY53HXwXPOuP9hd6iS-NUWV2tosQVRsbsXq6fZ6zMjv04gDNwc3fy8WgaboWsaqbSOzIHlfcPN8VeL5t2b0VEYhCcYdX3K1C88ie3xMr5YdHw8o884-fgC1rU79py0wZ0Llobc1BKJuF.

129. *Trump Calls Biden 'Stupid' and Harris 'Dumb as a Rock' at Arizona Campaign Event*, NBC News (Nov. 1, 2024), https://www.nbcnews.com/video/trump-calls-biden-stupid-and-harris-dumb-as-a-rock-at-arizona-campaign-event-223258693743.

130. Cheyanne M. Daniels, *Quarter of Young Black Men Say They Will Vote for Trump: Survey*, The Hill (Oct. 10, 2024), https://thehill.com/homenews/4949749-black-men-trump-vote-poll/.

131. Suzanne Gamboa, Nicole Acevedo, Daniella Silva, Carmen Sesin & Deon J. Hampton, *Record Voter Gains Among Latinos for Trump Mainly Boiled Down to Their Top Issue—The Economy*, NBC News (Nov. 6, 2024), https://www.nbcnews.com/news/latino/trump-economy-latino-vote-2024-election-rcna178951.

132. Tajfel & Turner, *supra* note 14, at 43.

> Tendencies to dissociate oneself psychologically from fellow members of low-prestige categories are known to many of us from everyday experience; they have been noted more systematically by Jahoda (1961) and Klineberg and Zavalloni (1969), among others, and indirectly by the whole literature on racial identification and preference. The most important feature of individual mobility is that the low status of one's own group is not thereby changed: it is an individualist approach designed, at least in the short run, to achieve a personal, not a group, solution. Thus, individual mobility implies a disidentification with the erstwhile in-group.

133. *Id.*

134. *Id.* at 40. Explaining, "Social categorizations ... provide a system for self-reference; they create and define the individual's place in society."

135. Luis Noe-Bustamante, Ana Gonzalez Barrera, Khaduah Edwards, Lauren Mora & Mark Hugo Lopez, *4. Measuring the Racial Identity of Latinos*, Pew Research Center (Nov. 4, 2021), https://www.pewresearch.org/race-and-ethnicity/2021/11/04/measuring-the-racial-identity-of-latinos/,

136. Tajfel & Turner, *supra* note 14, at 40.

137. Carter Sherman, *2024 US Elections Takeaways: How Female Voters Broke for Harris and Trump*, The Guardian (Nov. 6, 2024), https://www.theguardian.com/us-news/2024/nov/06/election-trump-harris-women-voters.

138. *Id.*

139. *Id.*

CHAPTER 11

Is Reform Unrealistic?

Sometimes our need to have hope prevents us from accepting the essentially human nature of systemic hierarchy. As previously mentioned, there is not, and has never been, a human society without systemic hierarchies. Despite this reality, there is a significant amount of Pollyannaish literature suggesting that changing demographics, multicultural exposure, and generative information environments will lead to reduced implicit bias, and consequently, reduced systemic hierarchy.[1] The truth is that this genre of literature, including my own previous article, is perhaps only an example of a reframed reality—one that palliatively seeks to distract us from the harsh reality of human societal structure.

Way back in 1956, Sherif concluded, based on his camp experiment described in Chapter 10, that competing groups in society will cooperate only when their cooperation is necessary for the well-being of both groups.[2] Sherif also demonstrated that merely exposing the groups to one another and providing opportunities for the groups to interact only increased the contention and animosity between the groups.[3] Instead, what was required, according to Sherif, for intergroup cooperation were situations where both groups needed the same result, but neither group could achieve it without the help and cooperation of the other.[4]

For example, Sherif told both groups at the camp that there was a loss of water supply to the camp.[5] The experiment involved water being delivered to the camp via a miles-long pipe system.[6] When the groups realized that there would be no water for any of them and that, due to the extent of the piping, it would take both groups working together to find the leak, they collaborated harmoniously.[7] Similarly, when Sherif mentioned to the campers that the truck delivering food to the camp was broken down, both groups worked together to pull the truck to try to get it started.[8] Sherif concluded that intergroup animosity is only reduced when both groups need each other to achieve a goal necessary for the survival of the all the groups.[9] Sherif's observations align perfectly with Derrick Bell's theory of interest convergence, which I mentioned in Chapter 2 in the context of the civil rights movement and the *Brown v. Board of Education* decisions.

The necessary condition for reducing intergroup animosity—the groups needing each other to achieve a mutually necessary goal—is a far cry from the idea that societal demographics changing or increased interaction and familiarity among groups will reduce implicit biases and structural inequity. I remind you here of my discussion in Chapter 8 about the Caribbean and the Brown Bag Clubs in New Orleans. According to Jost, once a society stratifies and establishes a systemic structure, all members of that society, even those disenfranchised by the structure, justify and reinforce it.[10] As previously discussed, while in the United States whiteness sits at the top of the social pyramid and system justification is rooted in race, there are countless other societies where human hierarchies are not based on race. Regardless of its genesis, systemic inequity is a universal human condition.

The studies suggesting that changing demographics and global integration will reduce implicit bias and systemic inequity all share one common feature: they rely on what I will describe here as a form of reverse intersectionality. Intersectionality, a term coined by Kimberlé Crenshaw, was originally applied to demonstrate that women of color were subject to a form of cumulative discrimination due their belonging to two distinct groups—females and people of color—both of which are subject to discrimination.[11] But intersectionality overlaps with the theory of "intergroup contact"[12] or deprovincialization in that both recognize the existence of discrete groups in society that are treated differently by other groups.[13]

Researchers argue that as more people become multiethnic or multiracial, we will eventually end up with a world where everyone considers themselves members of multiple groups, resulting in increased intergroup commonality or deprovincialization.[14] According to this research, this would extrapolate to a future where everyone views themselves as a member of a single group—the group of global citizens.[15] The existence of only one group would necessarily render intergroup competition and discrimination impossible.[16] Brewer frames this utopian concept as follows: "creating conditions that elicit identification with the global community has the potential for extending ingroup-based trust and sympathy to all humanity."[17] According to Brewer, the way to achieve this is by participating in worldwide cultural and social communities.[18]

In a similar vein, I proposed in a previous article that the internet could serve as the vehicle for achieving this feeling of membership in a global group of humans and the most efficient way to be exposed to multicultural perspectives.[19]

> [I]n the context of information, geographically defined communities are outdated in a generative information environment because people communicate and share information with people from all over the world via apps such as WhatsApp and Facebook. Perhaps even more so than they do with people in their own geographic environment. Information, unlike more tangible things like physical crime and noise ordinances, transcends geography because it is present everywhere internet access exists simultaneously.[20]

The difference between internet-based informational dissemination and information dissemination that existed before the internet is essential to understanding the suggestion that the internet is the most efficient vehicle for exposing individuals to multicultural perspectives.

Before the internet, the dissemination of information was controlled by the politically powerful in society because all information had to be filtered through established media corporations before it could be disseminated widely.[21] In the pre-internet era, media corporations—or entities with the ability to disseminate information on a large national or international scale—were limited to few discrete corporations that possessed the expensive, bulky, and sophisticated equipment necessary to transmit information broadly.[22]

For example, until the 1990s in the United States, the "big three"—NBC, CBS, and ABC—were the sole television corporations and essentially held a monopoly on the dissemination of information. If a random citizen called a news conference at the same time as the president of the United States or a renowned church leader, the networks would prioritize covering what the powerful or the famous had to say.

This led to a cycle of information dissemination control, resulting in the widescale dissemination of the viewpoints of those in power. The networks needed to capture the audience's interest, and people were more inclined to hear the views of the influential, powerful, and famous. In this way, the viewpoints of the powerful dominated the information highway until the 1990s.

The United States Supreme Court recognized this disproportionately larger access and influence over the media that public figures and government officials had as early as 1974 in the now-famous *Gertz*[23] opinion. The Court explained, "Public officials and public figures usually enjoy significantly greater access to the channels of effective communication," and, as a result, they can manipulate and control the predominant media message to a greater extent than private individuals.[24]

This reality of monopolistic access began to change in the 1990s because the internet created a "generative information environment."[25] A generative information environment is one in which individual members of the public generate the information that is consumed by the public, and everyone is free to contribute to the information repository, regardless of whether they are powerful, influential, or are connected to corporate media entities.[26]

Other technological changes in the 1990s also contributed to a shift in the information environment. Before the 1990s, recording equipment was bulky and expensive. Today, however, it is remarkably easy to record an event or occurrence on a cell phone, and simply pressing "post," "share," or the equivalent renders that information accessible to most of the world instantaneously. This change in recording technology, combined with the internet and the reduction in the cost of computer processing power, transformed the information environment from one where powerful people and corporate media monopolies controlled the dissemination of information to one where information dissemination became democratized.[27]

The importance of this information environment becomes clear when considering how difficult it was for a German citizen to hear viewpoints contrary to the message disseminated by the Third Reich during World War II. This was because the government exercised monopolistic control over the dissemination of information. Resistance movements, such as the White Rose, distributed dissenting opinions, but these groups were ruthlessly eliminated by the German government. Today, no matter where on the political spectrum you reside, the contrary viewpoint is almost inescapable because of the internet. For all intents and purposes, you had to be hiding in a sewer in Paris to hear a message contrary to Hitler's propaganda.

The effect of the internet was instantaneous. The 1990s saw an unravelling of many of the moral and hypocritical illusions the moral majority imposed on the population. For example, in 1991, the racism of the police became mainstream when a private citizen recorded the police beating of Rodney King on his "Sony camcorder"[28] and sent the footage to a local television station. Before the technological advancements that led to the development of camcorders, the reality of police racism was unbelievable to most people in the United States who were not themselves victims of police brutality or members of a minority population.

Given the information paradigm created by the internet, I initially wrote that it was the surest way to reduce implicit bias because it facilitated widespread exposure to multicultural perspectives. Anyone from any walk of life with any viewpoint could publish information consistent with their perspective or viewpoint. In 2019, I wrote:

> The internet provides an ideal medium for increasing exposure to multicultural viewpoints and differing narratives because "the content posted on the internet is less and less subject to filtering through [majoritarian] institutional policies and more and more gets there as a result of individual taste or thoughtlessness." There simply is no better, more wide reaching, prolific, and fertile source of differing viewpoints and multicultural perspectives than UGC on the internet.[29]

My error was in assuming that exposure to multicultural perspectives was enough to mitigate implicit bias, when, in fact, for implicit bias to be reduced, people must not only be exposed to different perspectives but also be motivated to incorporate those perspectives into their unconscious heuristics.[30] People are only motivated to rely less on unconscious processing heuristics when the results of those heuristics fail to explain what they are observing.[31] When unconscious processing becomes unable to explain what is observed, it creates dissonance, which engages the conscious mind to resolve the differences.[32] It turns out that the internet has reinforced stereotypes and hierarchies, making it easier to remain reliant on preexisting race-based heuristics. The reality is that after more than a quarter-century of the internet, we arrived at the second Trump presidency.

Multicultural experiences only mitigate bias and inter-group discrimination when those experiences are perceived as being inconsistent with the biases and stereotypes we previously held.[33] When such inconsistency occurs, we are forced to use our conscious brain to address the dissonance caused by observed results that conflict with the expected outcomes of unconscious processing. The theory suggests that this process leads to a reformation of the heuristic itself because, as humans, we have a fundamental need for things to make sense or to have answers for observed phenomena.[34]

Instead, what the internet provides is a plethora of information from both the right and the left that facilitates stereotyping and simplistic intergroup generalizations. The need for cognitive closure is satisfied, for example, by listening to Rush Limbaugh or Alex Jones if you are a right-leaning individual. It is much more comforting when anti-immigrant and anti-Black information reinforces the notion that immigrants and people of color are inferior, lazy, or less moral than white America. Because these biases are built into our social structure, when we hear narratives or make observations inconsistent with them, we experience cognitive dissonance.

It is much more comforting to internalize narratives that buttress our social inequities rather than experience cognitive dissonance and undertake the difficult cognitive task of incorporating new, non-conforming information to explain what we observe. People who find cognitive closure particularly comforting will actively avoid exposure to non-stereotype-conforming information to escape the discomfort of cognitive dissonance.[35] The generative information environment of the internet provides countless such comforting and reinforcing information sources.

I believe the reality is that people are only motivated to step outside of their cognitive comfort zones and become comfortable with lower needs for cognitive closure when their very survival depends on it, or they think they will benefit from it. Research shows, for example, that immigrants in a new country often finds ways to incorporate both the traditions of their old and new countries in order to reduce anxiety and depression.[36]

Cross and Turner suggest that immigrants in a new country have four mechanisms for coping with the social and cultural diversity they experience when moving to a new country. They can either assimilate, identifying almost entirely with the host country (seeing themselves as a citizen of only the new country); they can separate, identifying themselves solely as members of their original country while living in the new one; they can reject both the old and new cultures and remain marginalized; or they can assimilate and identify as a member of both societies[37]—these groups of immigrants are called bicultural or multicultural.[38]

I can relate to these four variations based on my own experiences. When I first migrated to the United States, I initially adopted the strategy of identifying only as American. I unconsciously accepted the preexisting narrative that framed the Caribbean as a backward, unsophisticated mecca of confusion and disorder, where people were hesitant to line up or follow rules. Palliatively, this was necessary for me when I was stuck on a factory trawler in winter, in the middle of the Bering Sea, while working as a marine biologist. To think of my island upbringing in the positive light that all cultures deserve would have been too painful. I did not associate or hang out with anyone from my home country when I moved to the United States. My unconscious mind, driven by its desire for palliative reframing, ensured that it was a clean break to minimize the pain and loss of the only life and cultural structure I had known before coming to the United States.

I also observed friends who went with the second option—separate and identify as members of their original country. They hung out only with people from Trinidad and cooked, ate, and drank only what was customary in Trinidad. They found comfort in a group of people who, like them, openly missed their homeland. While they recognized the unmatched economic opportunities in America, worked hard, and benefitted from this reality, they took pride in never fully assimilating. Today, 34 years after moving to the United States, I think I belong in category four and have become bicultural. I openly embrace both the cultural beauty of my home country and the wonder that the United States of America offers.

Bicultural individuals tend to be more tolerant of diversity, rely less on stereotyping, and seem more likely to consider multiple perspectives.[39] This may be true, but the code-switching[40] involved in being bicultural makes one feel mentally unstable, and it is always exhausting.[41]

When I hear people I love convincing themselves that voting for Trump has nothing to do with racism, I just stay quiet now, because it takes a diatribe the length of this book to even begin to make them receptive to the reality that they may be mistaken. Additionally, as I discussed previously, the truth is that it probably isn't possible to convince anyone about the reality of systemic racism.

Ultimately, Cross and Turner suggest that these cognitive mechanisms resulting in biculturality observed in immigrants can function the same way for the majoritarian groups in any country.[42] In other words, biculturalism is feasible for most white Americans as well. This is where I think they are incorrect. The current societal structure does not motivate people to make the uncomfortable cognitive adaptations that biculturality requires.[43]

As I described in Chapters 5 and 8—when discussing the racism inherent in the rescue of the Jewish Holocaust victims, the third verse of the national anthem, the inequitable application of the GI Bill, and the disorienting complexity of the gun and transgender sports debates—you likely felt significant dissonance and discomfort. This discomfort is reduced by "meh relegation," which we can now identify as the need for the comfort associated with cognitive closure that heuristic-based processing provides.[44]

There currently is no overriding benefit for the average white American to expose themselves to the cognitive dissonance required to restructure a heuristic. By contrast, during the Civil War, if white Southerners did not begin to change their assumptions about slavery and the impossibility of living without this institution, the South would have been decimated even more. They were forced to change their formerly unassailable viewpoint of a divine origin to the idea that Black people could never be free. The motivation to reform the cognitive pathways came only from the motivation to survive and not be killed by Union troops. There exists no such motivation to change cognitive structures regarding racism today, and as I have repeatedly said, at this point in our history, *I absolutely do not support or suggest any social violence or upheaval akin to the Civil War*.

In fact, the opposite motivation is true today. The information environment and the availability of echo chambers reinforce many of the reframed fantasies that support systemic racism. I, with all my research and knowledge on cognitive realities, cry when I am at a sporting event and the anthem plays, watching people stand with their hands on their hearts and face the flag of this amazing country. That is easier than constantly remembering we are playing a song written by a lawyer who enslaved people of African ancestry to enrich both himself and the nation that protected his property interest in human bodies. As a person of color, even my brain reframes this reality for my own well-being, even though I don't benefit from the privilege created by reframed realities to the same extent that white people do. If I succumb to the palliative reframing, even when that provides me relatively lower benefit than it does to white people, then is it unrealistic to ask them to stop reframing?

Unless and until the benefits of forming new cognitive pathways through experiencing cognitive dissonance outweigh the benefits of reframing reality, our very humanity will keep systemic racism entrenched and make it feel right. Cross and Turner emphatically state that unless the exposure to diversity causes you to experience inconsistencies in your stereotype-producing heuristics, diversity and exposure to diversity will create no change.[45] They further explain that if the person experiencing diversity is unmotivated to process cognitive inconsistencies, stereotypes persist, and exposure to diversity has no impact on changing perceptions.[46] As if this wasn't disheartening enough, for diversity exposure to impact stereotypical thinking, the exposure and discomfort has to be repeated frequently for any change in cognitive pathways to occur.[47]

If I were a white person, the truth is that, rather than suffer through all that cognitive disruption and discomfort, I would much rather have just listened to Rush Limbaugh and experienced the well-being and cognitive comfort of "keep it simple, stupid." I am not saying Limbaugh was stupid, but the simplistic, certain, and absolute narratives he generated catalyzed cognitive comfort in lieu of reality. The stakes simply aren't high enough to disrupt our current cycle of peaceful and palliative processing.

Additionally, it may be impossible for humans to sustain the cognitive load of constantly grappling with the intractable complexity of our world. According to Sapolsky, doing so would likely lead to depression.[48] This isn't just theoretical; studies have demonstrated that people of color experience mental health issues when facing or internalizing the reality of racism.[49] Not reframing our world is likely only sustainable when it is necessary for survival or provides some other significant benefit. The disruption of heuristic-based unconscious processing by incorporating conscious, non-conforming observations reduces cognitive closure, and it is exhausting.[50]

When people feel busy, pressured, or "uncalm," as most of us often do in the hustle and bustle of today's world, exposure to diversity has no impact on stereotype-based processing.[51] People need to feel that they are in a calm, focused state for the diversity experience to have any effect on reducing stereotyping.[52] In other words, as Subotnik suggested, if we didn't rely on bias and heuristic-based processing, we would still be cave-dwelling creatures.[53] The reality of human existence—navigating the effort of living in societies, conforming to rules, maintaining employment, searching for food, and simply surviving—makes the mental space and quiet needed for heuristic reform unlikely. Unfortunately, the truth is that we cannot be both human and also routinely find the time to sit in a pure, laboratory-like state of Zen, constantly devoting effort to rewriting our heuristics. Of course, when survival requires us to do so, the balance tilts in favor of heuristic rewriting, as I mentioned before.

Sherif was onto something in his camp experiments when he posited that we are only willing to disrupt intergroup hostilities when the different groups realize they need to get along for survival or to achieve benefits significant enough to warrant the disruption.[54] Other research in this area, particularly regarding the potential for deprovincialization, fails to consider that we have busy lives, and the disruption required for changes in heuristic-driven processing is not currently worth the cognitive discomfort it would bring.

The only time in American history when stereotypes about people viewed as minorities were modulated without a direct threat to our survival was during the efforts of the War Refugee Board.[55] The government engaged in sustained and massive information warfare to reduce antisemitism enough to make it politically expedient to resettle the Jewish victims of the Holocaust.[56] However, despite that unprecedented, large-scale government effort to combat antisemitism, the phenomenon of antisemitism has not disappeared.

Rather, the massive government-level effort seemed only to reduce antisemitism enough to permit the resettlement of Holocaust victims. And as Eric Goldstein pointed out, this was only possible because Jewish people were able to be included within the concept of whiteness.[57] This inclusion within whiteness is impossible for me, most immigrants from "shithole countries," most African Americans, and most American Natives. Understand, as I explain in the next paragraph, that post-2024, we now have a federal government that is doing the opposite for non-white immigrants and Americans of what the War Refugee Board did for Jewish people.[58]

The banning of critical race theory and the book bans, for example, are an attempt to make it impossible for people to be exposed to the very narratives that hold some hope for mitigating systemic inequity.[59] The current governmental reality for people of color is akin to what the reality would have been for Jewish people after World War II if the War Refugee Board prohibited Americans from being exposed to any information about Jewish suffering at the hands of the Nazis, rather than ensuring it was everywhere to be seen. The current governmental approach is to deliberately and decisively prevent the dissemination of information that accurately represents the inequality faced by people of color.

This is especially important because education seems to provide an environment where people are primed to receive repeated exposure to information that does not conform to stereotypes. Yet even here, only slightly more than half of the voters with college degrees supported the candidate that was not a convicted felon and a self-proclaimed xenophobe and racist. By reforming education to minimize the availability of counter-stereotypical narratives, such as those provided by critical race theory,[60] the stereotype-modulating impact of education will be reduced even further.

But a larger and more difficult question is ultimately at stake when we strive to achieve equality and egalitarianism: what does that actually look like? Nowhere in the entire history of humanity has there ever been a coherent illustration of equality and egalitarianism. What, then, are we truly aiming for? How will we know when we have arrived? Is the aim of antiracism simply to make continuous, incremental changes in societal disenfranchisement, or is it something more? If it is something more, what exactly does antiracism look like in practice? Is equality unattainable because currently it is merely an illusory and imagined target, one that humanity has never achieved? Before we can reach an end, we need to know what that end is. As scholars and antiracist advocates, perhaps we need to spend more time constructing this vision before we continue toward what is currently a phantom target.

This chapter is framed as a question because I am not sure that human societies can exist without creating hierarchies that conform to or support some form of implicit ordering and ranking. If we look throughout human history, we have always found ways to deploy *otherism* to devalue the lives of those we perceive as different from ourselves.

That separation can be by race, as in America, which this book has discussed; by birthright, as in the monarchies of Europe; or by caste, as in the societal structure in India. What is often uncomfortable to discuss, however, is the possibility that *otherism*—or the formation of different "us vs. them" groups—may be essential to human societal structure.

As mentioned before, cognitive load is significantly reduced when we rely on unconscious processing mechanisms.[61] Unconsciously forming groups to which we feel a sense of belonging is a cognitively efficient way to achieve group cooperation in areas such as defense, sourcing food, and even building dwellings or villages. Without the ability to unconsciously identify similarities between individuals and rely on those similarities for group functioning, human societies would never have developed as they did. *Otherism*, or the creation of "us" and "them," therefore appears essential to human social structure.

To reiterate, bias and discrimination are also the results of the same mechanisms that make human social structure possible. It may be that we cannot have one without the other. Consider that social norms and morality are only definable because of the existence of an "other" group—a group that does not conform to the same practices as the majority. We identify our societies and the groups to which we belong by the similarity of beliefs and behaviors.[62]

Muzafer Sherif explains that there is no simple explanation for intergroup conflicts, and we are far from being able to exist without them.[63] Tajfel and Turner suggest that categorization and grouping—such as furniture—is an essentially human attribute that enables us to think, speak about, and use those objects.[64] They argue that we apply the same categorization process to humans based on observable characteristics of such as race or language, such that a social group is, at its core, nothing more than a social category.[65]

Once social groups are established, people begin to self-identify as belonging to a particular group or not, and being a part of the group is established by commonality, whether that commonality is race, behavior, or some other phenomenon.[66]

The next stage in human societal structure is intergroup comparison, where members of individual groups begin comparing themselves with other groups. Once groups are formed, it is an essentially human characteristic to overvalue the behavior and worth of members of our own groups and to undervalue the members of other groups.[67]

This leads to another unavoidable aspect of human societies: the creation of social hierarchies based on groups. Each group perceives itself as superior in some regard to an out group based on one or more characteristics.[68]

On top of all these intergroup realities is John Jost's suggestion, through his theory of system justification, that all members of society become unconsciously motivated to defend the hierarchy of the groups. The reality, as Jost posits, is that the stability of human society can only be explained when all groups buy into the group hierarchy.[69]

The other problem with trying to minimize heuristic-based processing in favor of relying more on rationality is that it would slow down human decision-making to a degree that is inconsistent with our entire evolutionary history and has thus far been essential to our progress as a species. I again remind you here that Subotnik suggests that without bias we might still be a sub-apex species and residing in caves.[70] And as Daniel Kahneman points out, trying to make decisions without the heuristics that comprise bias would result in us not using vast swaths of our mental processing mechanisms.[71] This is simply not realistic for human beings.

These mechanisms that generate systemic inequity are essential for human societies to exist, and they are responsible for the efficiency of our species in developing and progressing. Asking for us to exist in a society where these implicit and unconscious mechanisms don't exist seems unrealistic. Rather, research suggests it may be possible to reroute or hijack the unconscious processing heuristics so the results and conclusions they produce are altered. Unfortunately, these hijackings have only been successful when human survival was at stake. Only in such situations are humans motivated to endure the cognitive discomfort necessary to rewire these unconscious processing shortcuts.

Humans have existed this way since the beginning of time. If we truly want to change and become more egalitarian, it's going to require massive social upheaval that forces us to reevaluate the fundamental but false tenets we continue to revalidate via "meh relegation." Ironically, I find comfort in the certainty that I—and most Americans—understand we may be long past accepting that level of upheaval as a society. Granted, there are racist and xenophobic individuals angry enough to consider another civil war to maintain white supremacy. I hope they are just a fringe element, though.

And I hope the majority of us believe and understand that, despite America's imperfections, we are, by many metrics, the greatest democracy that ever existed. Even the Chinese people's name for America is "mei guo," which translated from Mandarin means "beautiful country."[72] We got to this unique place in history by difficult and significant sacrifice. I hope the majority of Americans realize that this country is simply too precious and important to again resort to self-destructive internal violence simply because we appear to be at a state of significant flux and transition in our history. We *have no choice* but to discover another way to disrupt firmly entrenched systemic inequities.

Endnotes

1. *See, e.g.*, Carmit T. Tadmor, Ying-yi Hong, Melody M. Chao, Fon Wiruchnipawan & Wei Wang, *Multicultural Experiences Reduce Intergroup Bias Through Epistemic Unfreezing*, 103 J. of Personality & Soc. Psych. 750–772 (2012); Rory D. Bahadur, *Newsworthiness as an Internet-Era Mitigant of Implicit Bias*, 888 UMKC L. Rev. 1 (2019); Nancy R. Buchan, Marilynn B. Brewer, Gianluca Grimalda, Rick K. Wilson, Enrique Fatas & Margaret Foddy, *Global Social Identity and Global Cooperation*, 22 Psych. Sci. 821–828 (2011).

2. Muzafer Sherif, *Experiments in Group Conflict*, 195 Sci. Am. 54, 57–58 (1956).

3. *Id.*

4. *Id.* at 58.

5. *Id.*

6. *Id.*

7. *Id.*

8. *Id.*

9. *Id.*

10. John T. Jost, *A Theory of System Justification: Is There a Nonconscious Tendency to Defend, Bolster and Justify Aspects of the Societal Status Quo?*, Am. Psych. Ass'n (June 2017), https://perma.cc/LR7X-68MF.

11. Interview with Kimberlé W. Crenshaw, Columbia Law School (June 8, 2017), available at https://www.law.columbia.edu/news/archive/kimberle-crenshaw-intersectionality-more-two-decades-later; *see also* Council of Europe, https://www.coe.int/en/web/gender-matters/intersectionality-and-multiple-discrimination#:~:text=For%20example%2C%20a%20person%20who,often%20does%2C%20create%20cumulative%20disadvantage (last visited Jan. 24, 2025).

12. Marilynn B. Brewer, *Intergroup Discrimination: Ingroup Love or Outgroup Hate?*, in The Cambridge Handbook of the Psychology of Prejudice 90–104 (Chris G. Sibley & Fiona Kate Barlow eds., 2017) [hereinafter The Cambridge Handbook].

13. Thomas F. Pettigrew, *Deprovincialization*, in The Encyclopedia of Peace Psychology (D. J. Christie ed., 2011).

14. *See, e.g.*, The Cambridge Handbook, *supra* note 12, at 104. Explaining deprovincialization as:

> Redefining ingroup boundaries through recategorization or cross-categorization is effective in creating more inclusive ingroups (see Brewer & Gaertner, 2001). And taking advantage of our capacity for multiple social identities has the potential of reducing ingroup-outgroup distinctions and creating shared identity at a broad level of inclusiveness (Brewer, 2008, 2010).

15. *Id.*

16. *Id.*

17. *Id.*

18. *Id.*

19. Bahadur, *supra* note 1, at 35.

20. *Id.*

21. Jonathan Zittrain, *Law in a Networked World: Privacy 2.0*, 2008 U. Chi. Legal F. 65 (2008).

22. *Id.*

23. Gertz v. Robert Welch, Inc. 418 U.S. 323 (1974).

24. *Id.*

25. Zittrain, *supra*, note 21.

26. *Id.*

27. *Id.*

28. The Associated Press, *George Holliday, Who Shot the Video of Officers Beating Rodney King, Has Died*, NPR (Sept. 21, 2021, 9:37 AM), https://www.npr.org/2021/09/21/1039236256/george-holliday-who-shot-the-video-of-officers-beating-rodney-king-has-died#:~:text=King%20drowned%20in%20his%20backyard,unclear%20if%20it%20ever%20sold.

29. Bahadur, *supra* note 1, 26 (2019) (citing to Jonathan Zittrain).

30. *See* Tadmor et al., *supra* note 1, 752–53.

31. *Id.*

32. *Id.*

33. *Id.* at 753.

34. *Id.* at 752.

35. *Id.* at 753.

36. Richard J. Crisp & Rhiannon N. Turner, *Cognitive Adaptation to the Experience of Social and Cultural Diversity*, 137 Psych. Bull. 242, 244–45 (2011).

37. *Id.* at 244.

38. *Id.*

39. *Id.* at 245.

40. Nirupika Sharma, *Let's Talk About Code-Switching: A Double-Edged Sword*, Berkeley: Graduate Division (Nov. 14, 2023), https://grad.berkeley.edu/news/announcements/lets-talk-about-code-switching-a-double-edged-sword/. Code switching is defined as "the way people adjust how they present themselves is driven by societal expectations and norms. To align with the norms of different contexts, people may switch out of various identities, including race, ethnicity, gender, sexuality, age, socioeconomic status, and disability status."

41. *Id.* Code switching will "exact a mental toll, potentially leading to cognitive fatigue and burnout, as individuals remain hypervigilant to monitor their surroundings."

42. *Id.* at 245.

43. *Id. at* 251 (Explaining that people must be motivated to escape the comfort of stereotype-based processing or the cognitive adaptations will not occur.).

44. *See* Tadmor et al., *supra* note 1.

45. *Id.* at 258.

46. *Id.*

47. *Id.*

48. Robert M. Sapolsky, Determined: A Science of Life Without Free Will 387 (2023).

49. *See e.g.*, Mental Health America, *Racism and Mental Health*, https://www.mhanational.org/racism-and-mental-health (last visited Jan. 24, 2025) (explaining "Racism is a mental health issue because racism causes trauma. And trauma paints a direct line to mental illnesses, which need to be taken seriously."); *see also* David R. Williams, *Stress and the Mental Health of Populations of Color: Advancing Our Understanding of Race-Related Stressors*, 59 J. Health Soc. Behav. 466 (2018) (citing to Hughes et al. (2015) acknowledging "African Americans who had high levels of racial identity but also scored high on internalized racism were more likely to have lower levels of mastery and higher levels of depressive symptoms.").

50. *See* Tadmor et al., *supra* note 1.

51. *Id.*

52. *Id.* at 419.

53. Dan Subotnik, *Does Testing = Race Discrimination?: Ricci, the Bar Exam, the LSAT, and the Challenge to Learning*, 8 U. MASS. L. REV. 332, 398 (2013).

54. Sherif, *supra* note 2, at 57–58.

55. *See infra* Chapter 5 (explaining WWII as white privilege).

56. *Id.*

57. *See* ERIC L. GOLDSTEIN, THE PRICE OF WHITENESS: JEWS, RACE, AND AMERICAN IDENTITY 1 (Princeton University Press, 2019).

58. *See infra* Chapter 6.

59. *Id.*

60. *See infra* Chapter 6.

61. Tadmor et al., *supra* note 1, at 751.

62. *See* Marilynn B. Brewer, *Intergroup Discrimination: Ingroup Love or Outgroup Hate?*, in THE CAMBRIDGE HANDBOOK OF THE PSYCHOLOGY OF PREJUDICE 90–104 (Chris G. Sibley & Fiona Kate Barlow eds., 2017) .

63. *See* Sherif, *supra* note 2.

64. D. Robert Worley, *Tajfel and Turner Intergroup Conflict Theories 1997*, JOHNS HOPKINS UNIV. 1, 2 (January 2021).

65. *Id.*

66. *Id.*

67. *Id.*

68. Worley, *supra* note 64, at 2–3.

69. *Id.*

70. Erica Pandey, *America's Diploma Divide: States with Fewer Grads Went for Trump*, AXIOS (Nov. 7, 2024), https://www.axios.com/2024/11/07/college-degree-voters-split-harris-trump.

71. *See* DANIEL KAHNEMAN, THINKING, FAST AND SLOW (2011).

72. Alan Yu, *The U.S. and China: 2 Centuries of Infatuation and Disappointment*, NPR (Dec. 11, 2016, 2:48 PM), https://www.npr.org/sections/parallels/2016/12/11/504478025/the-u-s-and-china-two-centuries-of-infatuation-and-disappointment?utm_source=facebook.com&utm_medium=social&utm_campaign=npr&utm_term=nprnews&utm_content=2039&fbclid=IwZXh0bgNhZW0CMTEAAR0i_8SQj0majZwLlIbB4AEkH_PZ-B0Poi9SbxMdpWwlJbTRyKhB5aZodng_aem_BoRkEpK3HQJaYKJea4Iblw.

Conclusion

I began writing this book to understand and hopefully discover a way to improve systemic inequity, thereby finding a way to improve the country that adopted me and provided me with so much opportunity that could not be had elsewhere. When beginning this book, I desperately hoped I would conclude that Derrick Bell was wrong when he suggested that racism in America is permanent. According to Bell,

> Black people will never gain full equality in this country. Even those herculean efforts we hail as successful will produce no more than temporary 'peaks of progress,' short-lived victories that slide into irrelevance as racial patterns adapt in ways that maintain white dominance. This is a hard-to-accept fact that all history verifies.[1]

At the end of this book, I agree with Bell and admit that beyond just racism, all forms of systemic inequity might not only be permanent, but they may be essential to humanity. The same cognitive mechanisms that have made us an apex species with uniquely advanced societies are the ones that create systemic inequity.

These mental shortcuts that are essential to human success have only been hijacked and changed in the face of severe disruption such as the Civil War and the War of Independence where untold suffering and cruelty forced us to realize that our assumptions and conclusions drawn from these unconscious heuristics were incorrect. Reconstruction happened after the Civil War. I deeply hope most people would agree with me that America is past that level of disruption and social unrest.

While the reality is that America is a white dominated, Christian country with deeply entrenched systemic inequities buttressing that reality, it is also true that America is an aspirational beacon for most of the world. We are an imperfect species in an imperfect world, and I cannot deny that there is no place in that imperfect world, other than the United States that I, a non-white atheist, would choose to call home. This duality admittedly causes dissonance, but that dissonance is self-inflicted.

It may be that the error of my ways was beginning to research this topic. It was much easier when I could dismiss racism and racist actions as the actions of bad people. Instead, now I see racism and other forms of systemic inequity as a reality of our species and a core aspect of our humanity. Therefore, egalitarianism and equity are essentially the opposite of humanity. I find myself at a dark place of reckoning where it is possible that humans cannot simultaneously exist and be egalitarian.

I desperately hope I am wrong and that people much wiser than I can find a solution to systemic inequity that works for humans given the realities of the human brain. Until that day I am going to go back to smelling apple pie everywhere, seeing the American flag waving to the tune of wind created by angels, and focus on smaller stuff like what I will cook for the next Superbowl party.

The reality is that I am too exhausted trying to maintain resistance to systemic hierarchy and yearning for systemic reform. It seems much easier, and I think I am happier, when I acknowledge the reality that as a person of color there will always be impediments in my way and in the way of my biracial child. Instead of railing against this immovable reality I may just need to adapt my behavior accordingly and understand we will always have to work harder to get what we are entitled to. That's what I did to become a law professor; it's why I have published more than I needed to and worked way harder than was required. And it's why I made sure that even though it caused her great pain and anguish I burned this reality into my kid's psyche. Somehow, and perhaps it is from exhaustion, I am comfortable accepting that reality while simultaneously learning how to embrace the many opportunities provided to people like me to thrive in this amazing country despite the existence of systemic racism. I guess my only other option is dissonance-based insanity.

Neither I nor anyone else can change human biology. Once we accept the complexity and imperfection of our species, systemic racism, cruelty, and injustice can be understood as an essential component of humanity, rather than as a personal attack which we need to view through a lens of culpability. Yes, absolutely there is conscious racist conduct that is culpable and needs to be addressed directly and immediately. And it is frightening to accept that it is improbable we can both be human and not have systemic unfairness. The only control I have as an immigrant is to control my immediate circle, doing my best to ensure that my descendants will begin their adult life at a socioeconomic starting point that is higher than mine was and to make sure that we are all as happy as we can be. That entails working hard to take advantage of the opportunities America provides me, even if those opportunities are less than they otherwise would be if I had a different skin color, giving back to society and the less fortunate and celebrating every second I am surrounded by friends and family that care for me.

As demonstrated by my Chapter 5 narrative regarding World War II, systemic reform cannot be achieved without government-level reform, and even that may not be enough to achieve systemic equity for non-white people. At this point in time, government-level reform seems impossible given the nature of American politics. It may or may not change in my lifetime.

With that reality crystalized, I think I will go to the range, exercise my Second Amendment right, and do some target shooting with my two handguns, then I will go to a uniquely American grocery store and buy a bigger chunk of meat than most entire villages in the world will ever be able to share, put it on the smoker in my big-ass backyard and drink beer while trying to ensure I can be happy in the precious few remaining years I have on this earth.

Endnotes

1. Derrick Bell, *Racism Is Here to Stay: Now What?* 35 How. L. J. 79 (1991).

Index